RISK AND THE POLITICS OF PUBLIC HEALTH

| A Critical Review |

RISK AND THE POLITICS OF PUBLIC HEALTH

| A Critical Review |

Matthias Beck
Donnacha Seán Lucey
University College Cork, Ireland

World Scientific
NEW JERSEY • LONDON • SINGAPORE • BEIJING • SHANGHAI • HONG KONG • TAIPEI • CHENNAI

Published by

World Scientific Publishing Co. Pte. Ltd.
5 Toh Tuck Link, Singapore 596224
USA office: 27 Warren Street, Suite 401-402, Hackensack, NJ 07601
UK office: 57 Shelton Street, Covent Garden, London WC2H 9HE

Library of Congress Cataloging-in-Publication Data
Names: Beck, Matthias, 1964– author. | Lucey, Donnacha Seán, author.
Title: Risk and the politics of public health : a critical review /
Matthias Beck, Donnacha Seán Lucey.
Description: New Jersey : World Scientific, [2025] | Includes bibliographical references and index.
Identifiers: LCCN 2023039006 | ISBN 9789814689526 (hardcover) |
ISBN 9789814689533 (ebook for institutions) | ISBN 9789814689540 (ebook for individuals)
Subjects: MESH: Public Health--history | Risk Assessment--history | History of Medicine |
Social Problems--history | Policy Making
Classification: LCC RA418 | NLM WA 11.1 | DDC 362.1--dc23/eng/20231002
LC record available at https://lccn.loc.gov/2023039006

British Library Cataloguing-in-Publication Data
A catalogue record for this book is available from the British Library.

For any available supplementary material, please visit
https://www.worldscientific.com/worldscibooks/10.1142/9638#t=suppl

Desk Editors: Quek ZhiQin, Vanessa/Joy Quek

Typeset by Stallion Press
Email: enquiries@stallionpress.com

To the memory of Dr Caroline Hunter-Beck, 1957–2005, and
Joan Lucey, 1948–2021.

About the Authors

Matthias Beck is Professor of Management at Cork Business School, University College Cork, Ireland. He works in the area of risk management and health management. He has published over 100 articles and several books including *Risk: A Study of its Origins, History and Politics* (WSPC, 2014).

Dr. Donnacha Seán Lucey is the Research Manager in the College of Business and Law. His expertise lies in the history of health and health systems and has published extensively in these fields. His books include The End of the Irish Poor Law? *Welfare and Healthcare Reform in Revolutionary and Independent Ireland* (Manchester University Press, 2015).

Contents

List of Illustrations

Introduction

Risk and Public Health: An Uneasy Relationship

The outbreak of COVID-19, its speed and devastating impact, all have raised serious questions about public health as a discipline and its contribution to the mitigation of global health risks. These questions must be extended, by implication, to all steps of the risk management process in this area, ranging from risk identification, risk assessment, and risk mitigation, to the monitoring, reporting, and communication of public health risks. The emphasis of this book, is not on the causes of the COVID-19 outbreak, nor do we focus primarily on the failure of contemporary public health systems to anticipate or prevent this crisis. However, the core argument we explore is indirectly related to the latter issue. So what is our core argument? Our core argument is that, historically speaking, the relationship between our thinking about risk and our thinking about public health and medicine has always been an uneasy one. Risk thinking was slow to gain a place in medicine and public health, and once it did so it was far too easily hijacked by political interests rather than serving the public, or vulnerable groups which most needed health services.[1] This, in our view was no accident, but rather had to do with the hegemonic use and unequal

[1] Miles, Steven H., "Kaci Hickox: Public Health and the Politics of Fear," *The American Journal of Bioethics,* 15:4 (2015): 17–19; Roberts, Samuel, *Infectious Fear: Politics, Disease, and the Health Effects of Segregation*, Chapel Hill, NC, University of North Carolina Press (2009).

distribution of knowledge and uncertainty in health matters in Western societies.[2]

As to the contents of this book, we critically explore the gradual integration of risk terminology and concepts into medical and public health contexts (Chapters 1 and 2). Next, we adopt a somewhat unconventional structure where we investigate the risk and public health nexus around three themes. These three themes include areas where perceptions of risk have been central to the adoption of problematic public health policies. They include: "immigration" (Chapter 3), "race" (Chapter 4), and "war" (Chapter 5). Each of our three core chapters examines chronologically some of the key intellectual approaches to health risks around the respective themes and links these to policy actions or initiatives. In so doing, we do not exclude views or initiatives which later generations considered misguided or even shameful. Rather, each of our three thematic chapters places a strong emphasis (through the analysis of relevant primary sources) on the specific socio-political dynamics which allowed for, or encouraged, the emergence of specific social constructions of health-related risks. By examining these links, our book seeks to give the reader a detailed understanding of the changing philosophies which informed public health policy making over the past hundred years up to the present.

To round up this analysis of change in relation to the three core themes, our summary section then discusses a number of observations about the risk public health nexus, with a special focus on the role of misinformation and manipulation. Here we argue that the construction of social risks gains political momentum if it acquires an element of immediacy or urgency and if an issue is credibly described as crisis or at least described in crisis-like terms. Once a public health risk is viewed as urgent and a portrayal of it in crisis terms is widely accepted, the *status quo* is often no longer sustainable, requiring the existing pattern of "disorganised uncertainty" to be translated into forms of socially "organised

---

[2]Illich, Ivan, "Medical Nemesis," *Journal of Epidemiology & Community Health,* 57:12 (2003), 919–922; Illich, Ivan, "The Medicalization of Life," *Journal of Medical Ethics,* 1:2 (1975), 73–77; Illich, Ivan, "Clinical Damage, Medical Monopoly, the Expropriation of Health: Three Dimensions of Iatrogenic Tort," *Journal of Medical Ethics,* 1:2 (1975), 78.

uncertainty". This explains why certain health risks, such as novel infectious diseases, sometimes receive little attention, despite the fact that they could become regional or global threats, while minor threats, such as certain diseases transmitted by immigrants, are at times grossly exaggerated. We suggest that, in the absence of strong mechanisms of scientific, technical, and democratic accountability, a translation of risk perception into action can occur irrespective of the initial veracity or evidence base on which the claim of such a threat is based. One example of a translation of an unfounded threat claim into political action was the anti-Asian immigration movement of the United States of America, where proposed exclusion measures achieved significant popular and legislative support during the late 19th and early 20th century due to frequent references to public health threats. Less openly political responses to perceived crisis-like health risks can include the creation of formal or informal organisations and institutions, the emergence of new professions or professional specialisms, the creation of pseudo-academic disciplines such as eugenics, and the imposition of discriminatory testing regimes and qualification requirements on individuals.

Conversely, ignoring or underplaying relevant risks can take many forms, ranging from the invocations of techno-optimistic predictions that certain risks will disappear as hygiene standards improve, or the suggestion of optimistic scenarios, predicting for example the elimination of infectious diseases with novel pharmaceuticals were they to break out. One of the most striking examples of such a modern-day underplaying of major health risks is obviously the claim, which was popular up until the COVID-19 outbreak, that infectious diseases no longer posed a threat to public health. This claim was deeply questionable, when considering the ongoing discovery of new infectious diseases pre-COVID-19, as well as our increased awareness of mechanisms which accelerated and facilitated the creation and spread of these diseases.

One important characteristic of risk translation processes is that misguided initiatives of risk and threat identification or conversely failures of non-identification can weaken the reflective potential of key actors, whether this ultimately is judged as error of omission or error of commission. Errors of commission can include misguided political interventions, as exemplified by some early 20th century immigration legislation in the

United States or the more nuanced and ritualistic forms of some present day public private partnerships meant to combat global health problems. Errors of omission include delays or failures to develop, or provide, vaccinations in light of preventable diseases. The sophistication of corporate public relations campaigns has significantly increased the difficulties associated with the identification and prioritisation of genuine risks and poses increasing challenges to public health practitioners. In conclusion, we argue that this requires us to strengthen risk literacy and openness and equality in the communication of public health risks.

Chapter One

Beginnings

Risk, Probability, and Their Origin

Studies of the origins of risk as a concept of human thought typically relate its roots to the human occupation with games of chance. Board games and the throw of dice-like objects such as astragalus have been traced to ancient African and Middle Eastern cultures, including what is now modern Turkey and Egypt, from around 3500 BC.[1] This supports Huizinga's notion of the centrality of *homo ludens* — the human at play.[2] Florence N. David's history of probability suggests that, despite the popularity of game playing, it was many centuries before the "root mathematics" underpinning games were beginning to be appraised in Greco-Roman science and thence Aramaic, Arabic, and latterly, European mathematical conjecture. Yet, like Huizinga, she too gives these games a paramount position in the evolution of human thinking about uncertainty.[3]

---

[1] David, Florence Nightingale. *Games, Gods and Gambling, A History of Probability and Statistical Ideas*. London, Griffin (1962), pp. 4–5; Hacking, Ian, *The Emergence of Probability: A Philosophical Study of Early Ideas about Probability, Induction and Statistical Inference*. Cambridge University Press, 1975. pp. 1–10; Beck, Matthias and Beth Kewell, *Risk: A Study of Its Origins, History and Politics*, London, World Scientific (2014).

[2] See Huizinga, Johan, *Homo Ludens: A Study of the Play Element in Culture*, London, Routledge and Kegan Paul, 1949 [2014], P. 44; Huizinga makes use of ancient definitions of play taken from Greco-Roman, Norse, and Germanic sources, to argue that, whilst the delineation of frivolous play and serious play is axiomatically useful, in reality all forms of competitive interaction are "earnest" in terms of the spirit of contest they simulate.

[3] David, *Games, Gods and Gambling*, pp. 21–60.

The development of a "calculus of probabilities" attached to games of wit, speculation, and chance, is thought to have taken place after a long delay in Europe, following earlier inventions in India.[4] Europe's belated interest in arithmetical concepts of chance and probability, compared to the ancient Indian and the Arabic world, has been attributed to its relative intellectual isolation following the collapse of the Roman Empire in AD 455.[5] The late medieval nominalists of Italy, Germany, and Britain gradually overcame earlier barriers in the 14th century.[6] Translation of Brahmaguptan and Bhaskaran mathematics from 7th and 12th century Sanskrit into a newly flourishing Islamic mathematics disseminated gradually into Europe at that time.[7] Leonardo de Pisa (1170–1250) known as Fibonacci, made the Hindu-Islamic numeral system popular in his *Liber Abaci*; publishing what David described as "the first real mathematical treatise"[8] to capture the European imagination. Subsequent generations of Italian scholars are described by Cochrane as Fibonacci's inheritors.[9] They include Fra Luca Paccioli (or Paciolo) (1445–1517) and Celio Calcagnini (1479–1541) who wrote about "games" but not "the calculation of the chances involved" and Geronimo Cardano (1501–1576).[10]

Geronimo Cardano lived during the height of the renaissance with its zeal for rediscovery. According to historian Eric Cochrane, Cardano was inspired by Calcagnini whose non-calculative humanist treatments of chance are said to have influenced him.[11] Cardano's book, *Liber de Ludo Aleae*, or "Book on Games of Chance," written c. 1552 and published posthumously in Basle in 1663 was "the first serious effort to develop the

---

[4] Hacking, *The Emergence of Probability*, pp. 8–9.

[5] David, *Games, Gods and Gambling*, p. 27.

[6] Cochrane, Eric, "Science and Humanism in the Italian Renaissance," *The American Historical Review*, 81:5 (1976), 1044.

[7] See David, Gods, Games and Gambling, pp. 27–8.

[8] *Ibid.*, p. 31.

[9] Cochrane, "Science and Humanism".

[10] David, *Games, Gods and Gambling*, p. 41 and pp. 55–6; Hacking, *The Emergence of Probability*, p. 5

[11] Cochrane, "Science and Humanism".

statistical principles of probability."[12] Cochrane suggests that Cardano's fascination with the quandaries of chance and the algebraic probabilism shared little with the doctrines of Italian humanism that would have been taught at the Universities of Pavia, Bologna, and Pisa where he specialized in mathematics, astronomy, and dialectics.[13] These humanistic discourses focused on Platonic and Aristotelian philosophies, classic poetry, and sculpture.[14] Cochrane notes that "[i]t is not surprising, then, that students at Pisa in the 1570s, most of whom arrived at the university after a thoroughly humanist preparation in Florence, attended the debates [at Cardano's solicitation] only to be amused … ."[15] The historians, Florence N. David, Anders Hald, and the popular writer Peter L. Bernstein, have nonetheless each emphasized Girolamo Cardano's legacy.[16] Cardano established new proofs of principle in geometry and aleatory (or chance) mathematics around 1525 and revised his conjectures in 1563–1564,[17] some of which were shared with rival mathematician, Niccolo Fontana are called Tartaglia (1499–1557).[18] Cardano taught mathematics while seeking to obtain a license to practice medicine in Milan. He quit his teaching position in 1536 to focus on medicine, while continuing to be involved in discussions on mathematics.[19] Cardano's work had its own imitators.

---

[12] Bernstein, Peter L., *Against the Gods: The Remarkable Story of Risk*, New York, NY, John Wiley & Sons (1996), p. 48.

[13] Cochrane, "Science and Humanism", pp. 1040–1 and p. 1048. Cochrane states on p. 1040: "Humanism turned the minds of prospective scientists from facts to form, from substance to grammar, from empirical investigation to the adoration of ancient authorities."

[14] *Ibid.*, p. 1042.

[15] *Ibid.*, p. 1050.

[16] See David, *Games, Gods and Gambling*; Hald, Anders, *A History of Probability and Statistics and their Applications before 1750,* New York, NY, John Wiley (1990).

[17] David, *Games, Gods and Gambling*, p. 57.

[18] See principally David, *Games, Gods and Gambling*, p. 62; and also Long, Pamela, *Openness, Secrecy, Authorship: Technical Arts and the Culture of Knowledge from Antiquity to the Renaissance*, Baltimore, MD, Johns Hopkins University Press (2001).

[19] Ore, Øystein, *Cardano: the Gambling Scholar,* Princeton, NJ, Princeton University Press (2017).

By the early 17th to mid-17th century,[20] Galileo Galilei (1564–1642) discussed dice throwing in a paper likely written between 1613 and 1623, entitled *Sopra le Scoperte dei Dadi*, or "Concerning an Investigation on Dice."[21] This paper is said to recapitulate elements of Cardano's mathematical conjecture.[22] Researchers have suggested that Cardano's work influenced the resolution of unfinished card, dice, and balla games[23] (from which Paccioli's problem of points originated) as well as calculations relating to astronomy.[24]

Randomness and chance remained important themes for 19th century writers.[25] This built in part on earlier forays into probability theory which mostly involved French scholars.[26] They attempted to provide a first systematic exploration of how issues of decision making or measurement in the face of uncertainty could be investigated.[27] John Passmore's history of philosophy, accordingly, attributed a leap in the understanding of chance and probability to Laplace (1749–1827)[28] who, in turn, influenced later writings by George Boole (1815–1864). Boole was impressed by this and

---

[20] Rose, Paul L., "Humanist Culture and Renaissance Mathematics: The Italian Libraries of the Quattrocentre," *Studies in the Renaissance*, 20 (1973): 46–105, and Cochrane, "Science and Humanism"

[21] Hald, *A History of Probability and Statistics*, p. 41.

[22] David, *Games, Gods and Gambling*, pp. 62–4.

[23] Green, D. R. "Historical Topics: The Beginnings of Probability Theory." *Mathematics in School* 10:1 (1981): 6-8.

[24] David, *Games, Gods and Gambling*, p. 38; Bernstein, *Against the Gods*, p. 43

[25] Hacking, Ian, and Tim Hacking. *The Taming of Chance*. Cambridge, Cambridge University Press (1990), pp. 1–15.

[26] See, e.g., Laplace, Pierre-Simon, *Pierre-Simon Laplace Philosophical Essay on Probabilities: Translated from the Fifth French Edition of 1825 with Notes by the Translator*, Vol. 13. Cham, Springer Science & Business Media (2012).

[27] Long, Pamela O., *Openness, Secrecy, Authorship: Technical Arts and the Culture of Knowledge from Antiquity to the Renaissance,* Baltimore, MD, JHU Press (2001), p. 2, 27.

[28] It has been argued that there was a passion for probability around the time amongst European elites of scholars and theologians', including, among others, Pierre de Fermat (1601–1665), Blaise Pascal (1623–1662), Christiaan Huygens (1629–1695), Gottfried Leibniz (1646–1716) and Abraham de Moivre (1667–1695). See also Mesnard, Jean. *Pascal et les Roannez*, Paris, Desclee de Brouwer (1965); as well as Beck, Matthias, and Sara Melo, *Quality Management and Managerialism in Healthcare: A Critical Historical Survey*, Cham, Springer (2014), p. 33.

Quetelet's (1796–1874) accumulation of social statistics.[29] Accordingly, Boole thought that a combination of theory and data would allow scientists to make successful predictions, but cautioned that "the observation of social phenomena, does not in in general present to us probabilities in simple events, but of events occurring in particular connextions."[30] At the time of Boole's writing, sporadic efforts had indeed been made to apply the mathematics of probabilities to social data,[31] and also to exploit such knowledge commercially, for instance, through the sale of life insurance policies. As Weisberg notes, the links between observations, knowledge about the application of probability, and risk assessment, however, were still weak,[32] having been perhaps somewhat overestimated by some historians on account of the coterminous appearance of several key writings in 1662. These included the publication of the Port-Royal *Logic* in France

---

[29] Having founded the Royal Observatory of Belgium, Quetelet created or co-created a number of national and international statistical societies and journal. He collected measurements in many areas, including the human body, meteorology, demographics, and crime.

[30] Passmore, John, *A Hundred Years of Philosophy*, Harmondsworth, Penguin (1968), p. 129.

[31] One of the earliest examples of a limited quantitative and probabilistic analysis of mortality and birth data was Graunt's work on London Bills of Mortality: Graunt, John, *Natural and Political Observations mentioned in a following index, and made upon the Bills of Mortality. London. Republished as an introduction by B. Benjamin in Journal of the Institute of Actuaries* 90, (1662) [1964].

[32] Weisberg, Herbert I., *Willful Ignorance: The Mismeasure of Uncertainty*. New York, NY, John Wiley & Sons (2014) p. 82 makes the fascinating observation that "The mistaken belief that modern probability emerged full-blown around 1660 rests partly on an extraordinary coincidence. In 1662, the very year in which the Port-Royal *Logic* appeared in France, another publication of similar originality and significance was published. Whereas the *Logic* is often cited in connection with the emergence of probability, Graunt's *Observations on the Bills of Mortality* is considered the progenitor of statistics. Strange as it may seem, though, there was absolutely no connection between the ideas expressed in these two great works. The Logic made no reference to anything we would describe as statistical, and the *Observations* lacked any notion of a calculus of chance, let alone probability. This is not to say that core ideas of statistics pertaining to uncertainty and errors of measurement does not have long historical pedigree, dating back to Jacob Bernoulli (1654–1705), Abraham De Moivre (1667–1754), Pierre Simon Laplace (1749–1827), and Carl Friedrich Gauss (1777–1855). Likewise, we find an early advocacy of sampling in the works of Laplace.

and Graunt's *Observations on the Bills of Mortality* in London. Thus, commercial exploitation of information on death risks through the sale of insurance, at this stage, ha large been postponed, or carried out in a greatly simplified and hence commercially unsatisfactory manner.[33]

Risk and Medical Practice: The Beginnings

Karin Zachmann suggests that "while mathematicians in the era of scientific revolution and the enlightenment began to approach uncertainty as probability, the early-modern passion for gambling shaped notions of risk as genuine uncertainty and, therefore, precluded the early application of the nascent tools of probability."[34] This appears to have been the case, despite the fact that significant amounts of relevant data had been collected. They included the well-known *Bills of Mortality* of 1662 which described trends in plague deaths.[35] Stolley and Laskey note how John

[33] Halley (1656–1742) analysed 5,869 deaths from 1687 to 1691 in Breslau. See Halley, Edmund, "An Estimate of the Degrees of the Mortality of mankind, drawn from curious tables of the births and funerals at the city of Breslaw", *Philosophical Transactions Royal Society of London*, 17:196 (1693), 596–610. Halley developed the first life table, This, however, could not be used by English Life insurance, on account of the numerous assumptions he had made. These and related developments are explored in Rothstein's pioneering study of the risk factor as a concept in public health and medical thought. See Rothstein, William G., *Public Health and the Risk Factor: A History of an Uneven Medical Revolution*. Rochester, NY, Rochester University Press (2003). Like Rothstein's work, the latter part of this book relies predominately on North American material, largely due to the fact that a multitude of early debates around risk appeared in printed form in the US (much of which is now digitized).

[34] Zachmann, Karin, "Risk in Historical Perspective: Concepts, Contexts, and conjunctions," in Klüppelberg, Claudia, Daniel Straub, Isabell M. Welpe eds., *Risk A Multidisciplinary Introduction*, London, Springer (2014), 4.

[35] See Feinleib, Manning. "Health Statistics, History of," *Encyclopedia of Biostatistics,* 4 (2005). On p. 2 Feinleib notes how the City of London was amongst the first to collect death statistics, from 1538 onwards within the Church of England. Parish clerks submitted weekly reports (published from 1604 until 1842 when they were replaced reports from the Registrar General), which were examined by authorities to detect the onset of an epidemic while warning wealthy citizens to leave. These weekly Bills of Mortality were noted by the authorities who were to take actions if they detected the onset of an epidemic, gave wealthier citizens a warning to leave the city. Rothstein, *Public Health and the Risk Factor*, p.12 discusses the collection of this and similar data in other cities and regions, citing, among other sources. See also Daston, Lorraine, *Classical*

Graunt (1620–1674) and Sir William Petty (1623–1687) sought to draw "inferences about life expectancy and patterns of disease" from these data.[36]

Although highlighting the limits of early life tables and their commercial exploitation, Zachmann points to the role of deliberate risk taking among merchants and seafarers, who contributed to the use and creation of insurance as well as other risk-mitigation measures. This had been discussed in pioneering research on maritime insurance conducted by the historian Samuel Rosen in the 1930s.[37] In line with Rosen and Bonß, Zachmann describes the gradual evolution of the use of risk-language in relation to commercial ventures and describes the use of risk as a descriptive category within the discussion of activities. She argues that:[38] "risk was no longer seen only as danger and passively endured as fate, but taken as a challenge that could pay off if their calculations worked out."[39] She further highlights the slow but gradual creation of insurance markets which eventually came to facilitate the operation of these activities,[40] however, stating that initially "contractors relied on rules of thumb many forms of experience rather than statistical approaches."[41] Matters were similar in the area of medical

---

Probability in the Enlightenment, Princeton, NJ, Princeton University Press (1995) and Cassedy, James H., *Demography in Early America,* Cambridge, MA, Harvard University Press (2013).

[36] Stolley, Paul D., and Tamar Lasky, *Investigating Disease Patterns: the Science of Epidemiology*. New York, NY, Scientific American Library (1995), p. 27. The literature credits Graunt and Petty with a great deal, including the calculation of expectations of life and survivorship probabilities. However, it must be kept in mind that much of this observational analysis was speculative. Thus, Feinleib in "Health Statistics" reminds us that it was Antoine Deparcieux (1703–1768) who published the first correct life tables in two stages (1746 and 1760), albeit that core ideas such as the concept of competing risk can be traced to d'Alembert (1761).

[37] Rosen, Samuel, "The Origin and Development of the Modern Maritime Law." *Law Society Journal,* 6 (1934): 241–52.

[38] Bonß, Wolfgang, *Vom Risiko: Unsicherheit und Ungewißheit in der Moderne*. Hamburg, HIS Verlag-Gesellschaft (1995).

[39] Zachman, "Risk in Historical Perspective." p. 6.

[40] See also Daston, Lorraine, "The Domestication of Risk: Mathematical Probability and Insurance, 1650–1830," in L. Krüger ed., *The Probabilistic Revolution*, Cambridge, MA, MIT Press (1987), pp. 237–260.

[41] Zachman, "Risk in Historical Perspective," p. 6.

practice and observation, which underwent a first wave of professionalization with the publication of textbooks focusing on surgical techniques; albeit that there was no immediate link between risk taking and profit in this field. Risk as a concept appeared first in the early writings of surgeons. Here too risk was, for some time, seen as a qualitative concept for the description of the seriousness of an affliction, the difficulty of a procedure, or the danger associated with an error of omission or commission.

Specifically, we found some of the earliest of these "descriptive" medical uses of risk terminology in the writings of early Italian writers on surgery, such as Gabriele (also known as Camillo) de Ferrara (born about 1543 in Milan, died 1627 in Vienna). Ferrara studied surgery and then in 1591, joined a religious order of which he came to head by 1599.[42] He had his textbook on surgery entitled *Nova selva di cirurgia divisa in due parti* printed first in 1596 in Venice. In an early passage of this book, Ferrara discusses the risks of childbirth and measures which could be taken when there are no signs of life, some of which he concludes might "risk killing the child" [*rifchio d'uccider la creatura*].[43] Risk at this stage and in this context seems to have referred primarily to the risk of loss of life.

More frequent and specific use of risk terminology is made in later widely-read textbooks on surgery, such as the works of the Frenchman René Jacques Croissant de Garengeot (1688–1759). Garengeot came from a family of royal surgeons. He wrote his first textbook in 1720 entitled *Traité des opérations de chirurgie... avec les bandages qui conviennent à chaque appareil*, which appeared in English in 1723 as "A treatise of chirurgical operations, according to the mechanism of the parts of the experienced description of the instruments proper for chirurgical operations" (London: Printed for T. Woodward). Garengeot was widely respected and was inducted into the Royal Society in London in 1728, becoming Chief Surgeon of the Royal Infantry Regiment in 1742.[44] We

[42] Ferrara, Gabriele (Camillo) entry on the History of Vienna, webpage: https://www.geschichtewiki.wien.gv.at/index.php?title=Gabriele_Ferrara. Accessed November 2022.
[43] Ferrara, Gabriele (Camillo), *Nuova Selva di Cirvgia*, Venice, Giovanni Battista (1598).
[44] Garengeot, Rene Jacques de Croissant, entry on the Rare Book page, NYU dentistry, webpage: https://dental.nyu.edu/aboutus/rare-book-collection/18-c/garengeot.html, Accessed November 2022.

quote here from the French and English versions of his works to illustrate the use of the term "risk" as qualitative concept had evolved in both countries.[45]

Garengeot refers to risk, risks, and risking at several stages in his works. In most instances, these statements relate to the likelihood of an adverse outcome occurring. His discussion of Paronychia [Latin: Panaricium, French: Panaris], an infection of the finger, implies a concern that the potential severity of the condition was sometimes underestimated, which was a fair assessment given the lack of medications available at the time to fight the bacteria or fungus involved. The original French version reads, "le ne me reste plus pour finir lez traitemente de *Panaris*, ... don't les dolours sont si cruelles & si violentes, que le maladie **risqué** de predre la vie, si on ne lui donne un promt secours en evacuant la matierequi cause la maldie" (p. 175). We found this translated as follows in the English version as, "What remains, to make an end of the Cure of the several Sorts of Panaris ... the Pains whereof are so sharp and violent, that the Patient runs the **risk** of losing his Life, unless he is speedily relieved, by evacuating the Matter, which is the Cause of the Disease (p.146, emphasis)." On the obviously more serious matter of Quincy (or Squincy), a peritonsillar abscess, the English version of Garengeot's work again employs risk terminology to highlight the life-threatening nature of symptoms and complication. We read:

> The Respiration is almost suppressed: The Nostrils are very much dilated: The Patients can neither spit, nor lie down, without running the **risk** of being stifled: The Face is red and inflamed: The Eyes sparkle; and all those Accidents are generally attended with an acute Fever. The Prognoftick of that Disease is more or less dangerous, according to the Difficulty of breathing and swallowing for since Life is only preserved by the Air we breathe and by Food it follows that the more difficult the

[45] De Garengeot, René-Jacques Croissant, *Traité des Operations de Chirurgie: Suivant la Méchanique des parties du Corps Humain,* Chez Claude Robustel, ruë S. Jacques, au dessus de la fontaine S. Severin, à l'Image s. Jean (1720); Garengeot, René-Jacques Croissant de, *A Treatise of Chirurgical Operations, according to the Mechanism of the Parts of the Human Body*, London, Printed for Tho. Woodward (1723).

> Respiration and Deglutition are, the more dangerous the Disease will be. (P. 301, emphasis added).

Garengeot's work also uses the term "hazard" in conjunction with "risk," but again the terminology ascribes qualitative meaning to these concepts with no discernible differentiation. Here, we quote from a passage entitled "Of the Amputation of the Arm in the Joint" as it appeared in the English version of the same work:

> This is a very difficult and long Operation and therefore to remove those Difficulties, a Surgeon must never undertake it, without the Advice of Physicians, and other experienced Surgeons. Before he proceeds to that Operation, his Dressing must be ready ... When I say that he scrapes the Bone with the Point of the Needle, I mean, that he must pierce the Flesh by passing the Needle as near the Bone as possible but the Bone ought not to be grated; so that Operation would be extremely painful and the Point of the Needle being blunted, by striking against the Bone, would be no longer able to make an End of the Operation: Besides, if the Ligature was so near the Bone, the Surgeon would run the Hazard of cutting it, by separating the Bone from the Flesh, as I shall say hereafter. And if the Ligature was too far from the Bone, he would run the **risk** of palling the Needle through the Vessels, opening them, and occasioning a great Disorder. (pp. 521 and 522, emphasis added).

While the early usage of risk terminology in this type of surgical text largely sought to highlight levels of danger to life, subsequent semi-religious Spanish language texts touching on medical matters engaged in discussions of risks associated with an activity (or its avoidance) as compared to benefits; whereby we often find intermingled statements about tangible physical risks and spiritual risks. We would, however, be reluctant to attribute this more advanced use of risk terminology to the engagement of Spanish speaking elites in seafaring activities and their link to considerations of risk at several levels. Our view is based on two reasons: Firstly, the largely accidental reason which gave rise to these discussions, namely a religious tractate requiring priests to perform caesarean surgery on a dead or dying pregnant woman to save an unborn child. Secondly and relatedly, the semi-religious moral connotations attached to key aspects of these discussions, where risk was often associated with questions of moral trespass or wrongdoing rather than purely practical considerations.[46]

In 1745, the Sicilian born archpriest Francesco Emanuele Cangiamila (1702–1763) published a book advocating the performance of caesarean sections on dead or dying pregnant women, in order to allow for the baptism of the unborn child. Several clerics, including the Spanish Cistercian monk Antonio Rodriguez (1703–1777) and the Friar Francisco González Laguna of lima (1729–1799), reiterated Cangimilia's postulates in later publications and facilitated the wide dissemination of Cangiamilia's views. Francesco Emanuele Cangiamila (1702–1763) was born in Palermo. After studying and practicing law, he worked for the church and was ordained as priest in 1724, subsequently obtaining a doctorate in theology in 1728. He became archpriest of Palma, and upon returning to Palermo became director of the seminary in that city, where he published his highly influential *Embriologia Sacra* (English translation: Sacred Embryology) in 1745. Cangiamila's work aimed at promoting the performance of caesarean sections on dead and dying women in order to extract and baptize the fetus. One of Cangimila's key experiences apparently involved the extraction and baptism of a live fetus from a dead woman in 1736 in Palma. Cangiamila's writings and interventions were met with approval by the ruling members of the clergy and aristocracy. He was appointed in 1748 to canon theologian of the cathedral of Palermo,

[46] Efforts to employ probability considerations of one form or another to moral questions have a long pedigree in Catholic Spanish philosophical writing. Accordingly, the Dominican Bartolomé de Medina (1527–1581) who taught at the University of Salamanca held that If an opinion is probable, it is lawful to follow it, even though an opposing opinion is also, or even more probable. Controversies around probabilism were widespread, However, the Spanish Jesuit and Professor Juan Azor (1559–1603) who argued that "All the controversy here is about whether when there are contrary opinions it is permissible for the physician to treat the patient according to the opinion of others, against his own … . [I]f the opinion of the others is probable, even if it is not safer or more probable or common, the physician can follow their opinion with integrity because it derives from probable reasons and causa, which vacates imprudence and temerity, and for that reason the physician does not incur sin by admitting". See Schwartz, Daniel, "Probabilism Reconsidered: Deference to Experts, Types of Uncertainty, and Medicines," *Journal of the History of Ideas,* 75.3 (2014): 373–393. It is possible that Azor influenced Cangiamilia's work.

prebend of royal appointment, and then abbot of the abbey of SS. Giovanni and Ermete, as well as serving the inquisition in Sicily.[47] Cangiamila's suggestions were subsequently adopted by the king of the Two Sicilies, Charles VII in a law of 9 August 1749. When 10 years later, Charles VII of the Two Sicilies came to occupy the Spanish throne as Charles III, it took him two years until 1761 to pass a similar law and send a copy of his earlier law, along with a copy of the second edition of Cangimila's *Embriologia Sacra* (in Latin), to the bishops of Spain.[48] A Spanish cedula of 1804, later on ruled that transgressors (those failing to act on the demand to conduct a caesarean section on a dead or dying mother) would be guilty of homicide.

Theologically, Cangiamila has been described as Thomist, who, in line with Thomas Aquinas's teaching sought to protect human life. Thomistic tradition respected and sought to defend human life from the moment of its conception. This led Cangimila to believe that the eternal salvation of the unborn child should be of paramount importance to priests. Cangiamila was also concerned with abortions and miscarriages which he claimed had increased in number. Cangiamila thought the causes of this were often outside the control of mothers. In terms of contents, Cangiamila's *Sacred Embryology* advised priests on a range of topics, including how to give pastoral care to pregnant women, how to prevent abortions, how to baptize miscarried or grossly malformed fetuses, how to perform the caesarean operation, and how to assist the drowned. Cangimila's writing emphasized God's love for unborn children, expressed concerns with the limited qualification of midwifes and made suggestions on how to address this. He quoted other authors, explored issues of risk and uncertainty in relation to childbirth, and cited cases of successfully performed caesarean sections.[49]

---

[47] Cangiamila, Francesco Emanuele, entry in the Trecccani Insitute's Italian Encyclopedia of Sciences, Letters and Arts, webpage https://www.treccani.it/enciclopedia/francesco-emanuele-cangiamila_%28Dizionario-Biografico%29/ Accessed November 2022.

[48] Rigau-Pérez, José G., "Surgery at the Service of Theology: Postmortem Caesarean Sections in Puerto Rico and the Royal Cedula of 1804," *Hispanic American Historical Review,* 75:3 (1995), 385.

[49] *Ibid.* p. 384.

Despite acknowledging uncertainty and taking at times a caring stance, there was a sense of urgency and fanaticism in Cangiamila's writing that disquieted later theologians. Accordingly, Joseph F. Donceel, S.J. commented in a 1970 issue of *Theological Studies*:

> The complete title of the book is "Sacred embryology, or about the duty of priests, physicians, and others concerning the eternal salvation of the little ones who are in the womb." This is a strange and gruesome book. The author, a canon-theologian-inquisitor of Palermo, Sicily, is convinced that the human soul is present almost at once after conception and that unbaptized human beings cannot be saved. A great part of his book is about the need and the manner of practicing a caesarean operation on all pregnant women who die before delivery, so that the foetus may duly be baptized. The task is to be entrusted to a surgeon; if no surgeon is available, a barber or a midwife must take over. If none of these "experts" is at hand, the parish priest himself will have to do the job. Cangiamila's book explains how to go about it. The author inveighs against overzealous followers who do not wait until the woman is dead before setting to work. The good canon's Sacred Embryology must have led to a considerable amount of sacred butchery.[50]

This being said, Cangiamila's work on saving unborn life, included discussions about medical risk, uncertainty, and risk taking more generally, and therefore merits being examined in its original version, as do related works by his followers Rodriguez and Laguna. Here we quote from a later Spanish edition of Cangiamila's *Embriologia Sagrada* (itself translated from the original 1745 Italian Version), which was published in 1774 in Madrid. The passage below was translated by the academic historian Anthony M. Joseph into English:[51]

---

[50] Donceel, Joseph F., "Immediate Animation and Delayed Hominization." *Theological Studies,* 31:1 (1970): 76–105.

[51] Cangimila, Francesco Emanuele, and Joaquín Castellot, *Embriologia Sagrada Ó Tratado De La Obligacion Que Tienen Los Curas, Confesores, Médicos, Comadres, Y Otras Personas, De Cooperar Á La Salvación De Los Niños Que Aún No Han Nacido, De Los Que Nacen Al Parecer Muertos, De Los Abortivos, De Los Monstruos, Etc.*, Madrid, Pedro Martin (1774). Trans. Anthony M. Joseph, *The Unborn Child: A History* (http://www.history of the unbornchild.org/cangiamila). Accessed November 2022.

> This Compendium now published, it seemed necessary to add some precautions regarding the caesarean operation on living women that Mr. Brunel, well known in this Court for his judgment and skill in the obstetric art, communicated to me. They are the following: This operation should not be undertaken if the time of delivery has not arrived, as much as to not anticipate it too much as to avoid causing the death of the foetus, extracting it when it is not yet time. The section of the tegument must not be done, neither upon the white line that joins the two straight muscles nor upon the central part of the said muscles. For the said line being purely ligamentary, it could not be re-joined afterwards but with much difficulty, as there would be a danger of injuring the hypogastric artery which runs from the center of said muscles to be anastomosed with the external mammary. The section of the womb must be avoided by the side where the placenta is found attached to this viscera, on account of the copious effusion of blood which originates from this and the resulting great **risk** of losing the mother. (P. 16 in translation).

We find similar cautioning against risky actions in a later passage which we quote here from the first 1745 Italian version and then present it in translation, "Più anche pericolosa è giudicata l'incisione de la vessica … lo stesso Pietro Franco, che l'inventò, e gli riusci prosperamente in un Fanciullino; la condannò subito, come di grandissimo **rischio**, e quasi temerari: attribuendo il buon esito, ch'egli stesso ne avea osservato alla fortuna." (p. 190, emphasis added) This translates roughly as, "Even more dangerous is the incision of the vessica … which Pietro Franco, who invented it, and risked it successfully in a Child; immediately condemned, as of great risk, and almost reckless: attributing the good outcome, which he himself had observed, to luck."

Notwithstanding the questionable nature of Cangiamila's overall agenda, both passages show a progression of the use of risk terminology in connection with medical procedure. In the first passage, readers are cautioned against potential mistakes which would endanger the life of the pregnant woman. They are conducting the operation too early and performing a surgical incision incorrectly in the wrong place. In the second passage, another procedure is described as even more dangerous with the added evidence that a named medic, described it as risky to the level of being reckless. In other words, a key criterion for the use of a medical procedure is seen in its riskiness. Thus, surgical procedures were being compared according to riskiness and it was made clear that success of a procedure in a single case did not demonstrate that it was low risk or risk-free, as the outcome could be a chance result. Of course, the very fact that Cangiamila was fielding these ideas repeatedly in connection with his advocacy of the use of cesarean section to safe yet unborn children, implicitly reflected the questionable and potentially inhumane nature of his demand in relation to pregnant women. In other words, intense propaganda was needed to encourage priests and midwives to engage in acts of religiously motivated intervention and potential homicide, as well as to gain consent of relatives for the advocated procedure.

One of the disseminators, and presumably also modifiers, of Cangimila's views was Antonio Jose Rodriguez (1705–1781), a Benedictine monk, born in Merida, Spain.[52] Rodriguez wrote several works on medical and theological subjects. This included his *Nuevo Aspecto de Teologia Medico Moral,* a title which literally translates as New Aspects of Medico-Moral Theology. The first full version of this work (entailing all four volumes) was printed in Madrid in 1763.[53] We quote from this version. On page 85 in the section on births, under the subtitle "Customs in Cold Regions," we find the following advice, "La Medicina, como sabidora tan de cerca de estos peligros, ya tiene puestas sus respectivas precauciones para semejantes **riesgos**. Por eso manda, que la agua, v vino con que se

[52] Cook, Sherburne F., "Sarría's Treatise on the Cesarean Operation, 1830: Part I," *California and Western Medicine,* 47:2 (1937), 107–108.

[53] Rodríguez, Antonio José. *Nuevo Aspecto de Theologia Medico-moral y Ambos Derechos, o Paradoxas Fisico-teologico-legales…*, Imprenta real de la Gaceta (1763); Warren, Adam, "An Operation for Evangelization: Friar Francisco Gonzalez Laguna, the Cesarean Section, and Fetal Baptism late Colonial Peru," *Bulletin of the History of Medicine,* 83:4 (2009), 647–75. Warren mentions that Rodriguez published a first version of his work in 1742. It is doubtful that this was fully comparable to Cangimilia's Embryologia, since subsequent legal edicts refer to Cangimila's 1745 *Embryologia Sacra* instead of Rodriguez's *Nuevo aspecto;* Pardo-Tomás, José, and Àlvar Martínez-Vidal, "The Ignorance of Midwives: The Role of Clergymen in Spanish Enlightenment Debates on Birth Care," in O.P. Grell and A. Cunningham, eds., *Medicine and Religion in Enlightenment Europe*, London, Routledge (2017), pp. 49–72. This essay noted that Rodriguez felt that Cangimilia's *Embryologia Sacra* had moved the piety of Italians although it did not acknowledge its debt to him, see p. 54.

lavan, se entibien." This roughly translates as, "Medicine, knowing so closely about these dangers, already has its respective precautions for such **risks**. That is why it is commanded that the water and wine with which they wash be warmed, regardless of the climate." In this paragraph danger and risk are both used by Rodriguez, with danger denoting adverse events that can occur without specific human (medicinal) intervention and risk pertaining to adverse events which can be avoided through human action, namely the warming of water and wine, and hence constitute a risk in the sense of being a potential error of omission. On page 139, Rodriguez then uses risk terminology to speculate about the morality of past practices and present recommendations, including the use of the caesarean section. We quote from the original, "Esto mismo deben afirmar hoy todos los Thelogos, y Canonistas qué lieven la contraria, y es la razon muy conforme. Antes se ignoraba el modo de baptizar al infante, y de su valider dentro del ùtero; y como la vida espiritual que tanto vale, estaba en evidente **riesgo**, dictaba la piedad por el abandono de la temporal de la madre." This roughly translates as, "This same thing must be affirmed today by all the theologians and canonists who believe the contrary, and the reason is very much in agreement. Before, the manner of baptizing the infant and of its validation in the womb was unknown;[54] and since the spiritual life, which is so valuable, was in evident **risk**, piety dictated the abandonment of the mother's temporal life." Our understanding of this text, which can be interpreted in several ways, would be as follows: in the past, it was not understood that the unborn child could be baptized in the womb. Therefore, the risk to that child's spiritual life made it "moral" to abandon the temporal worldly life of the mother (which presumably

[54] *Ibid.*, p. 52-3, here the latter authors discuss Rodriguez's view that 'recent advances in Physica and Medicine in the last century' had shown 'experimentally' that the embryo was animated from the very first day of conception. Interestingly Rodriguez deviated from Cangiamila's advocacy of the caesarean section as vehicle for baptism in all cases (dead or mortally ill mothers). Rodriguez recommended intra-uterine baptism where the mother was alive: "Once the position of the head of the foetus had been detected or, failing that, of its chest, the surgeon or the midwife had to inject, by means of a syringe, the baptismal water while reciting the canonical formula for this sacrament". In the case of the death of the pregnant woman, however, "caesarean section always had to be carried out, so that the still alive foetus could be baptised."

refers to her potential death resulting from a caesarean section). In other words, Rodriguez argued that past belief about spiritual risk to the unborn justified certain actions. In writing this, he implied that this moral justification no longer existed now that it was understood that the unborn child could be baptized in the womb.

An interesting case of the dissemination of Cangmila's ideas and the associated risk terminology can be found in the work of Friar Francisco González Laguna. The historian Adam Warren examined how, by publishing a medical-theological treatise in 1781, Friar Francisco González Laguna of Lima initiated a campaign to train Andean priests[55] to perform post-mortem caesarean sections for the purpose of baptizing the fetus.[56] Laguna's writing is of interest here, because of its references to risk and uncertainty. Little is known about Laguna other than that he worked in Lima and was well respected in his field. Thus, a government functionary gave a positive evaluation of his 1781 work *Elzelo sacerdotal para con los niños no-nacidos*[57] to the ruling viceroy which subsequently inspired multiple government decrees requiring priests to learn and perform the caesarean section in Peru.[58] Risk is referred to by Laguna in several instances, mostly in connection with potential threats to a fetus's or mother's life. Accordingly, he warns against the risky punishment of a pregnant female slave, stating that the unborn child is not made of bronze (p. 181). Particularly interesting is his use of risk terminology in connection with breast feeding. Here he states that "No se niega que haya en ocasiones causas legitimas para evadir la lactaction, de que hacen mencion los Doctores. Primera: si la Madre padece alguna enfermedad contagiosa, que pueda trascender á el hijo. Segunda: si es tan debil de complexion, que con el alimento del Infante desfallezca demasiadamente,

---

[55] Blum, Anne S., *et al.*, "Women, Ethnicity, and Medical Authority: Historical Perspectives on Reproductive Health in Latin America," Center for Iberian and Latin American Studies, San Diego (2004), p. 20. This suggests that it is unclear how many caesarean sections were performed outside of Lima.

[56] Warren, Adam. "An Operation for Evangelization".

[57] Francisco González Laguna, *El Zelo Sacerdotal para con los Niños No-Nacidos ...* Lima, Imp. de los Niños Expósitos (1781).

[58] Warren, "An Operation for Evangelization." pp. 647–8.

con **riesgo** conocido de su Salud." (p. 251, emphasis added) This roughly translates as:

> It is not denied that there are sometimes legitimate causes to avoid the lactation mentioned by the Doctors. First: if the mother suffers from some contagious disease, which can spread to the child. Second: if she is so weak in complexion, that with the nourishment of the Infant she becomes too weak, with known **risk** to her health.

In this paragraph, Laguna essentially attempts to provide a risk assessment as to when breast feeding would not be recommended. His advice relates to two types of risks, risk to the infant, resulting from a contagious disease and risk to the health of the mother, due to her own weakness or ill health. In other words, potential risks to infant and mother are meant to guide practical decisions on breast feeding, instead of medical dogma or religion.

Laguna's work exerted some influence on medical practice in Peru and helped the church regain ground as provider of medical advice and service, against the increasing secularization of these activities which we observe in other countries.[59] As Warren notes, Laguna's works served as basis for further instructional writings published in the region. In later writings, which were mostly addressed at clerics, risk terminology was frequently employed in discussions of the danger of moral wrongdoing (or trespass), shifting in this sense away from the contexts of medical advice.[60] Some documents also indicate that the influence of Catholicism on legislation pertaining to obstetrics in the American colonies and perhaps to a lesser degree in Continental Europe was quite strong.

The support for caesarean sections to save or baptize unborn life, meanwhile, did not find support in protestant contexts.[61] Apparently

---

[59] *Ibid.*, p. 650–1.

[60] See especially Arrese, Pedro José de. *Rudimentos Fisico-canonico-morales,* Nueva Guatemala, De Arevalo (1786).

[61] Schäfer, Daniel, "Medical Practice and the Law in the Conflict between Traditional Belief and Empirical Evidence: Post-mortem Caesarean Section in the Nineteenth Century." *Medical History,* 43:4 (1999): 485–501.

protestant writers rarely worried about the salvation or rescue of the unborn, while being concerned with the fate of the mother. Here, emphasis was placed on the risk that a pregnant woman might only appear to be dead. Practitioners and local ordinances hence generally advised against the use of caesarean sections and recommended the use of forceps for the extraction of a fetus from a sick, dead, or dying mother, while the fear of persons only appearing to be dead was evidenced for example in the 1811 prohibition by the Prussian state of early autopsies.[62]

By the late 1700s and early 1800s, "risk" as a term and concept within medical writing, was loosely established, with different but similar qualitative meanings being given to it in different contexts. Thus, we find a well-known publication on the Yellow Fever outbreak in Philadelphia (a viral disease spread by mosquito bites) with the title *An Account of the Risk, Progress, And Termination, of the Malignant Fever lately prevalent in Philadelphia*, published in 1793, the year of that outbreak. Risk in this publication refers to a mix of infection risks (likelihood of infection) and mortality risks, as they were faced by individuals and groups of populations.[63] Again, the use of risk terminology in this report is largely qualitative, with risk being primarily used to describe dangerous or adverse events which were likely to occur.

At the end of the 1700s, risk terminology appeared repeatedly within the English language medical and surgical literature, with the term "risk" being typically used in connection with dangers associated with certain medical conditions or with the employment of particular surgical procedures. Here we cite from a leading English language textbook of the time, which is James Latta's (1754–1804) *A Practical System of Surgery*. Latta was admitted to the Royal College of Surgeons in 1783, which also listed him as Fellow.[64] His textbook on surgery was published in several forms, including a two volume version in 1793/4 and a three volume version

[62] *Ibid.*, p. 488.

[63] Carey, Mathew, *A Short Account of the Malignant Fever, lately prevalent in Philadelphia*, Philadelphia, J. Johnson (1794).

[64] Latta, James entry in The Royal College of Surgeons of Edinburgh Digital Collections, webpage: https://archiveandlibrary.rcsed.ac.uk/surgeon/3770400-james-latta. Accessed November 2022.

which appeared in 1795, reflecting the rapid growth of knowledge in the area at the time.[65] Between 1794 and 1800, a total of 12 editions of his work were published in English and German, and Worldcat listed 27 English language versions for the period from 1793 and 2005.[66] Latta applied the term "risk" to the context of adverse events resulting from a disease or injury, quite frequently and highlighted avoidable risk from a poorly carried out surgical procedure (that is an action or mistake he advises against). In this sense, Latta's use of risk terminology closely follows the precedent of Garengeot, albeit that Latta's use of the word "risk" was more frequent. Here we quote a few passages from the 1795 edition of his work, which is the first of the three volume (or full) version of his work. An early section on sutures (p. 53, emphasis added) states, "Half an inch in most cases will be sufficient; and in none perhaps will it be necessary to perforate at more than an inch distance from the lips of the wound. Some have directed a single knot, with the ends put twice through the ring, as sufficient for securing the lips of a wound; but this seems doubtful; and, considering the very little trouble there is in tying a knot, it can never be eligible to run any **risk** to avoid doing this." In other words, Latta recommends limited intervention in terms of perforating tissue, but points to the risk of not securing sutures with a proper knot which is outside the wound. Similarly, he comments on the procedure he proposes for a Hernia operation (p. 273, emphasis added). "Indeed, considering the little **risk** which attends the performance of this operation, it deserves to be considered, whether the mere circumstance of the extreme pain suffered by the patient be not a sufficient reason for operating as soon as possible, even independent of any other consideration." Latto also used risk terminology when describing what he considered difficult procedures. Hence, he states in connection with the operation of a bladder stone (p. 460, emphasis added), "Thus the urine which escapes from the urethra will have a free passage but, during the time of operating, it will be necessary for an assistant to keep the testicle out of the way of the knife; as, unless care be taken in this

---

[65] Latta, James, *A Practical System of Surgery*, Edinburgh, G. Mudie & Son, A. Guthrie, and J. Fairbairn; and London, for J. Johnson, and Ogilvie & Speare (1795).

[66] Latta, James surgeon in Edinburgh, entry in OCLC Worldcat Identities, webpage: https://worldcat.org/identities/lccn-nr92030342/. Accessed November 2022

respect, it will run a great **risk** of being wounded." Latto, in other words, was cognizant of risks of commission and omission in surgical contexts and used risk language to delineate the boundaries of what he believed to be the proper action of surgeons in different contexts.

The US medical literature presents us with similar uses of risk terminology. Apart from texts on surgery, this can be found in connection with the literature on midwifery and pregnancy, whereby the literature from the 1800s is more advanced and less tainted by religious dogma than the texts we discussed earlier. Here we quote from a well-known book on midwifery which was published in New York in 1807.[67] A sub-section entitled *Natural Labour* states:

> There is, however, no absolute criterion, by which false pains can certainly be distinguished from true labour pains; but by examining the effect which the pains have upon the internal orifice of the womb. Every midwife, every mother knows the nature of this examination: I shall only observe, that it is most conveniently made whilst the patient lies on her left side, with a pillow between her knees; the midwife sitting behind her is to make the examination with the utmost caution and deliberation, carefully avoiding all rudeness, by which the parts may be irritated; and above all things, taking care to run no **risk** of bursting the membranes, if the internal orifice of the womb should be found more open, and the membranes more advanced through it than she expected. (P. 70, emphasis added).

Here, the word risk is employed in connection with the avoidance of iatrogenic damage occurring during an examination and the identification of the potential riskiness of the examination is underpinned by the warning that the midwife might find the body of the patient in a different than expected stage.

Outside the mainstream surgical literature, "risk" was also referred to in connection with life-style habits that could have an adverse impact on

[67] Bard, Samuel, *A Compendium of the Theory and Practice of Midwifery: Containing Practical Instructions for the Management of Women, During Pregnancy, in Labour, and in Childbed. Illustrated by Many Cases, and Particularly Adapted to the Use of Students*, New York, NY. Collins and Company (1807).

aspects of health. This is illustrated in the following passage from a then popular book on eye health written for general readers and medical practitioners which appeared in 1822 in English but drew on an earlier German manuscript.[68] Here we read:

> The tightness of our neck-cloths presents a serious obstacle to the return of the blood by the jugular veins; and, in order to get rid of a pale countenance, we **risk** the swelling of the glands, lymphatic tumours, vertigoes, and even apoplexy itself. The present state of human knowledge ought never to reconcile itself, in particular, with that most barbarous and destructive custom of tight lacing, to which both sexes at present submit; but it is to no purpose to expatiate on its deleterious effects, as the false desire of pleasing, and the clamour of prejudice, will always drown the voice of reason. (P. 91, emphasis added).[69]

In the mainstream medical literature, meanwhile, the utilization of risk terminology in medical discourse expanded, particularly in connection with controversial issues such as vaccination, about which much was written in the late 1700s and early 1800s.[70] Thus, the 1808 issue of *Medical Communications of the Massachusetts Medical Society* included a critical correspondence on the effectiveness of a specific vaccination

---

[68] Beer, Georg Josef, *Art of Preserving the Sight Unimpaired to Extreme Old Age: And of Re-establishing and Strengthening it when it Becomes Weak; with Instructions how to Proceed in Accidental Cases which Do Not Require the Assistance of Professional Men, and the Mode of Treatment Proper for the Eyes During, and Immediately After, the Small-pox; to which are Added Observations on the Inconveniences and Dangers Arising from the Use of Common Spectacles*, London, Henry Colburn (1822).

[69] An interesting unrelated example of disease spread through fashion relates to primarily Western demand for fur of the Manchurian Marmot in the early 1900s, the hunting of which triggered a widespread epidemic of pneumonic plague. Shen, Yubin, "Pneumonic Plagues, Environmental Changes, and the International Fur Trade: The Retreat of Tarbagan Marmots from Northwest Manchuria, 1900s–30s," *Frontiers of History in China,* 14:3 (2019), 291–322 and also the early analysis by, Lien-Teh, Wu, and Frederick Eberson. "Transmission of Pulmonary and Septicaemic Plague among Marmots," *Epidemiology & Infection,* 16:1 (1917), 1–11.

[70] Rothstein, *Public Health and the Risk Factor*, p. 15.

technique known as Sutton's method. Risk terminology plays a central role in this contribution, and it is worthwhile examining this, as it reflects early advances in the qualitative understanding of risk. The corresponding author of this contribution states that[71]

> [the] youngest son had taken the natural smallpox, after having been vaccinated, I think it but justice to contradict the report; and to state, for your satisfaction, the real circumstances of the case, which are as follows: When he was about two months old, he was inoculated for the smallpox, in the Suttonian method, by a physician in Ireland, who has been very generally successful in inoculation, and pronounced by him to be perfectly free from the **risk** of infection; notwithstanding which, he caught the infection, about a fortnight since, and is now recovering from the natural smallpox. (p. 202, emphasis added).

The corresponding writer refers to Robert Sutton Senior's modification of an existing vaccination technique which involved a minor stab through the skin with a sharp lancet and the use of cause cow pox infected material.[72] Robert Sutton's son, Daniel, with his brothers and several other partners, set up a chain of franchises across England, parts of Europe and North America which offered the "Suttonian Method." Daniel apparently inoculated 22,000 people between 1763 and 1766 with only three deaths and profited from this. Sutton's contemporaries in the Royal College of Physicians found it difficult to emulate this approach and described the Suttons as "men of confined abilities." In 1796, Daniel Sutton published his observations and ideas concerning smallpox inoculation in an autobiography entitled *The Inoculator*, which was part instruction manual and part advertisement. Later research indicated that Sutton's cowpox virus was transmitted by contact and probably could only infect through cuts or scratches in the skin.[73]

---

[71] Massachusetts Medical Society, *Medical Communications of the Massachusetts Medical Society*, Boston, Published by the Society (1808).

[72] Boylston, Arthur. "The Origins of Vaccination: Myths and Reality," *Journal of the Royal Society of Medicine,* 106:9 (2013), 351–2.

[73] *Ibid.*, p. 353.

What is particularly interesting about the short report to the Massachusetts Medical Society mentioned above, is the writer's statement that "a physician in Ireland, who has been very generally successful in inoculation [with the Suttonian method], ... pronounced [his son] free from the **risk** of infection." In other words, the vaccination was declared to create an absolute freedom from the possibility of a future infection with smallpox and the term risk was used for expressing this. The correspondent then identified further uncertainties, which he also described in terms of risk terminology:

> It remains for us to describe the methods which have been proposed to obviate the few evils, which may arise in the practice of vaccination. These evils are the two following, for there are not any others worthy consideration. The first is the **risk** of the inoculator's relying on imperfect vaccination. The second the **risk** which every individual incurs of his liability to smallpox a second time, or what is the same, of smallpox after cowpock. (P. 226, emphasis added).

Although the case is not entirely clear, we can surmise that the writer alludes to the possibilities of skin penetration being insufficient or the vaccine material (cowpox scab) being faulty or insufficient. In the second sentence, the writer is more likely to refer to the nature of the infecting agent itself having changed. These scenarios are thus seen as risks or uncertainties around an ordinarily well-working or "risk-free" treatment.

By the early 1800s, we thus have a reasonably well-established repertory for the use of risk terminology in connection with medical activities. Firstly, this includes, at probably the simplest level, the use of the term "risk" or "risky" in surgical texts and pamphlets where it serves primarily as a qualitative indicator for the dangerousness of a condition or procedure, and later on also a qualitative indicator of the level of the danger associated with different procedures or conditions. Second, in the context of infection, vaccination/inoculation, "risk" is used again as a qualitative indicator to describe the likelihood of acquiring an infection (which might be characterized as high or low risk) or avoiding it (such as the no risk expectation falsely attributed to the Sutton method in the case above). Thirdly, in the case of Spanish and Italian semi-religious texts (some of which also appeared in Latin), risk terminology can occur in a somewhat strangely mixed form, where it is used to describe both hazards of surgery or disease, as well as dangers of moral trespass ("irregularidad" in the Spanish originals) associated with certain actions or their commission or omission.[74]

However, a more in-depth exploration of the potential of risk assessment as an analytical concept in medicine, medical care, health care, and public health, which would combine insights from statistics, probability, medicine, and medical observation, had to wait until the late 1800s, notwithstanding earlier sporadic applications. One such sporadic application, concerns the important use of the idea of risk as a means of investigating the health of occupational groups, rather than individuals *per se*, in the work of the Italian physician Bernadino Ramazzini (1633–1714). Ramazzini studied medicine in Parma, where he developed an interest in occupational medicine.[75] He taught in Modena and then from 1682 onward in Padua. His main work *De Morbis Artificum Diatriba* was published in Latin in Modena in 1700 and identified the ill-health effects of a number of occupational pursuits.[76] We quote here from a faithful 1822 French translation of Ramazzini's *De Morbis Artificium*, which has been credited with popularizing Ramazzini's work in France and Germany.[77] Ramazzini's use of risk as concept was generally qualitative and occupation specific. Thus, we read under *Diseases of Wigmakers and Hairdressers*, "Les coiffeurs actuels doivent faire attention aux cheveux dont ils se

[74]The tendency to describe issues of moral trespass or sin as risk in parallel with medical dangers or illnesses was not a unique feature of the Spanish literature of the time. Dubos, René, *Man, Medicine, and Environment.* Harmondsworth, Pelican. 1968, p. 89 notes that the Scottish anatomist and neurologist Charles Bell stated as late as 1805 that insanity was the result of sin.

[75]Pope, Malcolm H., "Bernardino Ramazzini: The Father of Occupational Medicine." *Spine* 29:20 (2004), 2335–8.

[76]See Ramazzini, Bernardino, *De Morbis Artificum Diatriba...*, J. Corona, Modena (1700), sought to identify health risks faced by workers employed in specific occupations on a largely observational basis. William A. Guy (1810–1885), collected much data of relevance to occupational and public health but felt mathematics had very limited application to the results of observation. See Feinleib, "Health Statistics", p. 3

[77]Ramazzini, Bernardino, *Traite des Maladies des Artisans.* transl. and edited by Ph. Patissier, Paris, J.B. Baillière (1822).

servent pour la confection des perruques: s'ils proviennent d'un individu galeux ou teigneux, ils courent le risque de contracter la gale ou la teigne." (P. 293) This is translated as, "Current hairdressers must be careful about the hair they use for making wigs; if they come from a mangy or scabby individual, they run the **risk** of contracting scabies or ringworm." A later passage refers to illnesses of service workers, such as waiters in inns or cabarets. Here Ramazzini states, "Séjournant habituellement dans des endroits don't la chaleur est souvent étouffante et l'air altéré par maladies des miasmes de tout genre ... lemonadiers risquent de contracter une foule de maux." (P. 26) Which we freely translate as, "Usually staying in places where the heat is often stifling and the air altered by diseases of miasmas of all kinds, innkeepers and waiters risk contracting a host of ailments such as headache, difficulty in breathing, loss of appetite, nausea." In other words, Ramazzini believed that certain occupations presented specific types of health risks to workers, which was the task of medics to identify and, where possible, to treat or prevent. Although largely qualitative and observational in nature, Ramazzini's work had a major impact on the recognition of health risks associated with a number of occupations.

The Russian economist and statistician Ladislaus Josephovich Bortkiewicz's (1868–1931) provided an early quantitative application of statistics and probability theory to risk analysis, or more precisely, accident analysis. His work too related to occupational context, this time involving soldiers' deaths from horse kicks. Bortkiewicz's work represents an early application of probability theory and statistics to medical (accident) data, where probability theory is applied to observational data in order to draw conclusions about a series of accidents. Specifically, Bortikiewicz showed that the fatal accident data presented to him followed a random pattern in line with a distribution discovered earlier by the French mathematician Siméon Denis Poisson (1781–1840). Bortkiewicz's analysis, which he published in a short book in 1898,[78] answered the question whether the observed horse kick deaths involving

[78] von Bortkiewicz, Ladislaus, and Vladislav I. Bortkevič, *Das Gesetz der Kleinen Zahlen.* Leipzig, BG Teubner (1898). pp. 23–5.

122 soldiers over 20 years were due to chance/randomness or systematic factors such as inadequate experience or similar factors.[79]

Notwithstanding the exception of pioneers like Ramazzini and Bortkiewicz, who used risk terminology and risk thinking to investigate and describe illnesses or accidents of occupation groups, such applications were relatively unusual at the time. The reasons for the delay in the coming together of mathematics, statistics, and medicine included a number of practical factors. The late 1600s and the 1700s obviously marked the beginning of political arithmetic,[80] i.e. the collection of data with the purpose of making generalizations about groups of populations, which in theory could have included investigations of health, life expectancy, mortality, or morbidity risks. In reality, however, a number of obstacles made this difficult. Some of the most obvious obstacles included the presence of a large number of small states in much of Continental Europe. Pre-Napoleonic Germany during the mid-1700s comprised of around 300–350 states. This meant that state agencies which could have collected even straightforward statistics on births and deaths were often too small to do so effectively. Data collection, moreover, was often delegated to individuals of limited reliability or professionalism. Graunt himself had described the female parish searchers who provided the data for the *Bills of Mortality* as drunk and incompetent.[81] Meanwhile even minor population movements between territories could have a major impact on population distribution, while few territories provided rigorous systems for the registration of residents. This was paralleled by archaic practices of data registration, where information on births and deaths and general resident data was

---

[79] Mises, R. V., "über die Wahrscheinlichkeit seltener Ereignisse," *ZAMM-Journal of Applied Mathematics and Mechanics/Zeitschrift für Angewandte Mathematik und Mechanik,* 1:2 (1921): 121–4.

[80] Schiøtz, Aina, "Medical Statistics and Epidemiology–the Early History," *Norsk Epidemiologi,* 25, 1–2 (2015) dates the replacement of the term political arithmetic, to 1749 to the German Philosophy professor German Gottfried Aachenwall (1719–72) who derived the term statistics (from the Italian word *stato*) to depict all political, social and economic conditions in the state.

[81] Vaught, Jennifer C, "Reckoning Death: Women Searchers and the Bills of Mortality in early modern London," in M. Crane, H. S. Turner eds., *Rhetorics of Bodily Disease and Health in Medieval and Early Modern England*, London, Routledge (2016), pp. 135–150.

collected on a household or even estate basis, rather than for individuals. These problems affected the depth, penetration, and quality of data acquisition. As if this was not enough of a problem, there were problems relating to the limited medical expertise of those who collected data, which militated against the collation of accurate mortality or morbidity figures.

The medical statistician, Horst Fassl, lists four main factors which stood in the way of an integration of data collection with the analysis of risk and probability in medicine and public health.[82] One group of problems concerned the absence of agreed upon classifications of illnesses. Existing early classifications were problematic and not widely agreed upon.[83] It was not until the late 1700s that the work of Cullen was widely disseminated for this purpose in parts of the UK, but even then, few comparable systems existed in other countries.[84] Another major problem concerned the fact that the determination of causes of deaths and diagnoses of illnesses frequently relied on unqualified observers and, hence, was not reliable.[85] This problem was aggravated by the fact that population or census figures which could serve as basis for the calculation of frequencies for risk assessments were often unknown or flawed. Lastly, for some medical phenomena, like the occurrence of certain rarer illnesses, the small size of observable individuals militated against the possibility of accurate descriptions or comparisons on a mass observation basis.

---

[82] Fassl, Horst, "Geschichtliche Spekte," In H-J., Lange, J. Michaelis, K. Überla eds., *15 Jahre Medizinische Statistik und Aocumentation*, Berlin, Springer (1978), pp. 25–33.

[83] See Platter, Felix, *Praxeos Seu de Cognoscendis, Praedicendis, Praecavendis, Curandisque Affectibus Homini Incommodantibus Tractatus,* Vol. 1. Waldkirchius 1602/3; and de Lacroix, Francois Boissier de Sauvages. *Nosologia Methodica Sistens Morborum Classes,* Vol. 1. sumptibus fratrum de Tournes (1763).

[84] Cullen, William, *Apparatus ad Nosologiam Methodicam*, Amsterdam [Edinburgh, 1769] (1775). See also Cullen, William, *Nosology: or, a Systematic Arrangement of Diseases... Translated from the Latin of W. Cullen,* Edinburgh, William Creech (1800).

[85] Feinleib, "Health statistics", p. 4 highlights that it was not until 1893, that Jacques Bertillon (1851–1922) proposed a system that became the International List of Causes of Death (see International Classification of Diseases (ICD)). Prinzing, Friedrich, *Handbuch der Medizinischen Statistik*, Jena, G. Fischer (1931) questioned the accuracy of diagnoses of death some time ago, and like Feinleib, noted the temptation of practitioners to obscure or falsify the cause of death to save respectable families embarrassment in certain sorts of death.

Some of these problems were more fully understood, on a theoretical level, once greater clarity had been gained about issues such as the law of large numbers. However, on a practical level, the collection of statistics in virtually all areas of public life improved only slowly.[86] Pioneers who attempted to use observational data systematically for therapeutic strategies included the Royal Navy surgeon James Lind (1716–1794)[87] and the French doctor Pierre Charles Alexandre Louis (1787–1872).[88] Like others, Louis faced significant opposition from the medical establishment of his time for his advocacy of data collection and analysis.[89] Fassl summarizes this concisely as consisting of frequent assertions that each person had individual characteristics and that medical treatment required instinctive engagement with the totality of an individual.[90]

Nonetheless, the year 1829 saw the publication of a first English textbook on medical statistics by F. Bisset Hawkins (1796–1894) with the grand title of *Elements of Medical Statistics; Containing the Substance of the Gulstonian Lectures Delivered at the Royal College of Physicians with Numerous Additions Illustrative of the Comparative Salubrity, Longevity, Mortality, and Prevalence of Diseases in the Principal Countries and Cities of the Civilized World.*[91] Hawkins contribution, as it stood, was very

[86] Fassl, "Geschichtliche Aspekte," p. 28 credits Abraham de Moivre (1667–1754), Pierre-Simon Laplace (1749–1827) and Johann Carl Friedrich Gauss's (1777–1855) with early theoretical advances.

[87] James Lind (1716–1794), carried out a clinical trial in 1747, where, seeking to cure scurfy he fed sailors different treatments and determined beneficial effects of limes and oranges. Although comparable trials were carried out thereafter, it took until 1946/7 that systematic andomized controlled trials were carried out. See Doll, Richard, "Controlled Trials: The 1948 Watershed," *British Medical Journal,* 317:7167 (1998), 1217–20.

[88] Louis's work on typhoid and diphtheria used patient data to show that bleeding was not beneficial in their treatment. Louis, Pierre Charles Alexandre Examen de l'examen de M., *Broussois, Relativement a la Phthisie et à l'Affection Typhoid,* Paris (1834).

[89] See also Bollet, Alfred Jay, "Pierre Louis: The Numerical Method and the Foundation of Quantitative Medicine," *The American Journal of the Medical Sciences,* 266:2 (1973), 92–101.

[90] Fassl, "Geschichtliche Aspekte," p. 28.

[91] See Feinleib, "Health Statistics", p. 3. who notes that these efforts were inadequate, lacking in four major areas; (i) a theory of probability and mathematical statistics; (ii) the analysis of uncertainty and errors of measurement (i.e. Measurement Error in Epidemiologic

limited and did not help the discipline progress. Meanwhile, more serious contributions were made to the discipline of medical statistics and risk analysis by Florence Nightingale (1820–1910) and her close friend and Oxford-professor Benjamin Jowett (1817–1893) who were both interested the field and discussed establishing a chair in the field.[92] Nightingale herself was elected the first female member of the Statistical Society (now the Royal Statistical Society) in 1858, just two years after returning from the Crimea.[93] Nightingale was a staunch advocate of data collection and the use of medical mass observation. This involved her designing forms for hospitals for the collection of patient data, and inventing techniques for visual data presentation which are still in use today.

Studies); (iii) design of experiments (i.e. Experimental Design) and sample surveys; and (iv) the collection, summarization, display, and interpretation of observational data (i.e. Observational Study) which are jointly required to underpin a full understanding of epidemiological data and medical risk.

[92] Schiøtz, "Medical Statistics", p. 4.

[93] Florence Nightingale provided pioneering statistical diagrams for Martineau's book. See Martineau, Harriet. *England and Her Soldiers*, London, Spottiswoode (1859).

Chapter Two

Transition

Early Expansions of Risk Thinking in Public Health Research

The systematic application of risk thinking and related statistical techniques of analysis[1] to public health can be attributed to several interacting drivers. Key drivers identified in the literature differ according to the thematic or locational focus of researchers.[2] Here we suggest, without any claim to novelty or authoritativeness, that three key developments drove medical practice, medical research, and epidemiology[3] to embrace these concepts. These drivers included the sanitation movement, the emergence of the dispensary system, and early studies of mortality risk conducted predominantly by insurers in the US.

---

[1] The introduction of basic ideas of risk and chance, is in fact part of modern statistics, so that these disciplines can be seen as interlinked. See, e.g., Everitt, Brian, *Chance Rules: An Informal Guide to Probability, Risk and Statistics*, New York, NY, Springer (1999).

[2] See, e.g., Magnello, Eileen M., "Victorian Vital and Mathematical Statistics." *BSHM Bulletin* 21.3 (2006), 219–229; and Fang, Jiqian, and Ying Lu, eds., *Advanced Medical Statistics*, Singapore, World Scientific (2003).

[3] Berkman, Lisa F., Ichirō Kawachi, and M. Maria Glymour, eds., *Social Epidemiology*, Oxford, Oxford University Press (2014), p. x. define epidemiology as follows: "A major purpose of epidemiology is to contribute information relevant to the prevention of disease and the promotion of health. To accomplish this goal, epidemiologists study the distribution of disease in populations and attempt to identify the factors that explain that distribution."

The sanitation movement involved researchers studying mortality rates across different regions, cities, districts, and areas[4] in order to identify the influence of sanitation, housing, economics, and social status on health. Prominent researchers included William Farr (1807–1883) working in London, Louis René Villermé (1782–1863) working in Paris, and Theodor Weyl (1851–1913) working in Berlin.[5] Findings from their studies and similar works were disseminated during a series of 14 International Sanitary Conferences which were held from 1851 to 1938 across Europe, as well as in Constantinople and Washington. These conferences contributed significantly to the growth of knowledge in the area of health risks, public health, and sanitation.[6] The activities of the sanitation movement also encouraged the creation of modern systems for the collection of health statistics,[7] and the creation of institutions concerned with public health in the broadest sense.[8] Another major impetus for the examination

---

[4] The usefulness of location-centered approaches was demonstrated by Snow's (1813–1858) pioneering 1854 research which showed that a cholera epidemic in London had been caused by contaminated sewage water from a pump (on Broad Street). Cholera epidemics of similar origin had spread across Europe throughout the early 1800s, with further waves in 1847, 1853, and the 1860s. See De Syon, Guillaume P., *Science and Technology in Modern European Life*, St Barbara, CA, ABC-CLIO (2008).

[5] See Schlich, Thomas, "Objectifying Uncertainty: History of Risk Concepts in Medicine," *Topoi* 23:2 (2004), 211–219; and also Schlich, Thomas, and Ulrich Tröhler, *The Risks of Medical Innovation: Risk Perception and Assessment in Historical Context*, London, Routledge (2004).

[6] Howard-Jones, Norman, *The Scientific Background of the International Sanitary Conferences*, 1851–1938, Geneva, World Health Organisation (1975). Agnoletti, Mauro, and Simone Neri Serneri, eds., *The Basic Environmental History*, Vol. 4. Cham, Springer (2014), p. 221, note how "The non-appropriation of excremental materials and the absence of monitoring of industrial activities increased the sanitary risk of waste. The situation was made worse by equipment dating from the colonial period, often unsuitable within the local context. At the same time, the so-called informal sector played a major role in on-site handling, collection, sorting, recycling, and recovery."

[7] Sheynin, Oskar B., "On the History of Medical Statistics," *Archive for History of Exact Sciences* 26:3 (1982), 241–86 provides a detail analysis of the influence of these and related developments on the creations of medical statistics.

[8] Feinleib, "Health Statistics," p. 6 highlights improved mortality statistics collection in the 1880 and 1890 US censuses under John Shaw Billings (1838–1913). The Vital Statistics Division of the Bureau of the Census was transferred to the Public Health Service in 1946,

of medical risks together with success rates of interventions, treatments, and therapies was the creation of the British hospital and dispensary movement of the late 1700s.[9] These early providers of medical care to working people, were interested in which types of treatments worked best and helped manage or stave off the risks of long-term illness or invalidity. Lastly, the attempts of insurers to identify mortality risk factors, which commenced in the US in the early 1900s, encouraged the examination of risk factors which affected the mortality of individuals[10], and helped medical research to transition from infectious to chronic and risk factor disease epidemiology.[11]

In parallel with these three key drivers, several factors kept discourses on epidemiology, risk, and public health alive and repeatedly revived their importance over several decades leading up to risk factor epidemiology in the 1970s.[12] Thus, advances and innovations in medicine and bacteriology of the 1850s[13] and the Edwardian period,[14] brought

---

becoming the National Office of Vital Statistics, with Halbert L. Dunn. (1896–1975) as Director. In 1960, NOVS was combined with the National Health Survey to become the National Center for Health Statistics with Forrest E. Linder (1906–1988) as Director.

[9] See Loudon, Irvine S., "The Origins and Growth of the Dispensary Movement in England," *Bulletin of the History of Medicine* 55:3 (1981), 322–42 and also Schlich, "Objectifying Uncertainty," who argues that these organisations encouraged doctors and lay sponsors to examine recovery and death rates within these institutions which shifted focus from individuals to whole populations or population groups.

[10] Rothstein, *Public Health and the Risk Factor*, p. 179 ff.

[11] Kuller, Lewis H., "Relationship Between Acute and Chronic Disease Epidemiology," *The Yale Journal of Biology and Medicine,* 60:4 (1987), 363.

[12] Schiøtz, Aina, "Medical Statistics," p.5 speaks of four overlapping phases in the development of epidemiology: 1. The Era of Sanitary Epidemiology from the 1850s. 2. The Era of Infectious Disease Epidemiology from the 1880s. 3. The Era of Chronic Disease Epidemiology from the 1950s. 4. The Era of Risk Factor Epidemiology from the 1980s. In line with the idea of overlap, we would date the beginnings of Chronic Disease epidemiology in the early 1900s and the beginnings of Risk Factor Epidemiology to the 1970s.

[13] Carter, K. Codell, "Ignaz Semmelweis, Carl Mayrhofer, and the Rise of Germ Theory," *Medical History,* 29:1 (1985), 33–53.

[14] Porter describes the complex effect of advances in bacteriology on procedures of disease control. Specifically, Porter argues that: "The new shift in public health during the Edwardian period began to categorize individuals into 'risk populations.' The 'sanitary era' had treated the health of an undifferentiated 'public.' It possessed a generalized concept of

early changes to perceptions of health risks. Subsequently, statistics and biometry expanded as academic disciplines in the 1930s and 40s, paving the way to modern evidence-based clinical research. Key figures promoting evidence-based approaches were Paul Martini (1889–1964) und Sir Austin Bradford Hill (1897–1991). The rise of medical statistics, meanwhile, also supported the creation of modern safety science in the 1970s and 1980s, which systematized accident analysis and helped define what could be considered acceptable safety levels. Medical statistics also helped improve efforts to measure the quality of healthcare and encouraged the systematic assessment of levels of iatrogenic risks. This was supplemented by works seeking to improve decision making in complex medical contexts by utilizing knowledge about risks and improve risk assessment. Lastly, a series of works originating in the 1970s sought to investigate links between lifestyle risk factors and medical outcomes, creating the new field of risk factor epidemiology. Overall, an emphasis on risk marked several areas of medicine in pronounced ways as medicine and public health progressed, leading to synergistic applications in a range of areas.

We will attempt to briefly summarize and disentangle some of these influences, in the hope that this will help clarify some aspects of the occasionally bewildering relationship between medicine, healthcare, public health, and risk. For practical reasons, our narrative does not follow a strict historical chronology, but instead highlights the role of individual pioneers and emphasizes themes which overlap in terms of time frames and topics. Also, a separate section on the link between risk thinking and applied statistics as it evolved in the 1930s and 1940s will be presented outside our chronology, in order to allow us to discuss key shifts in epidemiological thinking from infectious to chronic disease, and on to risk factor epidemiology sequentially.

---

the population as well as a generalized theory of disease propagation … During the 1890s, preventive medicine divided the population into TB victims; potential sufferers of post-partum puerperal fever; infants at risk from diarrhea; and schoolchildren vulnerable to diphtheria. This pattern became increasingly pronounced as new concerns developed about the physical deterioration of the nation during the early years of the twentieth century." Porter, Dorothy, *Health, Civilization and the State: A History of Public Health from Ancient to Modern Times*, London, Routledge (2005), p. 140.

Risk Within Infectious and Chronic Disease Epidemiologies

We start by exploring the understanding of health risk during the era of infectious disease epidemiology when it was considered important to examine identifiable microorganisms associated with contagious diseases via laboratory techniques.[15] Key discoveries related to cholera, tuberculosis, typhoid, syphilis, and malaria.[16] Broadly speaking, this disease epidemiology saw health risks as being primarily associated with microorganisms rather than the material conditions of various groups in society. This view soon matured and by the late 1800s and early decades of the 1900s,[17] increased attention was paid to the interaction of infectious diseases and environmental factors such as poverty, destitution, and battlefield conditions.[18] A subsequent phase, saw chronic disease epidemiology expand as a field.[19] Lucey documents that in Ireland between

---

[15]Schiøtz, "Medical Statistics", p. 6. See also Gaynes, Robert P., *Germ Theory: Medical Pioneers in Infectious Diseases*, New York, NY, John Wiley & Sons (2011).

[16]Barreto, Mauricio L., Maria Glória Teixeira, and Eduardo Hage Carmo, "Infectious Diseases Epidemiology," *Journal of Epidemiology & Community Health,* 60:3 (2006), 192–5.

[17]The First World War created significant demand for compounds that would avert typhus and tetanus (penicillin did not exist yet) and accelerated drug developments. The continued importance of infectious diseases was highlighted drastically by the outbreak of the Spanish flu which the Summer 1918, when troop movements and civilian malnutrition created particular vulnerabilities. Estimates of deaths from this pandemic vary between 25 to 50 million worldwide. See De Syon, *Science and Technology,* P. 120.

[18]Prinzing, Friedrich and Harald Westergaard, *Epidemics Resulting from Wars*, Clarendon Press; H. Milford, Oxford, London (1916) authored a detailed and authoritative survey of outbreaks of epidemics during conflicts. This work had been commissioned by the Carnegie Endowment for International Peace under the leadership of John Bates Clark.

[19]Weisz, George, *Chronic Disease in the Twentieth Century: A History*, Baltimore, MD, Johns Hopkins University Press (2014), p. xi argues that, notwithstanding the traditional distinction between acute (short term) and chronic (long term/recurring) disease, the latter was primarily an American policy construct during the first half of the twentieth century. Weisz, however, acknowledges that chronic disease is "about a meta-concept that has been exceptionally elastic and fluid" (p.2) that "has covered different diseases and conditions depending on the time, place, and goals of those utilizing it." Weisz (p. 6.) also notes that as medical research progressed the notion of chronic disease "became less useful within

December 1904 and November 1905 workhouse infirmaries admitted a total of 79,800 patients. Of this figure 33,836 cases were classified as acute, 21,427 as chronic and 2,366 received midwifery services. Surgical attention was needed in 22,178 cases. There were 6,446 cases of tuberculosis or phthisis patients and another 5,635 received treatment for infectious diseases in workhouse fever wards.[20] Some of this reflected an increasing recognition of the importance of environmental, social, and occupational factors. The British hospital and dispensary movement had become sufficiently well established for medics and lay sponsors to count recovery and death rates in a way which shifted the traditional individualistic approach of medicine to a focus "on the wellbeing of the whole population or specific groups within it — such as the laboring poor, soldiers, women, children..."[21] Health risk was now seen as being both group and person specific. However, there was sufficient commitment to statistics and observational methodology, as methods for studying biological patterns to know that many disease patterns were not random.[22]

As medicine witnessed further developments in modern physiology (Bernard), anesthesia (Morton), antisepsis (Lister and Semmelweis), x-rays (Roentgen), and germ theory (Pasteur and Koch), data collection and mass observation became ever more important, even though the methodology of clinical trials had not yet been fully developed.[23] Here we quote from the 1889 edition of a once popular book on hospital construction and management by Mouat and Snell, who saw health risks in acute

---

elite mainstream medicine" while maintaining its relevance as "a term of administration and welfare, often serving as popular shorthand for more regulatory formulas like 'incurable, infirm, or elderly.'"

[20] Lucey, Donnacha Seán, "'These Schemes Will Win for Themselves the Confidence of the People': Irish Independence, Poor Law Reform and Hospital Provision," *Medical History* 58:1 (2014), 49. This indicates that at this stage, a significant portion of hospital patients were already officially classified as chronic, but that acute and infectious diseases together still accounted for a majority of patients.

[21] Schlich, and Tröhler, *The Risks of Medical Innovation.*

[22] Bartrip, Peter WJ., *The Home Office and the Dangerous Trades: Regulating Occupational Disease in Victorian and Edwardian Britain*, Amsterdam, Rodopi (2002).

[23] Mayer, Dan, *Essential Evidence-based Medicine*, Vol. 1. Cambridge, Cambridge University Press (2004).

form and as well as chronic "new pathological states" as arising from what the authors described as "conditions of life in all civilized communities:"[24]

> The present conditions of life in all civilised communities, impose a strain upon mind and body by day and by night which is extremely difficult to bear, without serious **risk** of premature decay and death. The ever-increasing dangers to life and limb from the continuous and progressive multiplication of mechanical contrivances to supplement and supplant manual labour, and to annihilate time and space, have ... [created] ...fresh forms of accidents and injuries,[25] and new pathological states." (P. 3, emphasis added).

Medical risk, described in these general terms, was recognized to differ by locations, occupations, social classes, and places of treatment. Mouat and Snell did not discuss in detail whether such differences were primarily a reflection of social or economic inequalities, and whether these differences also reflected potentially related inequalities in the medical treatment patients received. However, like Florence Nightingale, with whom both authors frequently communicated, Frederic Mouat and Henry Snell advocated the collection of treatment records, to ensure certain levels of treatment quality:

> The hospitals themselves, I consider, ought to have just so much of state control as to secure their proper direction, with the remedy of such defects as may be control as to secure their proper direction to secure their proper direction, with the remedy of such defects as may be shown to exist. I know of no good reason why the different hospitals of London, and other great cities, should exhibit such different **risks** to life in similar circumstances, diseases, and accidents, as they do now and have done for long past; and why a proper uniform system of hospital record, in all departments of their administration, should not be as compulsory as

---

[24] Mouat, Frederic John, and Henry Saxon Snell, *Hospital Construction and Management*, London, J. & A. Churchill (1889).

[25] The reference to fresh forms of accidents and injuries, presumably reflect the authors' recognition of growing demands for protection of workers and the need for legislative measures addressing industrial risks.

customs, trade, and other economic returns, in matters of far less general and scientific interest." (P. 9, emphasis added)

While new developments in medicine were taking place, statistics, or at least mass observations of disease and research more generally, became more fully integrated into medical practice. Again we quote from Mouat and Snell who describe the task of clinical hospitals as follows:

> By clinical hospitals I mean hospitals attached to medical schools, which need, therefore, to be fully organised for the purposes of practical instruction in all branches of medicine. They should be provided with physiological and pathological laboratories, and be armed with all the means of conducting scientific inquiries — be, in fact, schools of research, as well as of technical teaching. The difference needed in their structural and other arrangements, as respects the sick, are greater space in the wards for clinical teaching, more complete classification of disease, the careful selection of typical cases, and special provisions for nursing and the admission of students to learn their profession. All classes of cases should be admitted to them, except infectious fevers." (underlining not original, P. 60)

The adoption of statistics by medics, however, did not occur quickly, and when it started taking place, it did so with, at times, dangerous aberrations (such as forays into eugenics, which we will discuss in connection with the evolution of biometry in a later section of this chapter in greater detail). When chronic disease epidemiology gained importance during and shortly after World War Two, this was based on the greater medical understanding of certain ailments as well as the recognition that some complicated or difficult to treat conditions affected a great number of individuals; albeit that there was not always a clear or strict dividing line between acute and chronic condition.[26] One of the key study areas of chronic disease epidemiology centered on heart disease (which had been identified as affecting a large number of individuals in the US by the late

[26] Bernell, Stephanie, and Steven W. Howard, "Use Your Words Carefully: What is a Chronic Disease?," *Frontiers in Public Health,* 4 (2016), 159.

1940s).[27] The other area of major discovery of chronic disease related to cancer which is, among other contributions, associated with the work of the statistician Sir Austin Bradford Hill (1897–1991) and the physician Richard Doll (1912–2005) who illuminated the relationship between smoking, lung cancer, and other illnesses.[28]

Regarding heart disease, William Osler (1849–1919), professor at Johns Hopkins Hospital, had worked extensively on angina, indicating that it was a symptom rather than a disease. Based on this, the American cardiologist James B. Herrick (1861–1954) concluded in 1912 that the slow, gradual narrowing of the coronary arteries could be a cause of angina.[29] Since the development of many cardiovascular drugs predates that of other cardiological interventions,[30] we provide a brief discussion of the development of some prominent cardiovascular drugs as example of therapy development as a form of risk management for some of the most widespread chronic diseases.[31] Early dispensaries and hospitals were limited to a small number of drugs for the management of cardiovascular problems and chronic diseases more generally.[32] Concerning cardiac

---

[27] Oppenheimer, Gerald M., "Profiling Risk: The Emergence of Coronary Heart Disease Epidemiology in The United States (1947–70)," *International Journal of Epidemiology* 35:3 (2006), 720–30. It is unclear whether there was a genuine increase in heart disease. However, Agnoletti and Serneri, *The Basic Environmental History*, p. 160 note that "vehicle exhausts spewed millions of tons of toxic lead into the atmosphere (tetraethyl lead was used as an additive in petrol…) …. Other vehicle pollutants known to have direct or indirect adverse effects on human health include carbon monoxide, sulphur dioxide, fine airborne particulates and volatile organic compounds (VOCs) such as benzene, which contribute to the increase or severity of cardio-respiratory conditions and even pose a cancer risk to city dwellers."

[28] Schiøtz, Aina. "Medical Statistics," p. 7.

[29] Lewis, Thomas, "Diseases of the Heart Described for Practitioners and Students," *The Journal of Nervous and Mental Disease,* 79:2 (1934), 222.

[30] Charles Theodore Dotter (1920–1985) described angioplasty in 1964. See Payne, Misty M. "Charles Theodore Dotter: The Father of Intervention," *Texas Heart Institute Journal* 28:1 (2001), 28.

[31] Scholz, Hasso, "Some Historical Aspects of The Development of Cardiovascular Drugs," *Zeitschrift für Kardiologie,* 91:4 (2002), iv34–iv42.

[32] Mercer, Alex, *Infections, Chronic Disease, and the Epidemiological Transition: A New Perspective*, Martlesham, Boydell & Brewer (2014).

conditions, early medications included cardiac glycosides which were typically derived from foxglove, or *Digitalis purpurea* which had first been described in 1785 by physician and botanist William Withering (1741–1799).[33] The properties of this drug were examined mostly through case studies and experiments by several academics, until Albert Fraenkel (1864–1938) eventually developed a biologically standardized extract of *Digitalis purpurea.* The resultant medicine was named "Digipuratum" and was marketed from 1912/1913 onward.[34] This was followed by the development of therapeutically related highly efficacious loop diuretics which were developed in the 1960s.

Further progress was made in the mid-1960s with the testing and subsequent introduction of calcium antagonists which were, at the time, believed to be beta-adrenoceptor blockers. Synthesized in 1964 by the Scottish physician and pharmacist James Black (1924–2010), these drugs are prescribed to manage coronary heart disease and hypertension and are considered one of the most important contributions to clinical medicine and pharmacology of the previous century. Further progress involved, among many other studies, the Evaluation of Losartan in the Elderly (ELITE) study, which compared effects on renal function, morbidity/mortality, and tolerability of long-term treatment with losartan or captopril in patients aged 65 years and older with symptomatic heart failure. This study which involved 722 randomly assigned patients showed that among elderly heart-failure patients, treatment with losartan was associated with an unexpected lower mortality than that found with captopril, triggering a further trial on a larger number of patients.[35]

The evaluation of medicines and therapies, which had originated in the context of dispensaries and early hospitals, by the 1930s, came to rely on more and more advanced methodology, which facilitated the systematic

[33] Withering, William, *An Account of the Foxglove, and Some of its Medical Uses.*, Cambridge, Cambridge University Press [1785] (2014).

[34] Scholz, Hasso, "Some Historical Aspects," p. iv35.

[35] Pitt, Bertram, *et al.*, "Randomised Trial of Losartan Versus Captopril in Patients Over 65 with Heart Failure (Evaluation of Losartan in the Elderly Study, ELITE)," *The Lancet* 349:9054 (1997), 747–52.

development of therapies[36] aimed at targeting major acute and chronic diseases.[37] Meanwhile, a parallel set of methodologies facilitated identifying their causes. Interestingly, it took until 1965 that Austin Bradford Hill's (1897–1991) set of nine criteria to provide epidemiologic evidence of a causal relationship was published and became widely accepted.[38]

Risk Factor Epidemiology of the 21st Century

Despite progress in the testing of medicines and therapies, further progress in the treatment of major chronic diseases had to wait for what has been described as the next phase of research on medical risk, which is usually described as **risk factor epidemiology**. At its core, this phase focused on mass data relating to people's lifestyles in order to understand the causes of major chronic diseases and relied on the evaluation of mass observation studies in so doing. Three large scale studies stood out in identifying the leading causes of chronic disease and death:[39] the Framingham Heart Study, the Seven Counties Study, and the British Doctors Study. These studies highlighted the role of cigarette smoking, diet, physical inactivity, and high blood pressure as leading causes of death. Started in Framingham, Massachusetts in 1948, the Framingham

---

[36] See Schumacher, Martin, "Entwicklung Klinischer Studien von Paul Martini bis Heute," *Drug Research,* 66:1 (2016), S5–S7. Lesch, John E., *The First Miracle Drugs: How the Sulfa Drugs Transformed Medicine.* Oxford, Oxford University Press (2007) describes how sulfonamidesas (the first broadly effective antibacterials) were tested using randomization and related methodology and used systemically.

[37] Le Fanu, James, *The Rise and Fall of Modern Medicine*, London, Hachette UK, (2011), p. 13, specifically lists the inventions of penicillin, cortisone, chlorpromazine, open-heart surgery, kidney transplants, stroke prevention, childhood cancer cures, test-tube babies, and the discovery of helicobacter as cause of peptic ulcers as major accomplishments of modern medicine.

[38] Bradford, Austin, "Association or Causation," *Proceedings of the Royal Society of Medicine,* 58 (1965), 295–300.

[39] Remington, Patrick L., and Brownson, Ross C, "Fifty Years of Progress in Chronic Disease Epidemiology and Control," *CDC Morbidity and Mortality Weekly Report (MMWR),* 60:04 (2011), 70–7.

study is an ongoing cardiovascular cohort study of local residents. Conducted by the University of Minnesota from 1956, the Seven Counties study systematically examined relationships between lifestyle, diet, coronary heart disease, and stroke in different populations from different regions, highlighting how risk factors can be changed.[40] The so-called British Doctors study, conducted between 1951–2001 in Oxford, assessed the risks associated with tobacco use and its relationship to lung cancer by tracking 34,439 male doctors practicing in Britain and recording their smoking habits, while observing the development of diseases including lung cancer, other cancers, respiratory diseases, cardiovascular diseases, and mortality rates. It showed that individuals who smoked tobacco were more likely to develop chronic respiratory illnesses, including lung cancer, and cardiovascular diseases.[41]

Rothstein, summarized the intellectual developments triggered by these, and other studies as follows:

> By the end of the century, most people accepted the statistical evidence that specific behaviours and characteristics of healthy persons, called '**risk factors**,' can increase the probability of developing disease, especially chronic disease. Most people also believe that making appropriate changes in their lifestyles, a concept associated with risk factors, can reduce the probability of the occurrence of disease. To facilitate this process, they expect health professionals, agencies concerned with public health, and the media to inform and educate the public about risk factors. The acceptance of risk factors has produced changes in public health and medicine as profound as those that resulted from bacteriology and the germ theory of disease. The changes have been most evident in coronary heart disease, which was the major cause of death in the twentieth century ... Yet the impact of the risk factor has been much more uneven than the germ theory. The risk factor concept has been controversial because of its statistical methodology, its multifactorial

---

[40] It is worth mentioning that other researchers continued to investigate the relationship between risk factors and diseases, Remington, and Brownson, "Fifty years", p. 70.

[41] Doll, Richard, and Richard Peto, "Mortality in Relation to Smoking: 20 Years' Observations on Male British Doctors," *British Medical Journal* 2:6051 (1976), 1525–36.

concept of disease etiology, and its effect on the economic interests of commercial, professional, and health organizations. (P. xi)[42]

Risk factors now became a paramount or even the dominant concept in public health and Rothstein diligently identified the influences, institutions, and individuals that contributed to this long journey. Contributors were many and ranged from private commercial insurers, who researched relevant predictors of mortality in order to screen potential policy holders, to medics who identified the characteristics of heart disease in the early years of the coronary heart disease epidemic, on to statisticians who identified the ill health effects of smoking. In parallel with the changes, the language of risk and risk assessment was now given a central place in statements about public health. Here we give two sample quotes, one from a review report on the Framingham study and the other from an early paper relating to the British Doctors smoking study. The first quote is part of an abstract summarizing Framingham's rationales:

> Cardiovascular disease (CVD) is among the leading causes of death and disability worldwide. Since its beginning, the Framingham study has been a leader in identifying CVD **risk factors**. Clinical trials have demonstrated that when the modifiable **risk factors** are treated and corrected, the chances of CVD occurring can be reduced. The Framingham study also recognized that CVD **risk factors** are multifactorial and interact over time to produce CVD. In response, Framingham investigators developed the Framingham **Risk Functions** (also called Framingham Risk Scores) to evaluate the <u>chance or likelihood of developing CVD in individuals</u>. These functions are <u>multivariate functions (algorithms) that combine the information in CVD risk factors such as sex, age, systolic blood pressure, total cholesterol, high-density lipoprotein cholesterol, smoking behavior, and diabetes</u> status to produce an estimate (or **risk**) of developing CVD or a component of CVD (such as coronary heart disease, stroke, peripheral vascular disease, or heart failure) over a fixed

---

[42]Rothstein, *Public Health and the Risk Factor*. Rothstein's early acknowledgment of some of the controversial aspects of the risk factor concept is remarkable in that it predates more recent concerns which relate to the marginalization of relevance of economic wealth, social position, race, and ethnicity.

> time, for example, the next 10 years. These estimates of CVD risk are often major inputs in recommending drug treatments such as cholesterol-lowering drugs.[43] (P. 11, emphasis added)

Accordingly, the authors of this review paper identified the core purpose of the Framingham study as identifying risk factors for coronary heart disease, with the purpose of treating and correcting these, and thus reducing disease risks to individuals. They further noted that, over time, the Framingham researchers recognized interactions among these factors that allowing them to estimate the combined impact of risk factors, which they then described as risk functions which predicted the possibility (or risk) of developing cardiovascular disease and also provided input in treatment decisions. Interestingly, another paper related to the Framingham study pointed out that, although the term risk factor first appeared in a Framingham study article in 1961, the concept predated the heart study and appeared in publications during the 1950s.[44]

Conceptually, the British Doctors study started off relatively simply. Here too, the basic start-out points were observational:

> The original questionnaire in 1951 asked only a few questions about the individual's current smoking habits or, for ex-smokers, about the types and amounts of tobacco last smoked. These were elaborated in further questionnaires in 1957, 1966, 1971, 1978, and 1991, to which the response rates (after reminders) varied between 98% initially and 94% finally. Accounts of the questions asked have been reported previously, as have the trends in cigarette consumption. Only the 1978 questionnaire, which was limited to those born in the 20th century, sought information about a wide range of characteristics (height, weight, blood pressure, alcohol, etc. including medical history) and asked those who had stopped smoking whether they had done so because they had already developed some serious respiratory or vascular disease. The

[43] D'Agostino Sr, Ralph B., *et al.*, "Cardiovascular Disease Risk Assessment: Insights from Framingham," *Global Heart* 8:1 (2013), 11–23.

[44] Oppenheimer, Gerald M., "Framingham Heart Study: The First 20 Years," *Progress in Cardiovascular Diseases* 53:1 (2010), 55–61, who cites Rothstein, *Public Health and the Risk Factor.*

2001 questionnaire sought only to check that we had identified correctly the individuals we believed we had traced."[45]

The researchers who designed the British Doctors study initially wrote to all registered physicians in the UK, obtaining responses from about two-thirds. Over time, the research design of the study was refined, with new medical conditions and additional behaviors being taken into account. Overall, the study, which ran from 1951–2001 provided convincing statistical proof that smoking increased lung cancer risk as early as 1956, while analyses during later years (including follow-up questionnaires in 1957, 1966, 1971, 1978, 1991, and 2001) also concerned themselves with the impact of alcohol consumption and identified a range of smoking related health conditions affecting the cardiovascular and circulatory system.

Generally speaking, the accomplishments of risk factor epidemiology are widely acknowledged, and the approach is rightfully considered a logical extension of, and advance on, some key aspects of previous epidemiologies. However, there are concerns about problems associated with the risk factor approach — an issue we will return to at the end of this chapter. For now, we will step back in history by several decades to fill some gaps in our narrative around the revolution of risk thinking and applied statistics in the 1930s and 1940s. The three institutional drivers mentioned earlier, namely, the sanitation movement with its studies of differential mortality rates of cities, districts, and areas, early clinical studies on treatment effectiveness conducted by the British dispensary and hospital movement, as well as pioneering studies of risk factors conducted initially by US insurers and then on a grand scale by universities, had all contributed much to deepen the understanding of the risk-health relationship by the 1960s. In terms of intellectual development, however, a number of earlier conceptual ingredients had to be drawn into the mix. They included a deeper understanding of how ideas of risk could be meaningfully and critically interpreted in medical contexts, how statistics could be employed in research on risks and the identification of causes of

[45] Doll, Richard, *et al.*, "Mortality in Relation to Smoking," 1519.

disease,[46] and how ideas of risk management could be proactively used to inform care decisions over individuals' lifetime,[47] as well as how these methods could help in the assessment and monitoring of iatrogenic risks. The next section will take a chronological step back in time in order to look at these concepts in more detail. This excursion will highlight key aspects of the link between statistical- and risk-related reasoning. Accordingly, it must be understood that risk factor epidemiology, in particular, is built on an elaborate and developed understanding of the meaning and importance of risk, as well as a broad and well-developed sets of tools in the area of medical statistics.[48]

Risk, Statistics, and Biometrics: An Historical Excursion

The previous sections have followed an established custom of presenting infectious disease epidemiology, chronic disease epidemiology, and risk factor epidemiology in succession to each other. This involved a chronological leap, as we skipped over developments in the conceptual understanding of medical risk and medical statistics, which were essential to these developments. We will now briefly step back in time to describe a few of the concepts which underpinned the rise of risk epidemiology.

One of the central developments that facilitated progress in public health and the rise of risk factor epidemiology, was an increased understanding of risk quantification within the mathematical statistical analysis of the 1930s. This did not mean that health risks were always assessed rigorously on the basis of accurate data, especially when it

---

[46] Parascandola, Mark, "Causes, Risks, and Probabilities: Probabilistic Concepts of Causation in Chronic Disease Epidemiology," *Preventive Medicine,* 53:4&5 (2011), 232–34.

[47] The unavoidability of some lifetime risk factors over the life span ultimately raises questions about the traditional interpretation of chronic illness as individualistic phenomena. Accordingly, Barker, D., "A New Model for the Origins of Chronic Disease", *Medicine, Healthcare and Philosophy,* 4 (2001), 31–5 discusses the possibility that chronic illness is the manifestation of programmed changes later in life.

[48] Pearce, Neil, "Traditional Epidemiology, Modern Epidemiology, and Public Health," *American Journal of Public Health* 86.5 (1996), 678–83.

came to different demographic, ethic, or occupation groups. However, it meant that many researchers now had some awareness of what information would be needed in order to correctly assess certain health risks.[49] This aspect is, in a way, so simple and commonsensical that it has hardly been recognized by historians working in the field. Nonetheless, its relevance should not be overlooked in a timeline of the risk–statistics–health relationship. We could quote from any of a dozen of textbooks of the time to make this point, but we choose a particularly simple example form the popular 1930 textbook *Medical Biometry and Statistics*.[50] Here, the author states in connection with rates, ratios, and estimates of risks:

> It should be noted at the outstart of the discussion of rates that 'number exposed to **risk**' does not always, or indeed usually, mean precisely the same thing as "number living." For example, suppose that in a particular community, say New York State in 1900, 452 persons died of puerperal septicemia, and in the same state the same year there were living 7,284,461 persons. These facts do not imply that the true force of mortality of puerperal septicaemia was 452-7,284,461–.00006, or 6 per 100,000. The true force of mortality must be quite different from this because: (a) Males cannot have puerperal septicemia, and are, therefore, not at risk of dying from this disease. (b) Females under ten or over sixty years of age are not exposed to risk of dying from this disease, because they are outside the reproductive period of life. (c) Women not in the puerperium, i. e., who have not recently been pregnant, are not exposed to **risk** of death from this disease. So then it appears that from the figure of 7,284,461 living there must be subtracted at the start all the males, and then all the females except those in a certain physiologic state. The number of live births in New York State in 1900 was 143,156. Now, adding to this number 4 per cent, of itself, to correct roughly for stillbirths, multiple births, etc., the number 148,900 may be taken approximately to

[49] See Ingraham, Hollis S., "Statistics and Medical Knowledge," *American Journal of Public Health and the Nation's Health,* 48:11 (1958), 1449–59, for an early example of the implication for risk awareness arising from the correct observation of populations specific rates in a smoker/non-smoker comparison.

[50] Pearl, Raymond, *Introduction to Medical Biometry and Statistics*, Philadelphia, PA, W.B. Saunders (1930).

> represent the number of women who during that year were in the puerperal state. So then the figure for force of mortality from this disease becomes roughly somewhere in the neighborhood of 452 – 148,900 = .003, or 300 per 100,000, a very different figure indeed from the 6 per 100,000 with which we started. (pp. 204 and 205, emphasis)

Simple as this example may sound, it is reflective of a desire to develop and utilize reliable and meaningful approaches to the measurement of disease risks.[51] Medical statistics and its treatment and estimation of risk as it evolved in the 1930s and 1940s, of course, significantly advanced beyond attempts to define rates in relation to correct and appropriate population estimates, although the above example hopefully indicates that this could involve some complications. As noted by several authors, the development of medical statistics at the time was primarily driven by mathematicians and medics who worked with data broadly relating to health issues or in the bio-sciences more generally.[52]

The authors of a well-known and respected contemporary textbook on Biometry credit Francis Galton (1822–1911) with the creation of much of the basis for the discipline, while acknowledging that his research was motivated by dubious hypothesizing in the area of Eugenics.[53] Eugenics also influenced the highly productive mathematician and statistician Karl Pearson (1857–1936) who sought to study natural selection and drew on research by the zoologist W.F.R Weldon (1860–1906) who is said to have coined the term biometry.[54] Pearson laid the foundation for much modern

[51] See also *Ibid.*, p.239 where the author correctly notes that "the exposed to risk over the whole day is the integration of the number exposed to risk at each infinitesimal instant of time in the whole day."

[52] Magnello, Eileen, and Anne Hardy (eds.), *The Road to Medical Statistics*, Vol. 67, Amsterdam, Rodopi (2002).

[53] Sokal, Robert R., and F. James Rohlf, *Biostatistics,* New York, NY, Freeman & Co (2000), p. 4.

[54] Pearsons claimed that tuberculosis (usually a bacterial infection) was inherited. See Delzell, Darcie AP, and Cathy D. Poliak, "Karl Pearson and Eugenics: Personal Opinions and Scientific Rigor," *Science and Engineering Ethics* 19:3 (2013), 1057–1070. As noted by Agnoletti and Sereni, *The Basic Environmental History*, p. 144, "poor domestic air quality — with concentrations of harmful particulates high in cramped conditions — undoubtedly increased the risk of illness and death from chronic respiratory diseases".

descriptive and correlational statistics, and his work, in turn, inspired Ronald Fisher (1890–1962) who worked at Rothamstead agricultural experimental station where he developed tests to analyze crop experiments. Since these early years, medical statistics and statistics more generally have remained a very active field, having now largely dropped the racist-eugenicist bias.

To give an example of the more dubious past of the discipline, we mention a short paper by Karl Pearson and Margaret Moul entitled *The Problem of Alien Immigration into Great Britain, illustrated by an Examination of Russian and Polish Jewish Children* which illustrates the unfortunate facet of this innovator in the area of medical statistics. Here, Pearson and Moul state:[55]

> [Feldman]... supposes the general mortality rate in Jews to be at each age the same as that of the Gentiles of the whole of London. But since the whole of London has a much lower mortality rate than the districts inhabited by our Alien Jewish population, this increases the population at risk and gives a value much too low for the death-rate based on the observed mortality for a special disease like tuberculosis. (P.42, emphasis added)

This, and similar, statements had the potential to be inflammatory, precisely because Pearson was a well-known scientist with a vast reputation in the area of medical statistics.[56] Although he does not bear direct responsibility for this, he was often cited as academic authority by

---

[55] Pearson, Karl, and Margaret Moul, "The Problem of Alien Immigration into Great Britain, Illustrated by an Examination of Russian and Polish Jewish Children," *Annals of Eugenics,* 1:1 (1925), 42.

[56] Incidentally Porter reports that: "At the end of the First World War, tuberculosis accounted for about a sixth of all deaths in France and up to a quarter of mortality in some large urban centres. The Rockefeller Foundation targeted it in a public health campaign in 1917. The campaign used a dispensary system for tracing cases, assisting patients' families, providing disinfection, and disseminating public education about reducing the risk of spreading the disease.' See Porter, Health, *Civilization and the State,* p. 281. At the time of publication of the Pearson and Moul paper, the threat from tuberculosis had diminished while its bacterial origins were better understood.

individuals pursuing racist and other forms of discriminatory agendas.[57] It is unclear why Galton, Pearson, Fisher, and other leading figures in the development of statistics harbored sympathies with eugenics and what they called eugenic or "scientific racism," and this is an aspect of their thinking that filtered into several disciplines that cannot, and should not, be ignored.[58]

Medical statistics in the early phase, which lasted into the 1950s, was very much seen as being related to the conduct and interpretation of experiments, with observational medical data being often interpreted as lesser quasi-experiment. One respected textbook on medical statistics claimed that there was a clear line dividing classical and modern experimentation. The author stated that:[59]

> The classical experimental approach is characterized by the attempt to determine the effect of a single condition or factor in such a manner that any observed effect on the experimental subject(s) may be ascribed to the single possible source. The procedure involves the variation of only one factor (such as the employment of different levels) in any single experiment, all other conditions or factors being held constant ... Modern experimental procedures, as developed primarily in the science of agriculture under the leadership of R. A. Fisher, differ markedly from the preceding. First, as far as is practicable, those factors which are expected

[57] For example, Pearson was cited as scientific expert by various authors supporting anti-immigration groups. See, e.g., Hall, Lucyle Irby, *Immigration and Other Interests of Prescott Farnsworth Hall*, New York, NY, Knickerbocker Press (1922), which notes on p. 33: 'Recent investigations in eugenics show that heredity is a much more important factor than environment as regards social conditions — in fact, that in most cases heredity is what makes the environment. This is confirmed by the practice of the insurance companies which attach the chief importance to the hereditary characteristics of an individual. If this position is sound, education and distribution can only palliate the evils and delay fundamental changes. As Professor Karl Pearson says: "You cannot change the leopard's spots, and you cannot change bad stock to good; you may dilute it, possibly spread it over a large area, spoiling good stock, but until it ceases to multiply it will not cease to be."

[58] Pilgrim, David, "The Eugenic Legacy in Psychology and Psychiatry," *International Journal of Social Psychiatry*, 5:3 (2008), 272–284.

[59] Bateson, Herbert C., *Medical Statistics*, Washington, Army Medical Department Research and Graduate School (1950), pp. 7–8.

to affect the outcome are allowed to vary concomitantly within known limits within the individual experiment. This action is based upon the now recognized fact that the effect of variation in one factor frequently is dependent greatly upon concomitant variation in another factor or group of factors. This mutual dependence of the effect of factors commonly is referred to as interaction or discrepancy and results from the failure of one factor to exert a constant independent effect when associated with variation in another factor. Second in the modern experimental procedure, more emphasis is placed upon accurate estimation of error than is placed upon its minimization. This constitutes a change in the concept of error from an association of the term with mistakes or inaccuracies in observations and measurements to a concept of normally existing variation in the experimental subjects or material independent of the known factors of experimental interest.

Risk, Safety, and Decision Making

The increased sophistication of statistical technique was a prerequisite for later studies, whether they investigated environmental, occupational, lifestyle, or occupational risk factors. The application of statistics in medicine hence entailed much neutral and factual investigation, in ways which did not reflect the problematic beliefs of some of its founding fathers.[60] However, measurement and related assessments of health risk entailed other problems of a more complex nature which relate, among other issues, to the nature and origins of standard setting.[61]

Drawing on Gigerenzer *et al.*, Schlich eloquently describes the modern use of statistics in medical research as "part of the process of objectification through which science entered medicine in a big way."[62] For medical research and perhaps also clinical practice, this objectification

---

[60] Bodmer, Walter, *et al.*, "The Outstanding Scientist, RA Fisher: His Views on Eugenics and Race," *Heredity,* 126:4 (2021), 565–76.

[61] Cambrosio, Alberto, *et al.*, "Biomedical Conventions and Regulatory Objectivity: A few Introductory Remarks," *Social Studies of Science,* 39:5 (2009), 651–664.

[62] See Gigerenzer, Gerd, *et al., The Empire of Chance: How Probability Changed Science and Everyday Life*, Cambridge, Cambridge University Press (1990), p. 47 and Schlich, "Objectifying Uncertainty." p. 212.

represented an important means of coping with uncertainty. It facilitated the test of hypotheses with regard to the efficacy (or otherwise) of treatments and therapies and it supported estimates of the certainty with which results were gained, or about the likelihood of certain events. According to Schlich, this supported the applicability of risk thinking in medicine and healthcare in four key areas.[63] These areas included predicting of illness, estimates and assessments of environmental risk, the identification and evaluation of lifestyle-related risk factors, and the assessment of risks associated with medical innovation and intervention, which we describe later on in the context of our analysis of the evolution of thinking about iatrogenic risk. Schlich proposed that the modern idea of risk factors, as it gained prominence in public health debates in the 1950s and 1960s, benefitted from advances in the areas of coronary and cardiovascular research as well as the rapidly expanding area of cancer research. This meant that much medical research and many medical discourses fully embraced risk language while drawing on key concepts of risk thinking, such as risk assessment and the assessment of costs and benefits under uncertainty.[64]

In parallel with the growth of research in these areas and the related emphasis of risk and risk factors, the risk–health nexus also attracted interest from other, perhaps unexpected, areas of health studies. Here we briefly discuss three fields of study which link risk, health, and medicine in their own, if related, way. They include the area of patient safety and quality of care, where much worked focused on iatrogenics or patient harm, the related area of accident studies and safety science, and lastly the related fields of quantitative medical decision making.

Iatrogenic risks relate to the possibility that a medical intervention causes real or potential harm to a patient or, in other words, creates iatrogenic risks. Iatrogenic events can be defined as "any untoward or adverse consequence of a preventive, diagnostic or therapeutic regimen or procedure that causes impairment, handicap, disability or death."[65] Schlich

---

[63] Schlich, "Objectifying Uncertainty," pp. 212–7.

[64] *Ibid.*, p. 212. See also Jasen, Patricia. "Breast Cancer and the Language of Risk, 1750–1950," *Social History of Medicine,* 15:1 (2002), 17–43.

[65] Last, John M., "Medicine and Health: Reducing the Hazards of Health Care," *World Health Forum*, 6 (1985), 135.

problematizes ideas of iatrogenic risks around medical innovation, in line with the earlier work of important researchers.[66] He argues that framing potential dangers of medical innovation in terms of risk, offered advantages to medical practitioners in that it implied that side-effects of medical innovation could be addressed in a calculable way. This view described the modern management of iatrogenic risks, or of the so-called side effects of treatment, as a risk management challenge. In so doing, it established a link with the discipline of risk management which evolved in the 1970s and 1980s, i.e. at a time when the analysis of iatrogenic risks was systematized. Iatrogenic risks, of course, do not only materialize in connection with medical innovation, although innovative procedures can be particularly risk prone. Iatrogenic risks, however, can also be associated with the "ordinary" day-to-day practice of medicine and healthcare.[67]

It is worth recalling that some early medical-organizational research already concerned itself with error prevention, with much of this focus being part of broader discussions around how to improve the quality of care, thus giving us important early examples of research into patient safety. For instance, Florence Nightingale's 19th century book, *Notes on Hospitals*, discussed the influence of sanitary conditions on mortality in hospitals, making recommendations with regard to hospital design and construction.[68] The Hungarian medic Ignaz Semmelweis conducted research on the role of hygiene in preventing childbed fever while working in the Vienna General Hospital's First Obstetrical Clinic which he published in 1857.[69]

Patient safety as a modern discipline attracted the systematic attention of medics during the middly of the 20th century, when several large-scale studies were undertaken in the United States.[70] Areas of focus in the early phases of the research included iatrogenic events in areas such

---

[66] Schlich, "Objectifying Uncertainty," pp. 215. See also Pickstone, John V. ed., *Medical Innovations in Historical Perspective*, New York, NY, St. Martin's Press (1992).

[67] See, e.g., Skolbekken, John-Arne, "The Risk Epidemic in Medical Journals," *Social Science and Medicine,* 40:3 (1995), 291–305; and Weingart, N. Saul, *et al.* "Epidemiology of Medical Error," *British Medical Journal,* 320:7237 (2000), 774–7.

[68] Nightingale, Florence, *Notes on Hospitals*, London: John W. Parker and Son, West Strand (1863).

[69] Vincent, Charles. *Patient Safety*. New York, NY, John Wiley & Sons (2011).

[70] *Ibid.*

as anesthesia,[71] diagnosis, and therapeutic procedures.[72] Recent decades have seen a renewed growth of studies on iatrogenic risks with US research playing a lead role.[73] This renewed focus on patient safety can be attributed to a number of factors, including medical malpractice litigation,[74] the impact of certain important research reports, and media attention to high profile cases such as the Shipman case and the Bristol Royal Infirmary inquiries.[75] Important reports include "To err is human," which the US Institute of Medicine (IOM) published in 1999.[76] The IOM's "To err is human" had a major impact on US patient care, making iatrogenic risk and patient safety a focal point for reform.[77] Like other

---

[71] Beecher, Henry K., and Donald P. Todd, "A Study of the Deaths Associated with Anesthesia and Surgery: Based on a Study of 599,548 Anesthesias in Ten Institutions 1948–1952, Inclusive," *Annals of Surgery,* 140:1 (1954), 2.

[72] Barr, David P., "Hazards of Modern Diagnosis and Therapy: The Price We Pay," *Journal of the American Medical Association,* 159:15 (1955), 1452–6; Moser, Robert Harlan, "Diseases of Medical Progress," *Clinical Pharmacology & Therapeutics,* 2:4 (1961), 446–522; Kanjanarat, P., Winterstein, A. G., Johns, T. E., Hatton, R. C., Gonzalez-Rothi, R., & Segal, R., "Nature of Preventable Adverse Drug Events in Hospitals: A Literature Review," *American Journal of Health-System Pharmacy*, 60:17 (2003), 1750–9.

[73] See, e.g. Brennan, Troyen A., *et al.,* "Incidence of Adverse Events and Negligence in Hospitalized Patients: Results of the Harvard Medical Practice Study I," *New England Journal of Medicine,* 324:6 (1991), 370–376; Gawande, Atul A., *et al.*, "The Incidence and Nature of Surgical Adverse Events in Colorado and Utah in 1992," *Surgery,* 126:1 (1999), 66–75.

[74] Wilson, Lionel L., and Max Fulton, "Risk Management: How Doctors, Hospitals and MDOs can Limit the Costs of Malpractice Litigation," *Medical Journal of Australia,* 172:2 (2000), 77–80.

[75] Pringle, M., "The Shipman Inquiry: Implications for the Public's Trust in Doctors", *The British Journal of General Practice*, 50:454 (200), 355; Walshe, Kieran, and N. Offen. "A Very Public Failure: Lessons for Quality Improvement in Healthcare Organisations from the Bristol Royal Infirmary," *British Medical Journal Quality & Safety,* 10:4 (2001), 250–6.

[76] Kohn, Linda T., Janet M. Corrigan, and Molla S. Donaldson, "Errors In Health Care: A Leading Cause of Death and Injury," in idem eds., *To Err is Human: Building a Safer Health System*, Washington DC, National Academies Press (1999).

[77] Berta, Whitney Blair, and Ross Baker, "Factors that Impact the Transfer and Retention of Best Practices for Reducing Error in Hospitals," *Health Care Management Review,* 29:2 (2004), 90–7.

reports in the area, the IOM report emphasized the preventability of errors through prudent and systematic risk management. In fact, error prevention has become an important and fruitful area for improvement in medical care and contributed much to the reduction of risk to patients.

There has been much progress in the intellectual development of the partly related area of social risk assessment and management. This area drew heavily on the pioneering work of Chauncey Starr (1912–2007). Publishing in the late 1960s and early 1970s, Starr suggested that historical accident statistics in relation to automobile use and road safety could be used to estimate what a society considered to be an acceptable risk in certain areas of activity and thus inform decisions about the introduction of safety measures and investment as well as guide the introduction and utilization of risky technologies and interventions.[78] While acknowledging that historical data could serve as an informal yardstick for establishing levels and acceptability of risk for certain activities, Starr cautioned that such data represented what was traditionally acceptable rather than what was socially desirable. Studies following Starr's lead have been able to highlight that risk tolerance in medicine can differ across countries in surprising ways, thus highlighting deficits some healthcare systems had to, or may have wished to, address.[79]

By the early 1980s, several sophisticated approaches were proposed for the employment of modern risk management assessment methods in medical decision making. Some of this work sought to extend the theoretical approaches initiated by Starr and others. Peter G. Moore's book, *The Business of Risk*, describes an intriguing hypothetical example of a medical decision-making problem, where knowledge of probabilities is shown to help make a therapeutic decision. In this example, a patient was diagnosed as having a stomach ulcer via X-ray.[80] Moore assumed that the

---

[78] Starr, Chauncey, "Social Benefit Versus Technological Risk: What is our Society Willing to Pay for Safety?", *Science* 165:3899 (1969), 1232–8; and Starr, Chauncey, and Chris Whipple, "A Perspective on Health and Safety Risk Analysis," *Management Science,* 30:4 (1984), 452–63.

[79] Girdwood, R. H., "Death After Taking Medicaments," *British Medical Journal,* 1:5906 (1974), 501–4.

[80] Moore, Peter G., *The Business of Risk*, Cambridge, Cambridge University Press, 1983, p. 173.

		States of Health	
		Benign	*Malignant*
Treatment approach	*Medication*	U_{11}	U_{12}
	Surgery	U_{21}	U_{22}
Probability		P_1	P_2

Note: The decision then can be gauged as product of P and U with the maximum expected utility being: $P_1U_{11}+P_2U_{22}$

Figure 2.1 Sample decision-making matrix.

Source: Modified from Moore 1983, p. 173.

treating doctor would be able to estimate the likelihood of the ulcer being benign or malignant. If the ulcer was benign, this could be treated through medicines, and if it was malignant, surgery would have to take place. Moore suggested that this could be represented as a two-by-two payoff matrix which presented the utility for each of the two "States of health" (benign and malign) on the horizontal axis and "Treatment approach" (medication or surgery) on the vertical axis. The utility of each treatment approach (medication or surgery) could be assessed by multiplying the utilities of the first treatment row (u11 and u12) with the predicted probabilities (p1 and p2) and adding them up (p1 × u11 + p2 × u12); this would then be compared with the same calculation for the second treatment (p1 × u21 + p2 × u22) (Moore, 1983, p. 173). A comparison of these two sums would then identify the expected utility value for each treatment and thus facilitate rational decision making (Figure 2.1).

Moore explored how this approach could be refined by taking into account, for instance, additional information about the patient's state of health, gained for example from a biopsy, or data about the likelihood of iatrogenic events. He suggested that similar approaches could be utilized to guide medical decision-making provided that there would be sufficiently accurate estimates of outcome probabilities, data on the costs of treatment, and values with regard to patient utilities or preference. Moore recognized that these data were not always available or could be highly inaccurate and he also noted that costs "would have to be placed on a common scale with the patient's utilities," which could be technically difficult or ethically controversial or complex to decide.

During the 1980s, some writers assumed that new methods of risk assessment and management, together with decision analytic frameworks, could put medical decision-making on a more solid footing than reliance on the clinical knowledge and experience of medics. In this context, particular interest emerged in relation to the possibilities of employing applications of cost-benefit analysis to medical decisions. This, however, did not gain broad approval, in part because of concerns with the ethical and medical complexities of human life.[81] Objections also related to the observation that nuances of therapeutic effect were not always fully understood, while there were disagreements on the medical implications of concepts such as efficacy and efficiency.[82]

Ideas about risk management have nonetheless impacted medicine and healthcare on several levels. This was particularly the case during the 1970s, when attempts to utilize modern risk management and decision-making techniques in connection with medical practice, healthcare, and public health surfaced throughout the literature. These approaches often attracted considerable enthusiasm from health policymakers as well as planners. However, their impact on day-to-day medical practice remained limited, mostly because of opposition from clinicians and their professional organisations. The emerging discourse about risk, medicine, risk management, and decision analysis, however, exerted a strong influence on at least two areas of medical practice. Firstly, those researching iatrogenic risk recognized that a solid understanding of risk management and risks could help generate defensible choices against litigation and other forms of institutionalized. Secondly, discussions about cost and benefit of treatments fed hopes that cost reduction might be achieved with little or no reductions in the quality of services.

---

[81] Wardell, W., "Assessment of The Benefits, Risks and Costs of Medical Progress," in D. Taylor ed., *Benefits and Risks in Medical Care,* London: Office of Health Economics (1974), 93–104.

[82] Feinstein, Alvan, R., "The Need for Humanised Science in Evaluating Medication," *The Lancet,* 300:7774 (1972), 421–3.

Some Ambiguities of Risk Factor Epidemiology

Recent research on cancer and cardiovascular disease has highlighted interactions between environmental factors, heredity, and lifestyle risks, making it difficult to strictly separate these approaches. Research on breast cancer, for example, initially suggested that factors such as child-bearing or breastfeeding, together with demographic factors or ethnicity, crucially affected the likelihood or risk of a woman contracting this disease. As research into hereditary risk factors progressed, these assumptions became less certain.[83] Similarly for premature coronary heart disease, a positive parental history has been confirmed as a risk factor, and heredity can be shown to have an effect once lifestyle factors were controlled for, including smoking, demographic factors such as social class as well as physiological factors such as high serum cholesterol, elevated blood pressure, diabetes, and obesity.[84] Studies from about the 1980s onwards, meanwhile, have identified hereditary risk factors for cancers other than breast cancer, including prostate cancer[85] and some types of brain cancers.[86]

Taken together, this research cast doubt on the views of earlier writers that, due to the decisive role of lifestyle factors, chronic disease was to a large degree the responsibility of individuals. By the end of the previous century, cancer research tended to associate mixtures of demographic, ethnic, hereditary, and genetic risk factors together with lifestyle and environmental factors in connection with cancer epidemiology and aetiology. In other words, the idea that lifestyle risks and, hence individual responsibility were always decisive for the health of individuals or groups of individuals

---

[83] Lynch, Henry T., "Hereditary Breast Cancer," *Annals of Medicine,* 23:5 (1991), 475–7.

[84] Jousilahti, Pekka, *et al.,* "Body Weight, Cardiovascular Risk Factors, and Coronary Mortality: 15-Year Follow-Up of Middle-Aged Men and Women in Eastern Finland," *Circulation,* 93:7 (1996), 1372–9.

[85] Bratt, Ola, "Hereditary Prostate Cancer: Clinical Aspects," *The Journal of Urology,* 168:3 (2002), 906–3.

[86] Malmer, Beatrice, Roger Henriksson, and Henrik Grönberg, "Familial Brain Tumours — Genetics or Environment? A Nationwide Cohort Study of Cancer Risk in Spouses and First-Degree Relatives of Brain Tumour Patients," *International Journal of Cancer* 106:2 (2003), 260–3.

was sometimes seen as problematic and reflected political beliefs rather than empirical research. Mold *et al.* cite Dorothy Porter as stating that, "By the end of the twentieth century, states facing the inexorable rising costs of providing health services from increasingly aging and chronically sick populations transformed personal wellness into an individual contribution to the commonwealth."[87] As Mold *et al.* would put it: Public health in this new form required a new kind of citizen, one that lived in a prudent and vigilant way to guarantee their good health. More radical observers argued that the idea of lifestyles as primary health risks gained prominence as part of the rise of neoliberal anti-welfare ideologies which informed UK and US politics during the 1980s (following the elections of Thatcher and Reagan). As a commonality, this modified lifestyle risk approach focused on individual responsibility for health outcomes, and in so doing de-emphasized the role of environmental, hereditary, occupational, or social factors. As Diez-Roux noted, epidemiological risk awareness shifted away from a focus on environmental risk factors to individual-level factors.[88] This individualization of risk perpetuated the idea that risk is individually determined rather than socially determined, and in so doing, discouraged research into the effects of macro-level or group-level variables on individual-level outcomes. "Lifestyles" and "behaviors" were regarded as matters of free individual choice and disassociated from the social contexts that shape and constrain them. It can, and has been, argued that this approach was not politically neutral, but that its emphasis on subjectivity and rational action were prone to lend support for market strategies in healthcare and health promotion strategies.[89]

---

[87] Mold, Alex, Peder Clark, Gareth Millward and Daisy Payling, *Placing the Public in Public Health in Post-War Britain, 1948–2012*, London, Palgrave MacMillan (2019), p. 2. Citing Porter, Dorothy, *Health Citizenship: Essays in Social Medicine and Biomedical Politics,* Berkeley, CA, Univ of California Press (2011), p. 2 and Petersen, Alan, and Deborah Lupton, *The New Public Health: Health and Self in the Age of Risk*, London, Sage (1996).

[88] Diez-Roux, Ana V. "Bringing Context Back into Epidemiology: Variables and Fallacies in Multilevel Analysis." *American Journal of Public Health* 88.2 (1998): 216–222. P. 216.

[89] Glasgow, Sara Mae, *The Private Life of Public Health: Managing Chronic Disease in an era of Neoliberal Governmentality*, Baltimore, MD. University of Maryland (2005).

Another critique of the risk factor approach concerned the question as to when, and by whom, a potentially harmful phenomenon was considered a health risk. Schlich gives an intriguing example of politicized decision making in relation to radioactivity resulting in a level of largely arbitrary standard setting.[90] This may have resulted in considerable harm to communities and workers exposed to thresholds that were, with hindsight, much too high.[91] Initially radioactivity was not considered a health hazard. The first permissible exposure limit, which marked the highest dose considered safe at the time, was set by physicist Arthur Mutscheller at a meeting of the American Roentgen Ray Society in 1924. Mutscheller proposed a permissible dose of about 70 rem per year or 0.2 rem per day, which was based on one hundredth of the monthly dose which he believed could cause harm to physicians and technicians (specifically a reddening of the skin, called erythema).[92] Mutscheller's recommendation and its refinement by the US Advisory Committee on X-Ray and Radiation Protection, which yielded a broadly similar result, subsequently became a formal standard for protecting individuals from radiation. The proposed radiation limit had no genuine basis in scientific research and was based primarily on the fact that this standard was technically achievable without major complications. Schlich reports how this standard came into question many years later, eventually leading to a new standard, when research the US biologist Muller (1890–1967) indicated that X-rays could cause mutations in *Drosophila* flies, and when an analysis of the dropping of two atomic bombs in August 1945, and nuclear tests and accidents[93] alerted members

[90] Schlich, "Objectifying Uncertainty," p. 213.

[91] Brown, Kathryn L., *Plutopia: Nuclear Families, Atomic Cities, and the Great Soviet and American Plutonium Disasters*, Oxford, Oxford University Press (2013).

[92] Inkret, William C., Charles B. Meinhold, and John C. Taschner. "A Brief History of Radiation Protection Standards," *Los Alamos Science,* 23 (1995), 116–123.

[93] The Castle Bravo test done in the Bikini atoll (Marshall Islands) in 1954, was a military experiment that affected civilians and military personnel in peacetime. Agnoletti and Sereni, *The Basic Environmental History*, p. 237, also highlight: "the fire and the release of radioactive material into the surrounding environment that occurred in 1957 in the British nuclear central of Windscale and the steam explosion and meltdown of the Stationary Low — Power Reactor Number One (SL-1) occurred in 1961 in an experimental reactor of the United States Army."

of the public to the destructive power of these weapons.[94] In response to the concerns of scientists and members of the public, the US National Academy of Sciences decided to investigate the issue and created a new standard which was to be based on a maximum permissible dose over a period of 30 years. This dose was to be determined as follows: background radiation together with radioactivity in homes and food were expected to amount to 4.3 rem over the period, to which would be added 0.002–0.5 rem from then permissible weapons testing as well as 3 rem from medical radiation, which would amount to a maximum permissible dose of 10 rem (or double the assumed levels of background radiation) over the 30-year time period.

The regulation of radiation is only one of many instances in which societal approaches to environmental risk have evolved from political interests and the reification of technical expediency.[95] These behavioral patterns can have serious adverse effects on the acknowledgement of major environmental risks. This has been recognized, for example, in connection with the regulation of asbestos,[96] which has been marked by a long-term reluctance to accept the risk to human health posed by all types of this mineral. Therefore, statements about environmental risks in particular cannot always be taken at face value but sometimes must be viewed in connection with political, economic, and even security interest which influence official attitudes. This issue can be particularly serious when key environmental risks are downgraded on account of lifestyle factors, and industrial activity or the use of certain materials are assessed in terms of their relative impact on individual health.[97]

---

[94] Schlich, "Objectifying uncertainty," p. 213.

[95] Brand, Ulrich, *et al.*, *Conflicts in Environmental Regulation and the Internationalisation Of The State: Contested Terrains*. London, Routledge (2008) discusses these issues in connection with the global regulation of biodiversity politics through the UN.

[96] McCulloch, Jock, and Geoffrey Tweedale, *Defending the Indefensible: The Global Asbestos Industry and its Fight for Survival*, Oxford, Oxford University Press (2008).

[97] Watterson, Andrew, and Matthias Beck, "An Exploratory Study of Beryllium and UK Soft Touch Regulation: An Enduring Example of Weaknesses of UK Occupational Health and Safety Governance," *International Journal of Environmental Research and Public Health,* 19:12771 (2022).

Another related issue is that the amount of variability in disease occurrence and impact that is attributable to lifestyle-related risk factors is often very limited, in a way that makes it appear to merely distract from environmental factors. Accordingly, one of the leading contemporary textbooks on social epidemiology, concludes in relation to heart diseases that: "Dozens of ... risk factors have been proposed, but not everyone agrees about them: obesity, physical inactivity, diabetes, blood lipid and clotting factors, stress, and various hormone factors. Nevertheless, when all of these risk factors are considered together, they explain only about 40% of the coronary heart disease that occurs."[98] Perhaps even more important is the recognition, highlighted in a recent Center for Disease Control publication that "health continues to be affected by factors beyond the physical environment, medical care, and health behaviors. These include socioeconomic position, race/ethnicity, social networks and support, work conditions, economic inequality, and social capital."[99]

As observed by Schlich, proponents of the pure risk factor approach selectively interpreted research such as the Framingham study as indicating that factors mirroring lifestyles choice, such as being overweight or having hypercholesteremia, determined individual health. This went so far as to treat lifestyle risk factors as "if they were straightforward diseases,"[100] so that risk factors became "a central part of modern clinical, public and financial strategies for predicting and managing individual variation in predisposition and experience." Implied in Schlich's analysis is the suspicion that the risk factor approach not only crowded out research on other causes of disease, but also systematically ignored questions about the pressures and factors which led individuals to adopt certain life-style choices.

In summary then, risk discourses in medicine were not politically neutral. By emphasizing distinct categories of risks, some of these discourses indirectly supported specific technical, social, and political agendas.

---

[98] Berkman, Kawachi, and Glymour, *Social Epidemiology*, p. xi.

[99] See Remington, and Brownson, "Fifty Years", p. 70; Institute of Medicine, *The Future of the Public's Health in the 21st Century*, Washington, DC, National Academies Press (2002).

[100] Schlich, "Objectifying Uncertainty," p. 214.

Accordingly, a focus on hereditary risk could bolster medico-technical research agendas related to the identification of specific genetic aspects of diseases. Meanwhile, environmental approaches could lend support to research in this area as well as improve regulatory control of emissions. The risk factor approach lastly, presented perhaps the most convenient political agenda, as it placed responsibilities on the individual, while giving the state primarily the duty to inform and campaign, while also allowing it to question environmental and related agendas. These themes and facets of medical discourse continue to be revisited in different guises and contexts.

Researchers concerned with social aspects of epidemiology have pointed to other weaknesses of the classical risk factor approach. Thus, Berkman *et al.* cite research indicating that an individual's risk of illness cannot be considered in isolation from the disease risk of the population to which she belongs.[101] These sophisticated approaches, however, have yet to fully penetrate modern thinking about medical risk.

[101] Berkman, Kawachi, and Glymour, *Social Epidemiology*, p. 7.

Chapter Three

Immigration

Public Health and Immigration: A Problematic Legacy

This chapter focuses on immigration policies of the US during the period from the mid to late 1800 into the mid-1900s. Specifically, the center of our attention is on the use of public health-based justifications for immigration restrictions aimed primarily at potential Asian immigrants. The reason for this focus is that the US government created severe immigration restrictions for these population groups, which were often justified during campaigns or in the formal proceedings of lawmakers, on account of public health reasons. Relevant exclusionary acts of Congress included the Page Act of 1875, the Chinese Exclusion Act of 1882, the Scott Act of 1888, the Immigration Act of 1891, the Geary Act of 1892, the Immigration Act of 1903 (Anarchist Exclusion Act), the Naturalization Act of 1906, the Immigration Act of 1907, the Immigration Act of 1917 (Barred Zone Act), the Emergency Quota Act of 1921, and the Chinese Exclusion Repeal Act of 1943 (Magnuson Act).[1] The history of these activities, their

[1] See, e.g. Goldin, Claudia, "The political Economy of Immigration Restriction in the United States, 1890 to 1921," in Claudia Goldin and Gary D. Libecap, eds, *The Regulated Economy: A Historical Approach to Political Economy*, University of Chicago Press (1994), 223–58; and Lee, Erika, "The "Yellow Peril" and Asian Exclusion in the Americas," *Pacific Historical Review,* 76:4 (2007), 537–562; and Lee, Erika, "The Chinese Exclusion Example: Race, immigration, and American Gatekeeping, 1882–1924," *Journal of American Ethnic History* 21:3 (2002), 36–62.

underlying motivation, and even the role of health-related debates and justifications has been the focus of much work and generally Been well researched,[2] so in this chapter does not fill a major knowledge gap. Nonetheless, our focus on public health risks offers novel insights.

The principal purpose of this chapter thus is to give an insight into the fraught and often fraudulent public health arguments, which were made historically to restrict immigration to the US. In other words, again following a largely chronological set-up, this chapter seeks to portray the use and abuse of health-related arguments in relation to migrants, ranging from the narrow observational condemnations of sanitary conditions made in immigrant areas, to the conceptual fabrications relating to "race pollution" proposed by the eugenics movement and its key protagonists in the early decades of the 1900s. In so doing, our primary goal is to gauge the breadth of the often poisonous and hateful claims which were made in relation to immigration under the guise of addressing public health problems. This will serve as basis for a typology of distorted communication patterns around public health, which will form the backbone of our concluding chapter on detecting flawed types of risk communication.

Early United States Nativism and the Making of Chinese Exclusion

The origins of anti-immigration politics and nativism as it manifested itself at the end of the 1700s into the early decades of the 1800s are not

[2] Molina, Natalia, "Medicalizing the Mexican: Immigration, Race, and Disability in the Early-twentieth-century United States." *Radical History Review,* 2006:94 (2006), 22–37; and O'Brien, Gerald V., "Indigestible Food, Conquering Hordes, and Waste Materials: Metaphors of Immigrants and the Early Immigration Restriction Debate in the United States." *Metaphor and Symbol* 18:1 (2003), 33–47; and Ngai, Mae M., "The Strange Career of the Illegal Alien: Immigration Restriction and Deportation Policy in the United States, 1921–1965," *Law and History Review* 21:1 (2003), 69–108; Markel, Howard. ""The Eyes Have It": Trachoma, the Perception of Disease, the United States Public Health Service, and the American Jewish Immigration Experience, 1897–1924," *Bulletin of the History of Medicine* 74:3 (2000), 525–60; and Markel, Howard, "Cholera, Quarantines, and Immigration Restriction: The View from Johns Hopkins, 1892," *Bulletin of the History of Medicine,* 67:4 (1993), 691–95.

entirely clear. Building on Higham's seminal work from the mid-1950s,[3] Scharf proposes that nativist lobbying commenced following first efforts to restrict immigration through an extension of required residency from 5 to 14 years in the naturalization act of 1798. Specifically, she suggests that a form of persistent protestant nativism started asserting itself between 1825 and 1850, when immigrant numbers were still relatively low.[4] As latent element of colonial identity, this early nativism voiced concerns over the gradually increasing number of immigrants who practiced the catholic faith, which nativists viewed as conflicting with American freedoms and the nation's belief systems.[5]

Scharf states that opposition to immigration intensified toward the 1880s. At this time, work at railroads which employed many Chinese laborers was nearing completion and the "nascent labor movement [was] eager for them to return to their native lands, hence the support for the Chinese Exclusion Act of 1882."[6] The following part of this chapter will look at developments leading up to this legislation in greater detail, both because of the blatantly racist nature of this Act,[7] and because of the sheer intensity which with this legislation was promoted and enforced.[8]

According to an insightful and detailed historical account of events leading up to Chinese exclusion, published as early as 1912, the Californian population did not openly object to the first Chinese immigrants of 1848.[9] Problems first arose in the mines, where Chinese laborers were content with less than half the daily wage of whites: "In 1849 the Chinese were expelled from Chinese Camp, a mining camp eight or ten miles south of Sonora. In the Columbia district in Tuolumne County, no

[3] Higham, John, *Strangers in the Land: Patterns of American Nativism*, 1860–1925, New Brunswick, NJ, Rutgers University Press (2002).

[4] Scharf, Irene, "Tired of Your Masses: A History of and Judicial Responses to Early 20th Century Anti-Immigration Legislation," *U. Hawaii. Law Review,* 21 (1999), 131.

[5] Barry, Colman J., "Some Roots of American Nativism," *The Catholic Historical Review* 44:2 (1958), 137–46.

[6] *Ibid.*, p. 132.

[7] Lee, Erika, "The Chinese Exclusion Example", 36–62.

[8] Lew-Williams, Beth, *The Chinese Must Go: Violence, Exclusion, and the Making of the Alien in America*, Cambridge, MA, Harvard University Press (2018).

[9] Wellborn, Mildred, "The Events Leading to the Chinese Exclusion Acts," *Annual Publication of the Historical Society of Southern California,* 9:1/2 (1912), 49–58.

Asiatics or South Sea islanders were allowed to mine for themselves or others, and no one was allowed to sell a claim to an Oriental."[10] In parallel, anti-Chinese agitation took place in other parts of the state, particularly in San Francisco. The main target of this agitation was contract laborers or "coolies," whom propagandists associated with gambling, living in filthy places, and keeping opium dens.[11] Some unenlightened politicians latched on to this by claiming that the Chinese were a danger to American institutions, maintained secret societies, and refused to assimilate.

Mildred Wellborn's 1912 account of racial tensions and anti-Chinese animus in California summarizes its causes as follows: "The first objection … was that the presence of the Chinese reduced the wages of the laborers, but increased the profits of the capitalists. However, it is doubtful if the Chinese actually made any perceptible change in the labor market, except for a period of six to ten years from 1863 to about 1875, and then not because labor was too abundant, but because money was scarce. The more fundamental cause for the anti-Chinese sentiment is probably to be found in race prejudice … ."[12] John Bigler (1805–1871), a Democrat who ran on an anti-Chinese platform, became the third governor of California from 1852 to 1856.[13] In 1854, the California legislature sent a resolution to Congress, asking that a tax be placed on Chinese or Japanese immigrants to be paid by the importing vessel, which was stopped on constitutional grounds. As noted by Wellborn:

> … in the mining camps the opposition to the Chinese had been growing or was manifested by riots and attempted lynchings. Consequently, this same legislature of '55 raised the Foreign Miners' Tax from four to six dollars per month. … the following legislature raised the tax to eight dollars, the next session to ten and so on for each succeeding year. As a

---

[10] *Ibid.*, p. 49.

[11] *Ibid.*, p. 50; Schwantes, Carlos A., "From Anti-Chinese Agitation to Reform Politics: The Legacy of the Knights of Labor in Washington and the Pacific Northwest," *The Pacific Northwest Quarterly,* 88:4 (1997), 174–184.

[12] *Ibid.*, p. 51.

[13] Paul, Rodman W., "The Origin of the Chinese Issue in California," *The Mississippi Valley Historical Review,* 25:2 (1938), 181–96; and Caldwell, Dan, "The Negroization of the Chinese Stereotype in California," *Southern California Quarterly* 53:2 (1971), 123–31.

> result of this increase in the license tax, almost all the Chinese gave up mining.[14] Many of them returned to China, and others congregated in the cities ... [but] [t]he discovery of a new vein of gold was sufficient to draw many Chinese back to the mines in spite of the high tax ... In 1859 the anti Chinese feeling reached such a pitch among the miners that Governor Weiler had to send a company of the militia to put down riots in Shasta county.[15] During the years of the Civil War the people had their attention diverted from local to national affairs, and from contract coolies to negro slaves. But in spite of more urgent and important questions of the day, the Legislature of 1862 appointed a committee which conferred with prominent Chinese officials and reported that there were 50,000 Chinese in the state [who] were no contract laborers; that the Chinese were not inordinately immoral; that they had been the victims of a system of wrongs and outrages; and that it would be most advantageous for the United States to maintain friendly commercial relations with China.[16]

Following the end of the Civil War, anti-Chinese societies were formed by workers, and the strongly anti-Chinese Democrat Henry Huntly Haight (1825–1878) was elected 10th governor of California from 1867 to 1871.[17] Wellborn reports how following some years of economic turmoil, the mid-1870s saw "cruel and unjustifiable outrages that were perpetrated upon the Chinese," while the Democrats held mass meetings by way of directing the wrath of the people toward the unfortunate Chinese who were targeted by rioters of all kinds.[18] In 1876, the California Legislature appointed a committee to investigate Chinese immigration. Its report was published in an *Address to the People of the United States upon the Evils*

---

[14] See also Kanazawa, Mark, "Immigration, Exclusion, and Taxation: Anti-Chinese Legislation in Gold Rush California." *The Journal of Economic History,* 65:3 (2005), 779–805.

[15] See also Sandmeyer, Elmer Clarence, *The Anti-Chinese Movement in California*, Champaign, IL, University of Illinois Press (1991).

[16] Wellborn, "The Events Leading to the Chinese Exclusion Acts," p. 52.

[17] Bottoms, D. Michael, *An Aristocracy of Color: Race and Reconstruction in California and the West, 1850–1890*, Vol. 5., Norman, Oklahoma, University of Oklahoma Press (2013).

[18] Wellborn, "The Events Leading to the Chinese Exclusion Acts", pp. 53–4.

of Chinese Immigration, which were said to include prostitution, criminality, non-conversion, competition, and coolie-slavery. The proposed remedies entailed, among others: 1) Cooperation with Great Britain in suppressing the coolie trade, 2) Abrogation of all existing treaties which permitted Chinese immigration, and 3) Congressional enactment prohibiting more than fifteen Chinese to land at any one time and place.[19] Wellborn observed that this report showed great ignorance, for the coolie trade had already been prohibited by both Great Britain and the US. Wellborn cites the historian Theodore H. Hittell (1813–1917), stating that the main result of this publication was "to furnish anti-Chinese thunder for the demagogues of the San Francisco sand lots."[20]

Wellborn reports a turning point in terms of Federal support for the California legislators around 1880. In 1880, a Commission was appointed to negotiate a new treaty with China, with the Chinese Emperor being willing to restrict the emigration of laborers, criminals, prostitutes, and diseased persons. The new agreement included revisions to the old Burlingame Treaty and allowed restrictions to the admission of laborers. In 1882, further legislation was added to execute the provisions of this treaty, and this became the first of the series of provisions later known as the Chinese Exclusion Acts. In 1886, negotiations were begun for a new treaty which would absolutely prohibit the immigration of Chinese laborers for a period of 20 years.[21] As if this was not enough, the Geary Act of 1892 led to a *de facto* extension of anti-Chinese legislation for an additional period of 10 years, while placing the burden of proof of the right to remain upon Chinese immigrants.[22] In 1902, existing anti-Chinese legislation was extended to the islands belonging to the US, and Chinese on the islands were forbidden to come to the States except under the same conditions as applied to those coming directly from China.

As a concluding remark to her chronology, Wellborn observed that "we have almost forgotten the Chinese question and have turned to the

[19] *Ibid*, p. 54.
[20] *Ibid*, p. 55.
[21] *Ibid*, p. 56.
[22] Lee, Erika, *At America's Gates: Chinese Immigration during the Exclusion Era, 1882–1943,* Chapel Hill, NC, Univ of North Carolina Press (2003).

Japanese instead, as exampled by the School Question of 1907 and the Alien Land Law of 1913." She found these developments deeply questionable on account of the fact that anti-Japanese agitation now came to repeat much of the fear and panic mongering of earlier anti-Chinese policies. Following on from this, Wellborn's 1923 chronology of anti-immigration politics ended on an interesting note, where she stated that "it would be both impossible and unkind, at this time when China is looking to the United States for help and guidance in the formation of the new republic, to prevent the Chinese from coming to our country to travel and study and learn of us."[23]

Nativism, in the view of liberal members of the US political landscape, started presenting a contradiction as early as 1912 when Wellborn wrote her chronology: On the one hand there was a case for lawmakers to follow the democratic process and to implement the wishes of the public as articulated through the electoral process. On the other hand, if the US desired to be a global power whose political system was to be emulated by other countries, then it could not, as World War One was about to show, shut itself off against immigrants and global politics more generally. Remarkably, the Chinese Exclusion Acts were primarily the product of regional lobbying, with California playing a key role. Meanwhile, federal policy making was in the background, although Congress ultimately came to authorize some of the state's legislative excesses.

Lobbying for Exclusion and References to Public Health

Our brief and sketchy chronology of Californian nativism has mentioned some of the intensity with which this movement carried out its activities from the mid-1800s into the 1910s. This section will look at examples of the type of agitation which characterised this debate with a special focus on claims about the health impact of Chinese immigration. The presentation of our text examples will follow a roughly chronological order, with samples being chosen on account of their representativeness for the type of propaganda which was being disseminated during this period.

[23] *Ibid*, p. 58.

One of the first prominent anti-Asian publications authored by a medic, was entitled *Chinese Immigration and the Physiological Causes the Decay of a Nation*. It was published in 1862 in San Francisco by Arthur Breese Stout, M.D.[24] Stout (1814–1898) studied medicine at the College of Physicians and Surgeons in New York where he received a M.D. degree in 1839. He then visited Europe and upon returning to New York in 1848 accepted the position of ship's surgeon on steamship S. S. California. Stout went into practice in San Francisco in 1849. Apart from running his own medical practice as "one of the leading physicians in the city", he was Professor of Surgery from 1872 to 1874 in Dr. Hugh Toland's Medical School in San Francisco. Politically Stout was active in San Francisco's Vigilance committee, but this appears to have been less relevant to him than his writing. Apart from his work on Chinese immigration, Stout became known for books on cataract surgery[25] and sewage in San Francisco,[26] as well as his testimonial before Congress in 1877 on immigration and health.[27]

Stout's anti-immigration writing was as pompous and pseudo-intellectual, as it was spiteful and aggressive. Here we quote from the introduction to his 1862 book, *Chinese Immigration and the Physiological Causes of the Decay of a Nation*, where he states:

> The Medical men disseminated through a state, are proper censors of the public health. It is their high province not only to cure disease, but to study and to promulgate the principles of Hygiene. In preventing the invasion of disease, they fulfill a more lofty, because more disinterested function, than in eradicating maladies already engendered. Occupying a high and influential position their counsels and their teachings are all-powerful in contributing to improve the health, the strength, the vigor, both physical and intellectual, and also the endurance among nations of

[24] Stout, Arthur B., *Chinese Immigration and the Physiological Causes of the Decay of a Nation*. San Francesco, Agnew & Deffebach (1862).

[25] Stout, Arthur B., *A Thesis on the Cataract: With Some Remarks on the Eye*. New York, NY, Henderson Greene (1837).

[26] *Ibid*.

[27] Trauner, Joan B., "The Chinese as Medical Scapegoats in San Francisco, 1870–1905," *California History*, 57:1 (1978), 70–87.

their race. It is in this view that I propose to examine the various causes which combine to deteriorate the American people. (P. 1)

He then goes on to state somewhat predictably:

> The time to urge and impress the mind with the necessity of preserving the purity of race, is while the race is new, and thus close the door to amalgamations while the stock is pure and young. To permit the ingress of an inferior race is to strike at self-destruction. A government to protect its people should strive to preserve the purity of the race; and, irrespective of political theories, should guard it from every amalgamation with inferior types.
>
> No State of our Union is so exposed and threatened as California. At the very dawn of its existence it is menaced with the introduction of these pernicious elements; and if now the struggle for life be not commenced, it must forever be abandoned. The degeneration will pursue its course, in personal and individual antipathies finding its only check.
>
> I am led to these reflections from the contest now waging in regard to the Chinese immigration. ... By intermarrying with Europeans, we are but reproducing our own Caucasian type; by commingling with the Eastern Asiatics, we are creating degenerate hybrids. (pp. 8 and 9)

Stout's rhetoric becomes more alarmist as he moves on. Here we quote from a paragraph which is interesting because it anticipates some of the arguments of later writers associated with "scientific racism." Notably, he fields arguments about the balance of different racial groupings and the danger of the influx of non-white populations could pose to white Americans:

> ... when, in addition to the American Indian and Negro amalgamation, the Asiatic Indian shall have had free scope; when, in that time which for nationalities is short, the Chinese, Japanese, Malays and Mongolians of every caste, shall have overrun the land; when they, in their turn, have given origin to their countless varieties of hybrid creatures. As the locusts of California overrun the fields of the husbandman, will these swarms of beings degenerate our land. (P. 13)

Stout's concern with intermarriage or "hybrid creatures" probably bears little semblance to facts, yet it is interesting in terms of his anticipation of much later arguments of the eugenics movement which frequently spoke of "mongrelization." In other words, Stout already saw "racial pollution" as a major threat to the United States which he believed was especially vulnerable as a young nation. His next question then, was why resistance was limited, and it is here that he refers to a combination of well-rehearsed arguments about the docile, self-sufficient nature of Coolieism and claims about the public health risk they created:

> Let the Attilas of Asiatic despotism appear, and every freeman will prove to be a Meroveg; but against a Coolie who can struggle? … If the former drive back these hardy pioneers, who shall defend the land? Who shall whiten the plains with their homesteads? Who shall form the families of the Republic? The vigorous strength of Caucasian labor cannot be nourished with a handful of rice, nor will their intelligence for their own emolument, or their aspirations for their children, accept existence in a state of protracted Coolieism or serfdom. Reduce their wages to the rates of Coolieism and you degrade them, physically and morally, to the state of Coolies. (P. 14)

Having made his key political points, Stout discussed a few additional dangers posed by immigrants. These included "hereditary diseases, [such] as phthisis or consumption, scrofula, syphilis, mental alienation, and epidemic diseases"[28] (leprosy and smallpox are mentioned later on) as well as tobacco and opium addiction.

Stout's rhetorical excesses were not untypical of the agitation of the time, which tended to mix early eugenics-type arguments about race pollution and "mongrelization" with economic concerns over wage levels, throwing in other traditional anti-immigration arguments around communicable diseases or contagious addictions and habits (as in case of opium consumptions). Trauner reports that when a smallpox epidemic struck San Francisco (1875–1876), the city health officer ordered every house in Chinatown to be thoroughly fumigated, declaring that "the cause [of the epidemic] is the presence in our midst of 30,000 (as a class) of

[28] *Ibid.*, pp. 20–4.

unscrupulous, lying and treacherous Chinamen, who have disregarded our sanitary laws, concealed and are concealing their cases of smallpox."[29]

Stout's 1862 *Chinese Immigration and the Physiological Causes of the Decay of a Nation* was among the earliest publications by a medic which was aimed at agitating against Chinese immigration. As such it anticipated many of the arguments which subsequent publications and testimonials utilized. This applied, among other works, to the 1876 *Chinese Immigration-Testimony Taken Before a Committee of the Senate of the State of California.*[30] The Democrat William Irwin (1827–1886) was appointed 13th governor of California between 1875 and 1880, following the Republican José Antonio Romualdo Pacheco whose response to the state's anti-immigration lobby had been considered unsatisfactory. Following public demand and agitation, the California State Senate created a special committee to investigate the impact of Chinese Immigration, chaired by State Senator Creed Haymond. This committee conducted hearings in San Francisco and Sacramento with witnesses such as US diplomats with experience in China, American businessmen who employed Chinese workers, law enforcement officers, public health officials, medics, and educators.[31] Due to the overlap of some of these testimonies with Stout's narrative, we focus on one testimony only. This testimony took place on the eighth day of the proceedings (San Francisco, 20 April 1876) and involved Dr Toland, the founder of Toland Medical University who was also a member of the San Francisco Board of Health. Toland Medical College had been founded in 1864 and became affiliated with the University of California in 1873. Hugh Huger Toland (1806–1880) originally hailed from South Carolina and made a name as a successful surgeon in San Francisco. He eventually secured the merger of his private college with the University of California.[32] Toland was well known for his concern with the public health hazards

---

[29] Trauner, "The Chinese as Medical Scapegoats in San Francisco," p. 73.

[30] California Legislature Senate Special, *Chinese Immigration: The Social, Moral, and Political Effect of Chinese Immigration. Testimony Taken Before a Committee of the Senate of the State of California, Appointed April 3d, 1876*, Sacramento, State Printing Office (1876).

[31] Lutton, Wayne, "1876 California Report on Chinese Immigration," *The Social Contract,* 6:3 (1996).

[32] Gardner, Frances Tomlinson, "The little acorn: Hugh Huger Toland, 1806–1880," *Bulletin of the History of Medicine* 24:1 (1950), 61–9.

arising from saloons and similar establishments. As part of his testimony, Toland focused on sexually transmitted diseases he claimed originated from Chinese immigrant prostitutes. Toland said:

> There is scarcely a single day that there are not a dozen young men at my office with syphilis or gonorrhoea. A great many of them have not means to be treated properly and nine cases out of ten it is the ruin of them. I have treated a great many of them and I have treated the parents. Sometimes the parents would come and after going through a course of treatment would bring their children. ... ...
>
> [Q: To what extent do these disease come from Chinese Prostitutes]
>
> I suppose nine-tenth. When these persons come to me I ask them where they got the disease and they generally tell me that they have been with Chinawomen. I think that diseases contracted from Chinawomen are harder to cure than those contracted elsewhere, so they tell me as a matter of self-protection. I am satisfied, from my experience, that nearly all boys in town that have venereal disease contracted it in Chinatown. They have no difficulty there for the prices are so low they can go whenever they please. (P. 104)

Following Californian representations to Congress, in July 1876, a concurrent resolution was introduced and carried in the US Senate and House of Representatives authorizing a joint special committee to investigate Chinese Immigration.[33] Three members from each house were to proceed to the Pacific Coast, where they procured testimony. The committee was required to report to the next session of Congress.[34]

The group reiterated some of the points made in previous reports about prostitution by Dr Toland.[35] The report also included a description of Chinatown by Mr Frank Morrison Pixley (1825–1895), a journalist, attorney, and politician who had served as 8th attorney general of California from 1861 to 1863. When Pixley was asked during the

---

[33] Gold, Martin, *Forbidden Citizens: Chinese Exclusion and the US Congress: A Legislative History*. The Capitol Net Inc (2011).

[34] Sargent, Senator Aaron A., "Report of the Joint Special Committee to Investigate Chinese Immigration," *Senate Rept*, 689 (1877).

[35] *Ibid*, p. 14.

proceedings "in what way do they [the Chinese] live in the city [San Francisco]," he responded as follows:

> The mayor and chief of police will extend to the honorable commission an invitation to visit the Chinese quarter, under the protection and guardianship of our police, who are familiar with all these purlieus, and we believe, gentlemen, that you will see such a spectacle of squalor, filth, disease, wretchedness, and crime as you never before witnessed, and, as we believe, exists in no other portion of the civilized world. You will recognize that it is a misfortune and a disgrace to our city that it should be permitted to exist. You will go down into underground tunnels. You will see that they pass from street to street by underground excavations. You will find them living down two or three stories deep in the earth, under sidewalks, in rooms divided, as I understand it, in the garret, and on their roofs, and on their balconies. In what way do they live? You will be better convinced by personal observation, by seeing their sights, hearing their one-string fiddles, smelling their diverse smells, visiting their hospitals, and witnessing their sick, than by any evidence that we can produce to you except the evidence of photography. We hope to be able to lay before you a series of views which will illustrate somewhat the condition of these people in their homes. (pp. 21 and 22)

In another passage, Pixley blamed Chinese immigrants for a recent smallpox outbreak. He said:

> .. within a few days several others died, showing that the disease had existed in the Chinese Quarter prior to this time, I do not know how long. They may have had any number of cases there without a death. That made it positive that the first death occurred in that quarter. I do not think that is a matter of much consequence, however. During the winter-time we frequently have cases of small-pox imported from the Mast among the immigrants, but we do not regard that. Those cases are isolated or removed, and precautions are taken to prevent its spread. I do not think in any civilized or well-regulated community we ought ever to have an epidemic of small-pox. I do not believe we ever would, if the local authorities would take proper measures to prevent it; as they have taken every measure that it was proper for them to take during this epidemic. I do not think we would have had an epidemic here at all, if it had not

> been for the concealment of these cases in Chinatown. During the early part of the epidemic, probably three-fourths of the cases occurred among white people in that portion of the city who had to pass through Chinatown constantly, going to and from their business. Of course, after a while it became general: the whole atmosphere became poisoned with this contagion, and people in any portion were liable to take it. (P. 128)

Pixley's testimony represented a case of scapegoating in fairly pure form. Earlier testimony before the same committee had spoken of Chinese inoculation practices against smallpox and mentioned the healthiness and cleanliness of this immigrant population. Yet here, Chinese immigrants were blamed for a smallpox outbreak which primarily affected white populations. We can of course not reject with absolute certainty the claim that the San Francisco's smallpox epidemic originated from Chinatown, however, other claims about inoculation practices and the health status of this community should make us as at least suspicious.

The California Senate report of 1876 and the report of the Congressional Joint Committee of 1877 had barely been circulated, when yet another inquiry was conducted. This involved a report published in 1885 by the board of Supervisors. The President of the Board of Supervisors had appointed three members as a Special Committee to "inspect and report upon that portion of the city commonly known as Chinatown, with a view of ascertaining so far as possible whether a condition of things exist in such quarter injurious to the public health or public morals, and what measures it may be necessary to adopt, if any, to correct abuses and abate public nuisances commonly supposed to exist in such district."[36]

It may be worth quoting the opening page of the 1885 report in full, if only to convey the tenor of the city government of the time, with its persistent efforts to link Chinese immigration to health problems:

> The attention of the Board of Supervisors had been repeatedly called to the continued and persistent violation of the sanitary regulations in that

---

[36] San Francisco, Supervisors, Board of, *Report of the Special Committee of the Board of Supervisors of San Francisco on the Condition of the Chinese Quarter of that City*, San Francisco, CA, AL Bancroft & Company (1885), p. 163.

> portion of the city occupied by the Chinese. The foul and filthy condition of the premises in that quarter; the total disregard paid to the regulations for protection against fire by the erection and maintenance of wooden additions to buildings; the violation of what is known as the cubic air law, by the over-crowding of premises; the vicious and pernicious practices and occupations carried on and conducted surreptitiously in defiance of law; with the ingenuity of these people in heretofore successfully thwarting all attempts to eradicate the nuisances, practices and occupations complained of, were so manifest, that the Board of Supervisors were of the conviction that some inquiry should be instituted as to how those evils were permitted to exist and what corrective action should be taken.
>
> The dangers arising therefrom to the health and lives of the people presented the peculiar condition of this thickly inhabited part of the city so forcibly as to lead to the conclusion that there must be causes which could tolerate a state of affairs so inimical to the welfare of the community, which it was proper to ascertain so that they might be removed.
>
> The question naturally presented itself whether any additional legislation was required, or whether there were laches on the part of the executive officers or departments, or whether the available force of those departments were inadequate to enforce the regulations and duties which were observed and performed in other portions of the city. It had been conceded and was unquestioned that this portion of the city was a standing menace to the health of the community. With these views and believing it to be the imperative duly of the municipal government to intervene for the public welfare, and to ascertain and present clearly the facts in connection with the occupation and use of this portion of the city, so that effective means might be taken and enforced to have the regulations passed for the general welfare observed.[37]

The 1885 Board of Supervisor report marks perhaps the high point of anti-Chinese agitation, and it is probably not surprising that this period was also characterised by numerous acts of physical violence against this

[37] *Ibid.*

community.[38] San Francisco's Chinatown, meanwhile, was the target of numerous complaints, which linked its presence to health risks for the population of the city as a whole. Here we quote from an early section of the 1885 report:

> All great cities have their slums and localities where filth, disease, crime and misery abound; but in the very best aspect which Chinatown can be made to present, it must stand apart, conspicuous and beyond them all in the extreme degree of all these horrible attributes, the rankest outgrowth of human degradation that can be found upon this continent. Here it may truly be said that human beings exist under conditions (as regards their mode of life and the air they breathe) scarcely one degree above those under which the rats of our water-front and other vermin live, breathe and have their being. And this order of things seems inseparable from the very nature of the race, and probably must be accepted and borne with — must be endured, if it cannot be cured — restricted and looked after, so far as possible, with unceasing vigilance, so that, whatever of benefit, 'of degree,' even, that may be derived from such modification of the evil of their presence among us, may at least be attained, not daring to hope that there can be any radical remedy for the great, overshadowing evil which Chinese immigration has inflicted upon this people. (P. 166)

In addition to hateful agitation of this kind, a considerable portion of the report was dedicated to pseudo-technical discussions of problems of overcrowding and the use of fires. The issue of open fires formed a central part in the scapegoating strategies of the report's authors, where it was argued that they presented a violation of local laws and presented a clear and present danger, while also producing otherwise unmanageable disease spread on account of the fumigation or air pollution they provided. Thus, the report argued:

> There is not a day in the year in which this order is not violated in hundreds and hundreds of instance. At the same time, the point which has already been alluded to in this report, viz: that the constant fumigation

[38] Sandmeyer, *The Anti-Chinese Movement in California*.

> to which Chinatown is subjected from these open wood fires, may be the source of prevention of zymotic diseases, should not be lost sight of. But, conceding that such is the fact, and that the risk and evil of these open fires be tolerated and the fumigation process be thereby preserved rather than to risk the possibility of disease growing out of their suppression, the fact stands out none the less clear-cut and striking that the very presence of these people among us compels the admission of the proposition that we cannot enact laws general in their application to which they can safely be subjected. Nor can we, on the other hand, enact special laws that shall apply alone to this or any other race of people, nor can we by any legislative action constitutionally exempt them from subjection to the general laws to which all other classes and races among as are amenable. The paradox involved, then, in these contradicting propositions, is by the simple fact that in this, as in many other things, these people when they come among us are above and beyond the law, and so they must possibly remain. Stated briefly, the special point now under consideration is this: The Law prohibits these open fires; if they are not suppressed, they will constitute a standing menace from fire, and may at any moment involve the city in a disastrous conflagration. If they are suppressed, there is every probability that Chinatown will become the seat of zymotic or other diseases which may involve the public health of the city at large and the sacrifice, possibly, of hundreds of lives annually. It is a choice of two evils — evils that the presence of this race among us forces upon us and which never can be wholly avoided so long as they are among us. (pp. 182–3)

This analysis provided the city administration with a win-win set of arguments in relation to epidemic diseases: If an epidemic broke out, this would be attributed to Chinese immigrants. If contagious disease outbreaks were avoided, it was because Chinese immigrants operated illegal open wood fires that fumigated the area.

Scapegoating of the Chinese immigrant population in California and especially of San Francisco, was not solely the remit of sensationalist reports and accompanying press coverage. It also extended to supposedly respectable academic journals which served as publication outlets for senior academics. Accordingly, an 1886 article with the title *Chinese*

Immigration published in the *North American Review* described San Francisco's Chinatown as follows[39]:

> There are 150 gambling dives, the approaches to which are generally so barricaded as to defy police detection; that, while there is an "opium lay-out" in nearly every sleeping room, the public resorts are 26, with 319 bunks; that there are 35 dens of white prostitution, generally patronized by Chinese, and 69 of Chinese prostitution, patronized generally by whites; that among the latter especially the rates are extremely low, and that white boys, as young as even 8 or 10, are often enticed into them; that there is no city in the world where so many children are afflicted with secret diseases as San Francisco, and that nine-tenths of it is traceable to the excessively cheap prostitution of "Chinatown;" that the Chinese prostitutes are regularly bought and sold for terms of years, and that organized bodies of villains exist, as the Ye Tung Society, for the purpose of capturing and restoring to the owner fugitive prostitutes; that gambling, opium-smoking, and prostitution are so entrenched that the police force necessary to suppress them would bankrupt the city; that the course of justice is systematically baffled by the powerful guilds or secret tribunals; that, within these 12 blocks, there are 13 Joss Houses, where hideous idols squat upon the altars; and that for every Chinaman's soul rationally converted, scores of American souls are lost through the increase of vice. (P. 33)

Nayan Shah's modern analysis of public health and San Francisco's Chinatown succinctly summarizes the unique aggressiveness with which this immigrant community was treated.[40] According to Shah, "in San Francisco, no other social groups defined by race or nationality were unequivocally identified as health threats. The impulse to expel the Chinese and remove Chinatown from the city animated the nuisance declarations. The practice of scapegoating the Chinese in San Francisco demonstrated the public health strategy that specified aberrations in order to

[39] Gilliam, E. W., "Chinese Immigration," *The North American Review,* 143:356 (1886), 26–34.

[40] Shah, Nayan, *Contagious Divides: Epidemics and Race in San Francisco's Chinatown*, Berkley, CA, Univ of California Press (2001).

achieve reform. Health officials characterized the aberrant conduct of the Chinese and condition of Chinatown as polluting the entire city system and threatening the total population. ... By putting the normative and normalizing agenda at risk, the nuisance demanded immediate remedy."[41] Public health in this context lost its objectivity, never mind any claims to being linked to a science and became little more than an instrument for fear mongering, which was part of a ruthless political struggle by a white elite to prevent Asian immigration or assimilation. The immigrant community of the San Francisco's Chinatown was blamed for each and every imaginable health risk, ranging from contagious diseases of any kind, including leprosy, smallpox, and cholera to sexual transmitted diseases, as well as physical hazards like fire, air pollution, and structurally unsound buildings and passages.

From Local Agitation to Preserving the National Racial Stock

By the 1900s, anti-Chinese agitation had slightly ebbed off, but it had not gone away. Japanese immigrants and Southern Europeans, meanwhile, had become new targets of anti-immigration lobbies. The Californian agitators had got their way with the 1882 Chinese Exclusion Act and various follow-up measures which were aimed to ensure its implementation.[42] The Anti-immigration movement, as it existed at the time, now attempted to gather nationwide support, rather than focusing only on the West Coast and Asian immigrants. One its prominent leaders, Prescott F. Hall (1868–1921), was a Harvard graduate who had also obtained a Harvard law degree. In 1894, he became one of the founders and the first secretary of the Immigration Restriction League, which was a position he held until his death. Described as an early think tank, which introduced effective forms of lobbying and agenda mobilization to US politics,[43] the *League*

[41] *Ibid.*, pp. 53–4.

[42] Salyer, Lucy E., *Laws Harsh as Tigers: Chinese Immigrants and the Shaping of Modern Immigration Law*, Chapel Hill, NC, Univ of North Carolina Press (1995).

[43] Decker, Robert Julio, "Citizenship and Its Duties: The Immigration Restriction League as a Progressive Movement" *Immigrants & Minorities*, 32:2 (2014), 162–82.

initially drew on old stock Yankee upper-class leaders.[44] This initial Boston foothold was followed by the creation of branches in New York, Chicago, and San Francisco with an additional branch created in Princeton in 1922.

Here, we quote from one of Hall's early papers which he published in 1904 in *The Annals of the American Academy of Political and Social Science* under the title *Selection of Immigration.*[45] It is interesting to note Hall's initially measured tone, which he let slip relatively quickly into language, which closely mirrored that of some of the California reports we quoted earlier. Accordingly, Hall starts out with a, by then, well-rehearsed race compatibility argument:

> It does not, therefore, at all follow that because this country has been able to assimilate large numbers of kindred races in the past it can in the future assimilate vastly larger numbers of races alien in customs, traditions and ideals. Immigration in 1903 amounted to over 850,000 persons. In 1923 or 1943 it may be two million a year, and the mere fact that the two million may bear no large proportion to the total population of that day than the immigration did to the population in 1870 is no guaranty of our power of assimilating such a number of such races, especially when our total population will contain such a large proportion of these very races which are difficult of assimilation. Within the last year or two there has been a marked increase in the number of sailings from Europe, and especially from the Mediterranean ports. Recently, the White Star Line has established a Mediterranean service, the Cunard Line has a guaranty of 30,000 emigrants per year from Austria-Hungary, and a new line has been established between Odessa and New York, also the steamers which formerly ran between Austria and Central America now are to run to New York. (P. 172)

---

[44] Lee, Erika, *America for Americans: A History of Xenophobia in the United States*, New York, NY, Basic Books (2019).

[45] Hall, Prescott F, "Selection of Immigration," *The Annals of the American Academy of Political and Social Science,* 24:1 (1904), 169–84. Hall also wrote several monographs including one with an introduction by the prominent eugenicist Madison Grant (1865–1937).

Hall then reverts to at the time all too familiar arguments about slums and contagion:

> The concentration of these large bodies of ignorant foreigners in the slums of our Eastern cities is a serious matter. Forming racial settlements, they do not tend to assimilate, but, as Washington predicted, keep to their native customs and standards of living. They cannot even read the newspapers, board of health notices and trade journals printed in their own language, and as a necessary consequence are slow to become acquainted with any other standards except those of their immediate neighbors. The census of 1890 seems to show that, taking an equal number of the foreign element and of the native element, the foreigners furnish 1 1/2 times as many criminals, 2 1/3 times as many insane, and 3 times as many paupers as the natives. (P. 177)

In terms of tone, the 1894 Immigration Restriction League was not as aggressive or incendiary in its rhetoric as California's proponents of Asian Exclusion had been. However, concern with immediate public health risks now was gradually replaced with so called long-term public health concerns. In the 1913 revised second edition of his book *Immigration: and its Effects Upon the United States*, which had first been published in 1905, the same Prescott Hall stated[46]:

> An act passed in 1875 prohibited the immigration of convicts, except those guilty of political offences; or, as it is expressed in the present law, 'persons who have been convicted of a felony or other crime or misdemeanor involving moral turpitude,' provided, 'that nothing in this act shall exclude persons convicted of an offence purely political, not involving moral turpitude.' In 1904, out of over 812,870 immigrants, only 35 were debarred under this clause — a small percentage probably of the number who should have been excluded.

The very low number of those rejected on account of existing legal and public health-related restrictions presented a problem for the

[46] Hall, Prescott F., *Immigration and its Effects upon the United States*, New York, NY, H. Holt (1913).

Immigration Restriction League on several levels. Firstly, it indicated that the immigrants who arrived, including what the *League* considered to be undesirable Southern or Eastern Europeans where in fact in physically good shape. Secondly, it suggested that existing provisions which required carriers to only grant passage to healthy passengers had reduced the alleged risk of disease-carrying immigrants reaching the country. One obvious strategy for the *League* was to question the decisions of immigration officials to reject so few arrivals. However, there was a limit to this approach. If the *League* accused existing immigration services of incompetency, this, however could lead to calls for improved funding for these activities and an increase in staff. This was not what the *League* wanted as it generally believed in a small state and certainly did not wish to see large amounts of taxpayers' money devoted to the processing of immigrants (other than for educational testing). Some *League* officials, nonetheless, hinted at the possibility that state-side immigration officials did not do their job, but this was not an argument the *League* wished to fully engage in for the reasons we have already mentioned.[47]

However, there was a way out of this challenge. This was to deny that the health status of current immigrants mattered altogether and to focus instead on other "broader" issues. In line with this strategy, the *League* switched its arguments against immigration from concerns about the potential risks of contagious diseases imported by immigrants, to arguments about the long-term risks of "race pollution." Hall's 1913 book, *Immigration: And its Effects Upon the United States*, stated accordingly[48]:

> For the period from 1835 to 1890, the Baltic furnished 87 per cent., the Alpine 10 per cent., and the Mediterranean 3 per cent, of the total immigration. For the decade from 1890 to 1900, the Baltic furnished 53 per cent., the Alpine 32 per cent., and the Mediterranean 15 per cent. For the two fiscal years 1901 and 1902, the Baltic furnished 35 per cent., the Alpine 42 per cent., and the Mediterranean 23 per cent. It therefore appears that during 1901–2, as compared with 1835–90, the Mediterranean has

[47] They also appear to have lacked evidence to make this argument or make statements that immigration services were understaffed.

[48] Hall, *Immigration and its Effects upon the United States.*

> increased 7 times, the Alpine over 4 times, while the Baltic has fallen to less than one-half. … Apart from this deterioration, the ... effects of the change in immigration will be as follows: the skull will become more of the brachio-cephalic type, the average stature will be lower and the average complexion will be darker. (pp. 104 and 105)

The racist prejudices of the *League* became even clearer in a passage on the *Social Effects of Immigration*, where Hall stated that:

> The United States has had to suffer and is still suffering untold miseries from the reckless introduction for purposes of material gain of an alien people, to wit, the African negro. The same arguments were used for the admission of negro slaves that are now used for the admission of the cheapest European and Asiatic labor. Wherever a superior and an inferior race are brought together, one must rule; and one will withdraw itself socially and politically from the other. (P. 176)

Hall's 1913 book devoted a lengthy chapter to Chinese Exclusion, which, was praised as a model for immigration legislation. His book concluded on the theme of race-compatibility. Presumably not wishing to be seen as a pure and absolute anti-immigrationist, Hall's concluded:

> Let us, then, continue the benefits of that selection which took place in the early days of the nation by sifting the immigration of today, so that no discordant elements shall enter to imperil the ideals and institutions of our nation, and to the end that we may produce a still finer race to help the world in its progress. Such selection of immigration surely has the highest ethical sanction. (P. 323)

Hall was an early US advocate of eugenics and is known today primarily for his role in lobbying for the passage of what became the Immigration Act of 1917. This act imposed literacy tests and added new categories of undesirable persons, following in many respects the Chinese Exclusion Act of 1882. It also included an "Asiatic barred zone" from which people could not immigrate, including much of Asia and the Pacific Islands. Like other Eugenicists and "scientific racists" of the time, Hall made much of an alleged hierarchy of races and used this concepts as a key part of his anti-immigration lobbying.[49] Both the idea of racial hierarchy and that of risks created by racial mixing or the influx of non-nordic races more generally, are obviously somewhat reminiscent of some of the arguments of German National Socialism of the 1930s, which in fact paid great respect to these American agitators.[50] However, unlike the Nazis, members of the *League* did not see themselves as revolutionaries or radicals.

Instead, members of the Immigration Restriction League saw themselves as purveyors of an academically grounded discourse on human improvement and racial interaction. *League* members often associated themselves with then leading Eugenicists and one of their preferred publication outlets was the *Eugenics Review.* As part of this focus, the nature of anti-immigration discourse in the US changed considerably. The public health risks of immigration and the main risks posed by immigration more generally, were no longer associated with contagion by infectious diseases or the importation of undesirable behaviors such as opium consumption, gambling, or criminal behaviors. Rather, the arguments became more complex and related closely to then fashionable writings within the area of so-called "scientific racism," typically proclaiming the risk of a displacement or even the disappearance of "superior Anglo-Saxon racial stock."[51]

Well known "scientific racists" like William Z. Ripley (1867–1941), professor of economics at MIT and professor of political economy at Harvard University, warned about the long-term dangers of immigration. Ripley focused on differential birth rates by arguing that[52]:

> With us the danger lies in the fact that this low and declining birth rate is primarily confined to the Anglo Saxon contingent. The immigrant

[49] Ludmerer, Kenneth M., "Genetics, Eugenics, and the Immigration Restriction Act of 1924," *Bulletin of the History of Medicine,* 46:1 (1972), 59–81.

[50] Kuhl, Stefan. *The Nazi Connection: Eugenics, American Racism, and German National Socialism*, Oxford, University Press (2002).

[51] One of the then most prominent works expounding these views was Grant, Madison. *The Passing of the Great Race: Or the Racial Basis of European History*, New York, NY, C. Scribner's sons (1921).

[52] Ripley, William Z., "Race Progress and Immigration," *The Annals of the American Academy of Political and Social Science,* 34:1 (1909), 130–38.

> European horde, until recently at least, has continued to reproduce upon our soil with well sustained energy. Baldly stated, the birth rate among the foreign-born in Massachusetts is about three times that of the native-born. Childless marriages are one-third less frequent. (P. 133)

This argument of long-term risks to a superior racial stock was elaborated on at length in the works of Robert DeCourcy Ward (1867–1931). Ward was the first professor of Climatology in the US, working at Harvard, as well as being co-founder of the Immigration Restriction League. His 1910 paper *National Eugenics in Relation to Immigration* stated[53]:

> In the United States the low and falling birth-rate is principally confined to the Anglo-Saxon element, and the tendency to multiply more rapidly is found among the less intelligent, the most recent immigrants. This clearly operates to bring a tremendously rapid change of the race." (P. 60)

And

> the next best plan, ... although it would require legislation and considerable expenditure of public money (yet would not almost any expenditure, even on a huge scale, be a wise national policy in so important a matter?) would be to insist that each alien, on landing here, should undergo a very thorough mental and physical examination at the hands of our Public Health and Marine Hospital Service surgeons.
>
> These examinations would involve a stripping to the skin of each alien; the usual physical and mental examination; tests for syphilis and similar precautions. Is this too much to demand when the welfare of a whole new race is concerned? The eugenist is ready with his answer; he says, emphatically, No. We certainly ought to begin at once to segregate, far more than we now do, all our native and foreign-born population which is unfit for parenthood. They must be prevented from breeding. But the biggest, the most effective, the most immediate way in which we can further national eugenics is at the ports where this year over half a million alien immigrants will land. Our immigration officials are doing all in their power, under existing conditions, to select our immigrants. Our surgeons are doing a wonderful work, under tremendous disadvantages,

---

[53] De C. Ward, Robert, "National Eugenics in Relation to Immigration," *The North American Review,* 192:656 (1910), 56–67.

> in trying to detect the physical and mental disabilities which by law debar the aliens who have them. But it is nothing short of a crime to admit people, as often happens in a rush season, at the rate of 3,000, 4,000 or 5,000 in one day. (P. 65)

Ward's language is crass but phrases such as "examinations would involve a stripping to the skin of each alien" and "[aliens] must be prevented from breeding" were seen as justifiable by members of the immigration restriction establishment on account of the risk that they believed immigration presented itself to the racial health of the nation.

Eugenics was an international movement at this time[54] and the *League* received much support from non-US academics. One example of this was Andre Siegfried (1875–1959), professor of Social Studies in the Ecole des Sciences Politiques, Paris. In a paper published in 1926 in the *Eugenics Review* titled "American Emigration and Eugenics", which he also presented at the International Federation of Eugenic Organisations, Paris, Siegfried expressed his wholehearted support for US immigration restrictions and especially those aimed at Asians.[55] He said:

> The new immigration laws may possibly be regarded as a first type of Eugenic law, and they are aimed first at a newly voiced desire on the part of the Anglo-Saxons to maintain the purity of their race, of which the first indication caused prohibition against further intrusion of black and yellow peoples. But eugenic law has gone a step further in the United States and is now aiming at purging the degenerate elements within all races.
>
> Twenty-three States in all have passed sterilization laws. Purely eugenic in intention. While in regard to immigration, a scheme has already been proposed carrying the examination of the individual immigrant as to his fitness for citizenship, into his family stock, in order to learn whether be bears as a recessive, hereditary taints which will appear among his progeny. It is in fact harder to conceive of a wider application of scientific theory in social organisation, ranging from the careful study

---

[54] Kevles, Daniel J., *In the Name of Eugenics: Genetics and the Uses of Human Heredity*, Cambridge, MA, Harvard University Press (1995).

[55] Siegfried, Andre, "American Emigration and Eugenics," *The Eugenics Review,* 18:3 (1926), 217.

> of the character making up the individual as a potential parent, to the psychological attributes borne in the race as suitable or unsuitable contributions to the whole body politic. (P. 222)

By the end of World War Two, eugenics faced considerable criticism, not least because of the overlap of some of its agendas with views and actions of recently defeated powers. However, eugenics thinking had not disappeared from post-war politics.[56] References to race in debates about immigration became more subtle and terms like inferior and superior racial stock were avoided.[57] One approach taken by opponents of immigration now was to link immigration to the alleged global population explosion and to relate this to emerging discourses on environmental sustainability.[58] An example of this can be found in a 1966 letter to the editor of *Eugenics Review* which appeared under the title "Population Explosion".[59] The contribution was written by Professor Cedric Oswald Carter (1917–1984) a prominent medical geneticist. Carter used an initially measured tone and wrote:

> As has been pointed out in the editorial columns of the REVIEW the word 'explosion' is an exaggeration. The long-term excess fertility is perhaps of the order of 10 per cent, an average family size of 2–4 to 2–5 … . This is about 100,000 births per year. Gross emigration, welcome to Australia and Canada, is now of the order of 200,000 individuals per year, balanced by an immigration of much the same order. Much of the excess fertility could, if this was thought desirable, be simply met by a more restrictive immigration policy. Most members of the Society will, in contrast to Professor Titmuss, welcome the modest increase in average family size in the middle class (an increase which even now is perhaps only sufficient to raise their fertility to replacement level) and will

---

[56] Hanson, Clare, *Eugenics, Literature, and Culture in Post-war Britain*. London, Routledge (2013).

[57] Hanley, Anne, "Migration, Racism and Sexual Health in Post-war Britain," *History Workshop Journal*, 94 (2022), 202–22.

[58] Ummel, Deborah, "Dream or Nightmare? The Impact of American Eugenics, Past and Present," *CrossCurrents* 66:3 (2016), 389–98.

[59] Carter, C. O., "The Population Explosion," *The Eugenics Review,* 58.1 (1966), 53.

reject the implication that the more fortunately situated have been wrong to have more children. (P. 54)

In other words, Carter argued that if there were fears in a country that population expanded too quickly, this could be addressed simply by restricting the immigration of migrants, whose fertility typically exceeded that of native populations.

Meanwhile, there was a hard core of academics who believed that inequalities among population groups were persistent and could not be addressed through social policies, and these individuals also saw continued value in immigration restriction or the control of less desirable population groups in a country. Emily Klancher Merchant's history of population control describes views held by leaders of the Milbank Memorial Fund, a public health–oriented philanthropy based in New York City.[60] She notes how board member Thomas Cochran had grown frustrated with the outlays for the health of an expanding poor population in the United States. He suggested that the Fund's money could be better spent on control, reducing poverty by reducing the fertility of the poor. This attitude was easily extended to issues of global poverty and health needs. This allowed American eugenicists to turn to birth control as a more socially acceptable means of population engineering as compared to earlier and now largely discredited sterilization agendas. It also gave some eugenicists an opportunity to reinvent themselves as globally aware students of population dynamics, whose forward-looking work contributed to the sustainability of troubled regions. As part of this transformation, a new generation of demographic researchers frequently maintained close ties to global population control organizations.[61] One of the beliefs held within these new alliances was that "excess" third world population growth should be controlled locally and regionally, rather than through immigration to wealthy nations, which would only shift the problem elsewhere. The new mantra, as proposed in the 1960s by the Population

[60] Merchant, Emily K., "A Digital History of Anglophone Demography and Global Population Control, 1915–1984," *Population and Development Review,* 43:1 (2017), 83–117.

[61] *Ibid*, p. 84.

Council, the Ford Foundation and later on the United States Agency for International Development (USAID) as well as the National Institutes of Health (NIH) was that population growth was the major cause of global poverty and inequality, and that birth control was a key prerequisite for economic development.[62]

Nonetheless, it is probably fair to say that radical anti-immigration agendas no longer had any place in post-war Western politics, except in isolated discussions around questions of carrying capacity, food supply and sustainability, or conflict proneness of certain areas. Local anti-immigrant agitation, however, had sadly not disappeared from US political discourse but found a new target in Latin immigrant populations.[63]

Immigration and Public Health Risks: An Attempted Summary

Early anti-immigration rhetoric in the US appears to have drawn heavily on the idea that the US was a unique society where free individuals were able to articulate and pursue their personal beliefs. In this context, immigrants deferring to an external authority, such as the catholic church, were considered inferior and problematic. In parallel, existing health checks on immigrants encouraged the formulation of more urgent arguments against immigration, which viewed immigrants as a potential health threat to the native population. Meanwhile, on the West Coast, opposition to the immigration of Asians initially drew heavily on economic arguments. This, however, soon was replaced by recourse to mostly spurious public health concerns which helped underpin a hateful and inflammatory debate which reached a *crescendo* in the Chinese Exclusion Act of 1882. Lobbying for this act involved many populist state politicians, especially in California, who drew heavily on the expertise of medics, as well as flawed local testimony on disease outbreaks, sanitary conditions, and lifestyle habits.

Following drastic legislative intervention against Asian immigration, the focus of anti-immigration policy in the US shifted somewhat to the

[62] *Ibid.*, p. 96.

[63] Perea, Juan F. (ed.), *Immigrants Out!: the New Nativism and the Anti-immigrant Impulse in the United States*, New York, NY, NYU Press (1997).

East coast, where the Immigration Restriction League (founded in 1894) lobbied against the new wave of Southern and Eastern European immigrants. This agitation again initially focused heavily on public health issues with much being made of contagious diseases such as Trachoma, cholera, and typhoid fever. These concerns, however, did not provide sufficient ammunition to support the populist movement for stringent immigration restrictions envisaged by the League, primarily because immigration inspections rejected only relatively few arrivals on public health grounds. As an alternative, anti-immigration movements, such as the League, adopted eugenics-style arguments highlighting the immediate and medium-term dangers associated with miscegenation and hybridization, while elaborating on the imaginary threat of the long-term transformation of the country's racial make-up. This moved anti-immigration politics from the realm of a localized populist condemnation of specific immigrant groups, their culture, and habits, into the full-scale adoption "racial science" or "racialism," marking a shift where "clear and present danger" to public health arguments were gradually replaced by more elaborate racist constructs around perceived threats to the white Anglo-Saxon population. Both facets of anti-immigration rhetoric drew on public health rationales, although their precise incarnation differed. Both also offered advantages and disadvantages to their proponents. The immediate threat of contagious diseases argument helped raise levels of public fear and anger. However, it could easily lose its power when these problems lessened or did not materialize, which was increasingly the case as the sanitation movement and modern medicine advanced. The eugenics-type argument about "race-pollution" and "race-displacement" was harder to dispel but required more of an engagement and acceptance of racist categories by the population as a whole but was harder to dispel with reason and rational argument once eugenics had gained ground and gathered a certain momentum. On the whole, both links of anti-immigration thinking to public health; the contagious disease and the "race-mix effects" argument, show the dangerous side of discourses which utilized pseudo-scientific information in order to pursue agendas aimed at prioritizing the rights of the powerful over those of weak or under-privileged groups.

Figure 1. Portrait of Gerolamo Gardano (1501–1576) on his 48th year of life.

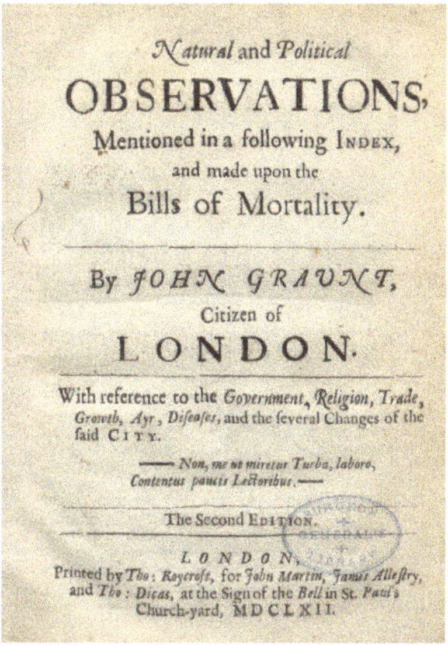
Natural and Political
OBSERVATIONS
Mentioned in a following INDEX,
and made upon the
Bills of Mortality.

By JOHN GRAUNT,
Citizen of
LONDON.

With reference to the Government, Religion, Trade, Growth, Ayr, Diseases, and the several Changes of the said CITY.

—— Non, me ut miretur Turba, laboro,
Contentus paucis Lectoribus.——

The Second EDITION.

LONDON,
Printed by Tho: Roycroft, for John Martin, James Allestry, and Tho: Dicas, at the Sign of the Bell in St. Paul's Church-yard, MDCLXII.

Figure 2. John Graunt's (1620–1674) Bills of Mortality (Lading), printed in London, 1662.

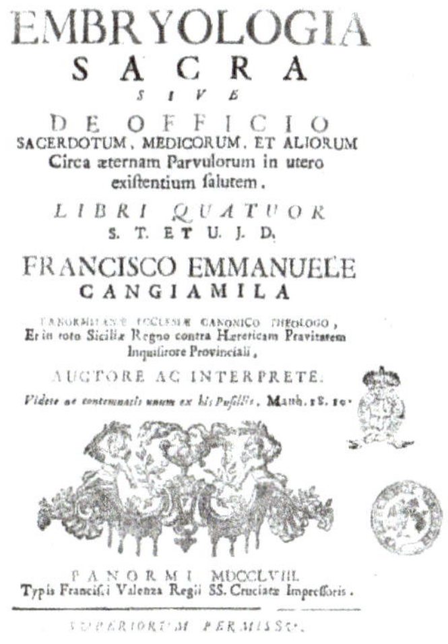
EMBRYOLOGIA
SACRA
SIVE
DE OFFICIO
SACERDOTUM, MEDICORUM, ET ALIORUM
Circa æternam Parvulorum in utero
existentium salutem.
LIBRI QUATUOR
S. T. ET U. J. D.
FRANCISCO EMMANUELE
CANGIAMILA
PANORMITANÆ ECCLESIÆ CANONICO THEOLOGO,
Et in toto Siciliæ Regno contra Hæreticam Pravitatem Inquisitore Provinciali,
AUCTORE AC INTERPRETE.
Videte ne contemnatis unum ex his Pusillis. Matth. 18. 10.

PANORMI MDCCLVIII.
Typis Francisci Valenza Regii SS. Cruciatæ Impressoris.

SUPERIORUM PERMISSU.

Figure 3. Italian version of Fransisco Cangiamila's (1702–1763) *Embriologia Sacra*, 1758.

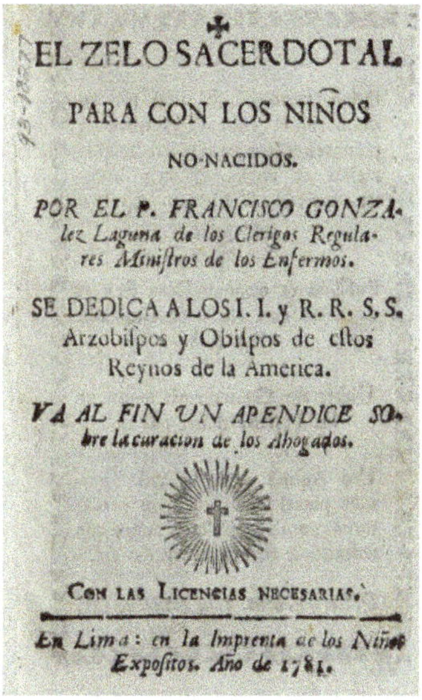
EL ZELO SACERDOTAL
PARA CON LOS NIÑOS
NO-NACIDOS.
POR EL P. FRANCISCO GONZALez Laguna de los Clerigos Regulares Ministros de los Enfermos.
SE DEDICA A LOS I. I. y R. R. S. S. Arzobispos y Obispos de estos Reynos de la America.
VA AL FIN UN APENDICE SObre la curacion de los Ahogados.

CON LAS LICENCIAS NECESARIAS.

En Lima: en la Imprenta de los Niños Expositos. Año de 1781.

Figure 4. Friar Francisco González Laguna's (1729–99) El Zelo Sacerdotal Para Con Los Ninos Non-Nacidos, printed in Lima Peru, 1781.

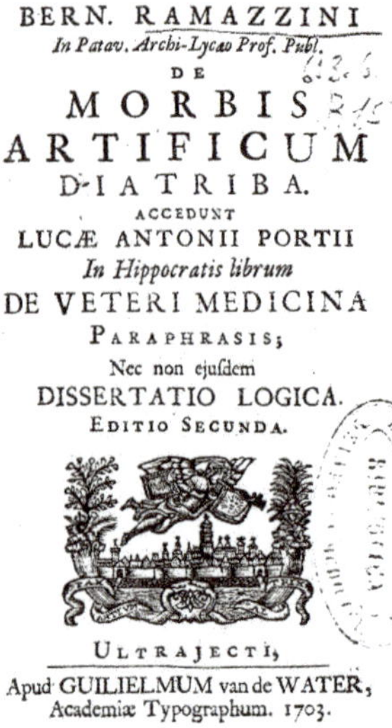

BERN. RAMAZZINI
In Patav. Archi-Lycæo Prof. Publ.
DE
MORBIS
ARTIFICUM
DIATRIBA.
ACCEDUNT
LUCÆ ANTONII PORTII
In Hippocratis librum
DE VETERI MEDICINA
PARAPHRASIS;
Nec non ejusdem
DISSERTATIO LOGICA.
EDITIO SECUNDA.
ULTRAJECTI,
Apud GUILIELMUM van de WATER,
Academiæ Typographum. 1703.

Figure 5. Second edition of Bernardino Ramazzini's (1633–1714) *De Morbis Artificum Diatriba* [Diseases of Workers] published in 1703.

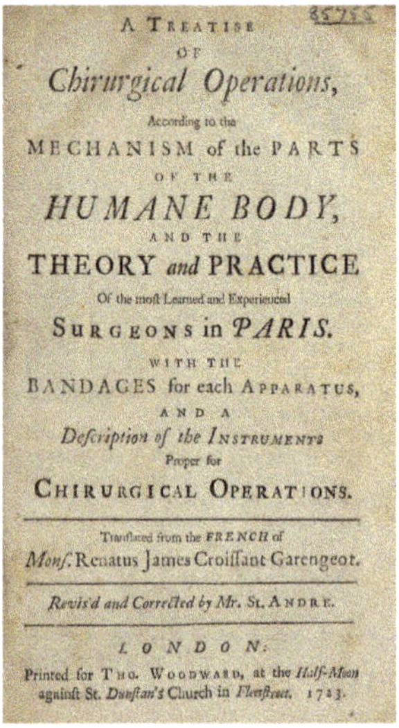

A TREATISE
OF
Chirurgical Operations,
According to the
MECHANISM of the PARTS
OF THE
HUMANE BODY,
AND THE
THEORY and PRACTICE
Of the most Learned and Experienced
SURGEONS in PARIS.
WITH THE
BANDAGES for each APPARATUS,
AND A
Description of the INSTRUMENTS
Proper for
CHIRURGICAL OPERATIONS.
Translated from the FRENCH of
Monf. Renatus James Croissant Garengeot.
Revis'd and Corrected by Mr. St. ANDRE.
LONDON:
Printed for THO. WOODWARD, at the Half-Moon
against St. Dunstan's Church in Fleetstreet. 1723.

Figure 6. René Jacques Croissant de Garengeot's (1688–1759) textbook of Surgery printed in London in 1723.

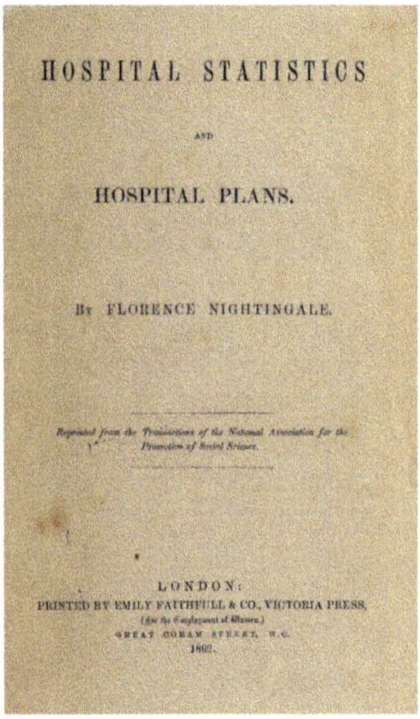

HOSPITAL STATISTICS
AND
HOSPITAL PLANS.
BY FLORENCE NIGHTINGALE.
Reprinted from the Transactions of the National Association for the Promotion of Social Science.
LONDON:
PRINTED BY EMILY FAITHFULL & CO., VICTORIA PRESS,
(for the Employment of Women,)
GREAT CORAM STREET, W.C.
1862.

Figure 7. Florence Nightingale's (1820–1910) work on *Hospital Statistics and Hospital Plans* of 1862 included forms for the recording of patient data as well as ideal plans for hospitals.

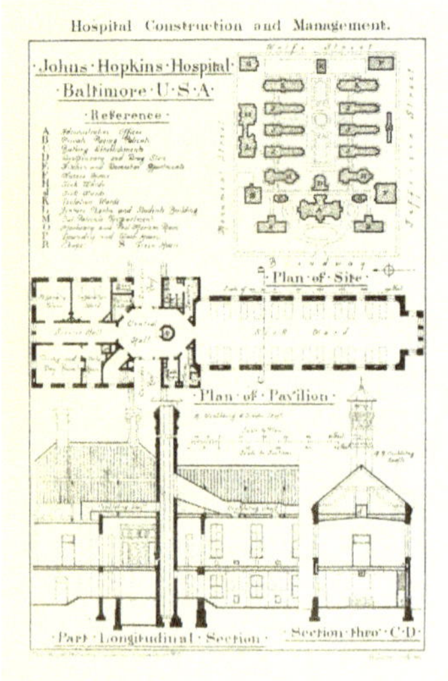

Figure 8. John Hopkins as example hospital from Frederic J. Mouat and H. Saxon Snell, 1816–1897; Snell, H. Saxon (1883) *Hospital Construction and Management.*

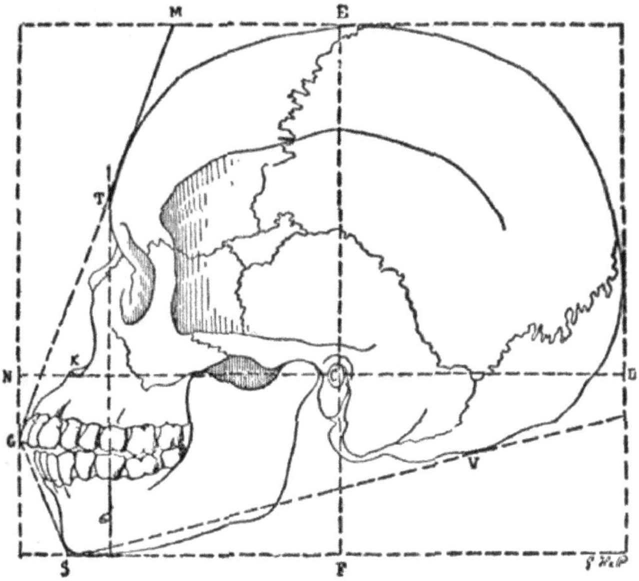

Figure 9. Daniel Garrison Brinton (1837–1899) published his *Races and Peoples: Lectures on the Science of Ethnography* in 1890. He was an advocate of Craniometry.

Prescott F. Hall

Figure 10. Prescott F. Hall (1868–1921) was one of the founders of the *Immigration Restriction League.*

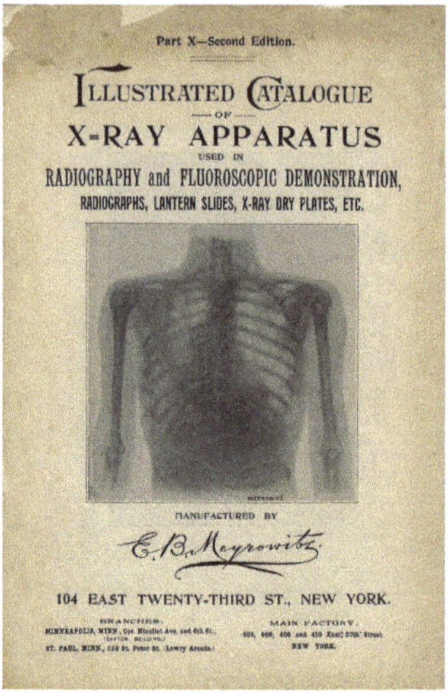

Figure 11. Advertisement of for Ray Machines, from about 1920.

Figure 12. A 1987 report by the US Army noted that more than 54,000 personnel had been exposed to nuclear tests.

Chapter Four

Race

Public Health and Race: Legacies of Oppression and Discrimination

This chapter touches on another well-researched topic, which is the establishment racism which dominated academia in the US for many decades, being variously termed "scientific racism," "race research," "racialism," or "eugenics."[1] Racism as a discourse entailing biased perceptions of human groupings, targeted mostly at non-white populations, has generally been well explored, albeit that its links to public health, or writing in the health field more generally, is less well known.[2] Again, this chapter focuses on

---

[1] Smith, Robert A., "Types of Mankind: Polygenism and Scientific Racism in the Nineteenth Century United States Scientific Community", Master's Thesis, Pittsburg State University (2014); Dewbury, Adam, "The American School and Scientific Racism in Early American Anthropology," *Histories of Anthropology Annual* 3:1 (2007), 121–47; Jackson, John P., Nadine M. Weidman, and Gretchen Rubin, "The Origins of Scientific Racism." *The Journal of Blacks in Higher Education,* 50 (Winter, 2005/06), 66–79; Tucker, William H., *The Funding of Scientific Racism: Wickliffe Draper and the Pioneer Fund,* Champaign, Illinois, University of Illinois Press (2002); Barkan, Elazar, *The Retreat of Scientific Racism: Changing Concepts of Race in Britain and the United States between the World Wars,* Cambridge, Cambridge University Press (1992).

[2] Notable exceptions include Byrd, W. Michael, and Linda A. Clayton, "Race, Medicine, and Health Care in the United States: A Historical Survey," *Journal of the National Medical Association* 93.3 Suppl (2001): 11S. Leslie, Charles. "Scientific Racism: Reflections on Peer Review, Science and Ideology," *Social Science & Medicine* 31:8 (1990), 891–905.

the US, primarily because we can draw on extensive historical source material. This is also the reason why this chapter focuses primarily on historical writings about African Americans who were for centuries the primary target of deplorable racist misrepresentations. The methodological approach underpinning this chapter largely mirrors that of the previous chapter on immigration, with which it partly overlaps. This means that we present and analyze key primary texts in rough chronological sequence, in order to highlight the evolution of key concepts and ideas around the themes of race, health risk, and public health. In so doing, we seek to highlight some surprising and lesser-known connections. Our analysis is largely exploratory in that we do not structure our historical survey on the basis of a preconceived understanding of how thinking about race and public health evolved during the time period we consider, which roughly extends from about 1890 to 1970.

Early Thinking on Race, Health, and Health Risks

Academic writing, which linked race to health, commenced with works which sought to identify the distinguishing characteristics of different racial groupings. One early contribution to this genre was the book *The Races of Men: Philosophical Enquiry into the Influence of Race Over the Destinies of Nations* by Robert Knox, M.D. The book *Races of Men* was first published in London in 1850 with the subtitle *A Fragment.*[3] It was then reprinted in 1862 in extended form with the aforementioned title.[4] The author, Robert Knox (1791–1862) was an anatomy lecturer in Edinburgh who achieved some notoriety through his connections with the Burke and Hare serial killings in the West Port district of Edinburgh in the 1820s. Knox denied this connection and it seems uncertain, although the body of a Mrs Docherty was discovered in Knox's cellar at Surgeons' Square; the site of his private dissecting room.[5]

---

[3] Knox, Robert. *The Races of Men: A Fragment.* Philadelphia, Lea & Blanchard (1850).

[4] Knox, Robert, *The Races of Men: A Philosophical Enquiry. into the Influence of Race Over the Destinies of Nations by*, London, Henry Renshaw (1862).

[5] The authorities doubted whether the cadaver had arrived there by a permissible method. Knox, like other anatomists, had difficulties in obtaining a supply of subjects and did not query their origin. A post-mortem showed Mrs Docherty to have been strangled. See

Knox, who was described as founder of pseudo-scientific British racism by a historian as early as 1965,[6] presented an at best strange view of race. His book essentially argued that human destiny was determined by immutable racial characteristics. Apart from being a surgeon, Knox was a student of anatomical variation. As such, he stepped into the footsteps of Buffon (1707–1788), Linnaeus (1707–1778), and Blumenbach (1752–1840), whose interest in craniometry he inherited.[7] Knox had planned to move to America but later abandoned the idea.[8] His work on race became well known in Britain and later on also in the US.[9] Here we quote one of the lesser known passages of the 1862 version of *Races of Men* where he espouses his idea that certain races could inhabit certain regions without health risk, as long as they employed members of other racial groupings as servants or laborers. Knox stated:

> France has much to do before Algeria can become a portion of the French empire, inhabited by able, healthy Frenchmen: Will this ever happen? Would it not have been better to have imported a Negro population as labourers? In India we have the Coolies and the labouring servile population of Hindostan. In Jamaica the Negroes. In the southern states of America our Saxon descendants employ the Negro; it is the same in Brazil, Cuba, and all tropical countries. In Morocco and Peru it was precisely the same: the coloured population alone could labour; the European was unequal to it. (P. 304).

This suggestion builds on the idea expressed earlier in his book that the anatomy of human races differed, making them uniquely suitable for certain tasks and climates:

Biddiss, Michael D., "The Politics of Anatomy: Dr Robert Knox and Victorian Racism," *Proc. Roy. Soc. Med.*, 69 (1976), 245.

[6] Davie, Neil, "Dissecting the Races of Men: Robert Knox, Anatomy and Racial Theory in Britain, 1820–1870," in Michel Prum, ed., *Sexe, Race et Mixité dans l'aire Anglophone,* Paris, L'Harmattan (2011), 19.

[7] In other words, he was hoping that measuring the skull housing the brain, would shed light on the intelligence and even moral characteristics of individuals.

[8] Budil, Ivo, "Robert Knox: Racial Imagination, Transcendental Anatomy and Western Colonial Expansion," č. 2, *West Bohemian Review of Social Sciences & Humanities* (2013), 14–36.

[9] Young, Robert JC., *Colonial Desire: Hybridity in Theory, Culture and Race*, London, Routledge (1995).

> Look more narrowly into the races of men, and you will find them to be subject to diseases peculiar to each; that the very essence of their language is distinct; their civilization also, if they have any. Trace the matter further, and you will find that transcendental anatomy can alone explain these mysterious circumstances. (P. 37).

It is not entirely clear what Knox meant with "transcendental anatomy," and this has given rise to some speculation about the meaning of some of his work.[10] What seems obvious, however, is that he believed human health, as well as physical and mental strength to be race specific. He further surmised that the ability to perform physical work differed by race and that it matched certain races to certain locations. Drawing on these ideas, Knox concluded that there were races who were naturally predestined to supervise the work of others, leading him to advocate various forms of colonial exploitation, forced labor, and even slavery as benefitting mankind.

Elements of Knox's thoughts were picked up by American writers like Daniel Garrison Brinton M.D. (1837–1899). He was an American surgeon and ethnologist who, after practicing medicine, became a professor of ethnology and archaeology in the Academy of Natural Sciences in Philadelphia in 1884, and then at the University of Pennsylvania in 1886.[11] One of Brinton's most well-known works was *Races and Peoples: Lectures on the Science of Ethnography* which was published in New York in 1890. Arguing along similar lines as Knox, Brinton proposed that races differed in terms of their physical health and endurance and also in terms of their mental ability. Moreover, he suggested that these aspects could diverge. Specifically, he claimed that black races possessed attributes of physical strength but were mentally inferior. Brinton's pseudo-scientific claims about the mental inferiority of the black races were the likely basis of his personal success, as well as the popularity of his book *Races and*

[10] Rehbock, Philip F., "Transcendental Anatomy," in Andrew Cunningham and Nicholas Jardine eds, *Romanticism and the Sciences,* Cambridge, Cambridge University Press (1990), 145 for example argues that this essentially romanticist notion was compatible with a wide variety of other biological, metaphysical, and socio-political doctrines.

[11] Baker, Lee D., "Daniel G. Brinton's Success on the Road to Obscurity, 1890–99," *Cultural Anthropology,* 15:3 (2000), 394–423.

Peoples.[12] Here we quote two contrasting paragraphs from *Races and Peoples*, both making reference to health and physical well-being. In his section entitled 'Disease and Races', Brinton initially stated:

> Exemption and liability to diseases differ noticeably in races. The white race is more liable to yellow fever, malarial diseases, syphilis, scarlet fever and sunstroke; the colored races to measles, tuberculosis, leprosy, elephantiasis, and pneumonia. Indeed, from the physical point of view, the pure white is weaker than the dark races, worse prepared for the combat of life, with inferior viability. This has been shown by the careful researches of statisticians. But in the white this is more than compensated by the development of the nervous system and the intellectual power. He can bear greater mental strain than any other race, and the activity of his mind supplies him with means to overcome the inferiority of his body, and thus places him at the head of the whole species. (P. 39).

Brinton elaborated on this idea when he wrote about the inferiority of dark races in a later section. His section on *High and Low Races*, accordingly, gives a less than positive description of "inferior races." Brinton states:

> We are accustomed familiarly to speak of 'higher' and 'lower' races, and we are justified in this even from merely physical considerations. These indeed bear intimate relations to mental capacity, and where the body presents many points of arrested or retarded development, we may be sure that the mind will also. There are two explanations of the presence of the inferior physical traits in certain races of men; the one, that of the evolutionists, that they are reversions or perpetuations of the ape-like (simian, pithecoid) features of the lower animal which was man's immediate ancestor; the other, that of the special creationists, that they are instances of surviving fetal peculiarities, or else deficiency or excess of development from unknown causes. ... Measured by these criteria, the

---

[12] *Ibid.*, p. 406 notes that "[w]hen Brinton described the various stocks and groups of black merely restated widespread racial stereotypes and validated them as facts. ... His scheme mirrors other schemes that position each race on a rung of the civilization. ... Brinton's style of ethnography was heartily embraced, and *Races and Peoples* received positive reviews on both sides of the Atlantic."

European or white race stands at the head of the list, the African or negro at its foot. (P. 48).

Brinton was not afraid of contradictions, especially when it came to justifying his overall social agenda which centered around the justification of slavery. "Dark races," might have good health and vitality, but their "mental inferiority," with its outward physical characteristics destined them to labor under the control of "superior" whites. Brinton, in other words, used pseudo-scientific argument about racial hierarchy, in order to justify slavery and racial exploitation as natural order. Brinton thus was an early and prominent exponent of pseudo-scientific racism who misapplied concepts from physical anthropology in order to develop deeply questionable classifications of human populations. Brinton believed in race as basis of legislation and opposed notions of the universality of the rights of men.[13]

Racial Health Inequalities Uncovered

The literature on race and health as it existed before 1900, however, could, at times, go beyond the narrow Knox-Briton type pattern of preposterous racist ranking and typecasting. One example of this is the 1896 publication *Race Traits and Tendencies of the American Negro* written by Frederick Ludwig Hoffman on behalf of the American Economic Association.[14] Hoffman was an American statistician who had been educated in Germany. *Race Traits* is a strange work, which espouses, apart from some careful statistical insights, some unusually progressive views alongside atrocious racist stereotyping. Thus, Hoffman deplores the relative decline of the African American population in terms of the overall population share, advocates interracial marriages as a means of refreshing blood of both "blacks" and "whites," and expresses concern for the high child mortality among African American children. Unfortunately, he also reiterates numerous racist stereotypes, which do not tally with his

[13] Lofgren, Charles A., *The Plessy Case: A Legal-historical Interpretation*, Oxford, University Press (1987).

[14] Hoffman, Frederick Ludwig, *Race Traits and Tendencies of the American Negro*, Vol. 11. No. 1–3, New York, American Economic Association (1896).

otherwise careful analysis of population and health data. The health focus of Hoffman's analysis, nonetheless, makes his book an important contribution to discussions about race and health in late nineteenth-century America, and we will quote at some length from both some of the enlightened and some of the less enlightened passages of his writing. Hoffman starts us off with the interesting observation of a low and declining birth rate among African Americans. He notes:

> The low vitality of the colored race in the North did not escape the notice of the officials in charge of the registration records .... Dr. Fisher, for many years the registrar of vital statistics of Rhode Island, refers to the subject in the second annual report of the state board of health, as follows: 'The circumstances favorable to the promotion of the physical health of the colored population are believed to be at least quite as favorable and ample in Rhode Island as in any other northern or eastern state. When we find that in a period of eighteen years the excess of births over deaths is only 42, and having full knowledge of the fact that the state is annually having accessions to the number of colored people by immigration and these accessions largely in the periods of life between twenty and forty years, we must conclude, however reluctantly, that the race is not self-sustaining in this latitude.' (pp. 35 to 36).

Hoffman further observes that for most southern cities, "the mortality among the colored exceeds that of the whites in each of the ten cities ... , which includes most of the principal cities of the South ...., For the ten cities combined the mortality of the negroes exceeds that of the whites by 12.49 per 1,000 of population or by 62.1 per cent." (P. 39)

Rejecting the idea that social and economic inequality could explain some of the low "black" birth rates and high death rates, Hoffman goes on to explore potential causes of this. This leads him to consider high infant mortality rates among African Americans. Specifically, he states, "... in the city of Washington out of a million whites born during the year 1880, 739,661 will survive to their fifth year, while only 499,169 of the colored population will survive, a difference of 240,492 lives. This represents an enormous economic loss." Hoffman's further identification of causes for high "colored" mortality is somewhat confused. He firstly argues that European physicians could not "successfully treat a colored person in view of the radical differences existing between the two races."[15] Secondly, he claims that there is a "neglect of children by negro parents,"[16] particularly as concerns illness and medical need. At this stage of his analysis, he then moves closer to established racial stereotypes of the time, by arguing that:

> The mortality from diarrhæal diseases is largely subject to sanitary conditions, which no doubt have some influence in producing a negro mortality rate nearly a hundred per cent higher than that of the whites. Deaths from inanition, debility and atrophy are largely the result of inferior organisms and constitutional weakness, which as we shall see later on is one of the most pronounced race characteristics of the American negro. (P. 66).

Hoffman's overall conclusion is that "It is not in the conditions of life, but in the race traits and tendencies that we find the causes of the excessive mortality."[17] From this, he easily descends into the reiteration of then established racial stereotypes, which essentially attribute the poor health of African American to lifestyle choices, albeit that he adds a cautious note at the outset of this section:

> Alcoholism, insanity and suicide are three important phenomena of the sociology of the colored race, to which frequent reference has been made in medical, anthropological and economic literature. But few facts have been brought forward to support one view or the other. This is largely due to a paucity of data; which, however, is no excuse for the expression of unwarranted opinions. 'Alcoholism among negroes,' we are informed by Dr Norman Kerr, ... 'differs materially from the same disease in the white and Indian races.' The negroes, with their vivacity and enthusiasm, from their nervous sensitiveness, are easily excited. Their drunkenness is more demonstrative than profound, but the anæstethic influence is less lasting. They may be characterized as more readily intoxicated than the white men of western countries. (P. 121).

---

[15] *Ibid.*, p. 61.
[16] *Ibid.*, pp. 62–3.
[17] *Ibid.*, p. 95.

Hoffman's analysis is likely to leave today's reader puzzled. Here is a researcher who supports interracial marriage, identifies glaring health inequalities, yet denies their material and social causes and resorts to blatant racial stereotyping when looking for explanations of these inequalities. Compared to the generation of eugenicists who followed him, Hoffman's work, nonetheless, can be seen as showing at least some readiness to openly engage with certain aspects of observational data on health inequality.

Early Eugenics

Eugenics is a set of beliefs which advocates the improvement of the human race through selective breeding. Eugenics typically supports restrictions on marriage and the reproduction of those considered inferior, while encouraging the propagation of those considered superior. It also typically disapproves of intermarriage between members of different races. Modern eugenics was created by Francis Galton (1822–1911), a British statistician and polymath, who supported the so-called scientific racism as well as social Darwinism.[18] He defined eugenics as: "the science which deals with all influences that improve the inborn qualities of a race; also with those that develop them to the utmost advantage."[19]

Eugenics was popularized widely in the US through the writings of Paul Bowman Popenoe (1888–1979), one of the most influential and toxic racist and eugenicist writers of the US. Having worked initially in agricultural research, Popenoe turned toward research on human breeding, and from 1913 to 1917 edited the *Journal of Heredity*. In 1918, he teamed up with Roswell Hill Johnson (1877–1867), then an instructor at the University of Pittsburgh, to author a college textbook on eugenics, with the title *Applied Eugenics*. The book was edited by the prominent economist Richard Theodore Ely (1854–1943)[20] and became hugely popular for

---

[18] Dennis, Rutledge M., "Social Darwinism, Scientific Racism, and the Metaphysics of Race." *Journal of Negro Education*, 64:3 (1995), 243–52.

[19] Galton, Francis, "Eugenics: Its Definition, Scope, and Aims," *American Journal of Sociology* 10:1 (1904), 1–25.

[20] The links between the US progressive movement and eugenics have been thoroughly researched. See, e.g., Leonard, T. C., "American Economic Reform in the Progressive Era:

several decades. Popenoe believed in compulsory sterilization and the removal of the "unfit" to rural institutions. One of the most influential aspects of his *Applied Eugenics*, however, concerned the authors' view on the health and social characteristics of African Americans, and the potential future impact of these aspects on the country as a whole. As regards, the health of Africa-Americans, *Applied Eugenics* restated some of the observations of earlier writers, including[21]:

> That tuberculosis is particularly fatal to the Negro race is well known. … That overcrowding and climate cannot be the sole factors is indicated by the fact that the Negro race has been decimated, wherever it has met tuberculosis. Despite all the efforts of medicine and sanitation, it is likely that the Negro death-rate from phthisis will continue high for some years, until … the race will possess a degree of resistance, or immunity, not much inferior to that of the whites among whom they live. (pp. 129 and 130).

To be clear, Popenoe and Johnson's *Applied Eugenics* did not claim that the presence of African Americans represented an immediate physical health hazard. In their view, the core of the "negro problem" related to the realm of social relations. This was in fact one of the core messages of *Applied Eugenics* and the authors deviously constructed their argument as a thought experiment, where they argued that:

> If the only differences between white and black, which cannot be removed by education, are of no real significance, — a chocolate hue of skin, a certain kinkiness of hair, and so on, — then logically the white race should remove the handicaps which lack of education and bad environment have placed on the Negro, and receive him on terms of perfect equality, in business, in politics, and in marriage. (P. 282).

This in their view, however, was not the case:

Its Foundational Beliefs and their Relation to Eugenics," *History of Political Economy,* 41:1 (2009), 109–41. Freeden, Michael, "Eugenics and Progressive Thought: A Study in Ideological Affinity," *The Historical Journal,* 22:3 (1979): 645–71.

[21] Popenoe, Paul, and Roswell H. Johnson, *Applied Eugenics*, New York, NY, Macmillan (1918).

> But what are these social differences, which it is the custom to dismiss in such a light-hearted way? Are they not based on fundamental incompatibilities of racial temperament, which in turn are based on differences in heredity? Modern sociologists for the main part have no illusions as to the ease with which these differences in racial tradition and custom can be removed. The social heritage of the Negro has been described at great length. Only a glance can be given of the subject here, but it may profitably be asked what the Negro did when he was left to himself in Africa. An elementary knowledge of the history of Africa, or the more recent and much-quoted example of Haiti, is sufficient to prove that the Negro's own social heritage is at a level far below that of the whites among whom he is living in the United States. No matter how much one may admire some of the Negro's individual traits, one must admit that his development of group traits is primitive, and suggests a mental development which is also primitive. If the number of original contributions which it has made to the world's civilization is any fair criterion of the relative value of a race, then the Negro race must be placed very near zero on the scale. (pp. 283 and 284).

The real threat of multi-racialism (where different races are given equal status in a society) in Popenoe and Johnson's view thus arose from two factors. Firstly, the possibility that these supposed differences were ignored, and race integration proceeded to the detriment of all involved. And secondly, from the weakening of the white race, which the authors already observed in terms of low white middle class birth rates. Despite these fears and their own racist alarmism, the authors of *Applied Eugenics* saw limited grounds for optimism, if only their racist beliefs were more widely embraced:

> The education of public opinion which, acting through the many agencies named, will gradually bring about an increase in the birth-rate of superior people, will not be speedy; but it has begun. The writers, therefore, feel justified in thinking, not solely as a matter of optimistic affirmation, but because of the evidence available, that the race suicide now taking place in the old American stock will soon reach its lowest limit, and that thereafter the birth-rate in that particular stock will slowly rise. If it does, and if, as seems probable, the birth-rate in some inferior

> sections of the American population at the same time falls from its present level, a change in the racial composition of the nation will take place, which, judged by past history, is bound to be of great eugenic value. (P. 279).

Popenoe and Johnson's strategy for crafting arguments around race and health did bear some similarity with the approaches of anti-immigration agitators at the later stages of that debate. Since it could not be shown that "undesirables" or "inferior races" presented a clear and present danger to public health, either in terms of contagion or through an interbreeding of their characteristics with those of "superior races," a third argument alleging long-term damage to the status quo or stability of society was constructed. In case of the eugenics-inspired phase of anti-immigration agitation, this involved the claim of an impending shift of the racial balance of the country from a predominantly white Anglo-Saxon majority to a multiracial society with an ever-diminishing old core. Popenoe and Johnson's arguments were similar but centered on the social sphere and were aimed at advocating forms of social containment or apartheid. The main source of danger in their view was the socio-political integration of African Americans whom they described as incapable of contributing to the social organization of a modern society.

Popenoe reiterated his racist claims in several contexts, including work published in the *Journal of Heredity* of which he had been an editor. Here we quote from a paper on *Negro Intelligence* where intellectual inferiority of African Americans and a resulting inability to organize society are presented as public health facts.[22] Popenoe states:

> As the conclusions of the army tests agree with those made under other auspices, it may be taken as certain that the negro is, as measured by intelligence tests, markedly inferior to the white men among whom he lives. Is this inferiority an innate and ineradicable condition, or is it, as some have supposed, merely a handicap due to unfavorable tradition and environment? Professor Johnson and I have elsewhere pointed out the historical indications that the negro's low mental estate is irremediable. ... The mental tests strongly support this conclusion; for they measure

[22] Popenoe, Paul, "Intelligence and Race: A Review of Some of the Results of the Army intelligence tests — II. The Negro," *Journal of Heredity,* 13:7 (1922): 295–298.

> traits which are largely independent of schooling. They point clearly to the fact that the observed inferiority of the negro is to a large extent one which no amount of education, or favorable environment can obviate. While there are many bright negroes, and many dull whites, the average of the two races is measurably different. The negro is mentally, therefore, eugenically inferior to the white race. All treatment of the negro, in the United States or elsewhere, must take into account this fundamental fact. (P. 298).

With Popenoe and Johnson's *Applied Eugenics,* and its many admirers, followers, and imitators,[23] racist thinking in the US as it related to public health, may well have reached its zenith. Local political interests as well as an international network of researchers,[24] meanwhile, kept some of the movement's core ideas simmering beyond the interwar period. They also expanded and even radicalized some of the movement's original ideas, particularly relating to the mixing of races.

Mature Eugenics

Apart from confirming and reiterating many of Popenoe's statements about *Negro Intelligence*, the British-American academic Reginald Ruggles Gates (1882–1962) expanded the list of predominantly black diseases and public health problems. Gates held a professorship at King's College London and was an associate professor at the University of California, reflecting the international nature of work in the area of eugenics. In 1923, he published his book *Heredity and Eugenics* with Macmillan in New York.[25] Regarding diseases of the "Black," he stated:

[23] Comer, Sue D., "The Growing Need for a National Eugenic Program." *Bios* (1936), 176–87. Darwin, Leonard, "The Eugenic Predicament," *The Eugenics Review,* 25:4 (1934), 266. Dachert, Alfred, "Positive Eugenics in Practice: An Account of the First Positive Eugenic Experiment," *The Eugenics Review,* 23:1 (1931), 15, Gosney, Ezra S., "Eugenic Sterilization," *Scientific American* 151:1 (1934), 18–53; Stoddard, Lothrop, *The Revolt against Civilization: The Menace of the Under Man*, New York, NY, C. Scribner's sons (1922).

[24] Turda, Marius, "Legacies of Eugenics: Confronting the Past, Forging a Future." *Ethnic and Racial Studies,* 45:13 (2022), 2470–7. See Whitman, James Q., *Hitler's American model: The United States and the Making of Nazi Race Law*, Princeton, Princeton University Press (2017).

[25] Gates, Reginald Ruggles, *Heredity and Eugenics*, Vol. 10. New York, NY, Macmillan Company (1923).

> That negroes are relatively lacking in resistance to tuberculosis and pneumonia is shown by the fact that the rate for tuberculosis was over twice as high among coloured troops, while for pneumonia it was two or three times as high. The rate for venereal disease is three or four times higher in coloured troops, epilepsy, hysteria, neuralgia, and hemorrhoids are about twice as frequent, addiction to drugs is more common, while skin diseases are less common than in white troops. (P. 235).

In hindsight, the disregard for the impact of social factors on health or test outcomes, which runs like a *leitmotiv* through most "race research," appears puzzling and sheds a negative light on the intellectual integrity of academics who were involved in this work.

Despite its obvious weaknesses, eugenics in the US retained its halo as an academic discipline for many decades to come. Many of the country's top universities continued to make professorial appointments in the field and contributed to the work of organizations such as the Eugenics Record Office at Cold Spring Harbor Laboratory (1910–1939).[26] One area of particular concern of eugenics was the issue of racial hybridization, which attracted the attention of some of the leaders of the movement. One example of this was a paper presented by Kenneth B. Aikman, M.D. M.R.C.P in 1933 to the Eugenics Society and published in 1933 in the *Eugenics Review* with the title "Race Mixture". Aikman was a then well-known British trained medical researcher, who worked in London's prestigious Harley Street as an independent physician and maintained strong contacts to UK and US eugenicists. Aikman argued[27]:

> It may be said that the bulk of medical opinion is against hybridization between the Primary Races and that the best eugenic opinion is definitely against it. ... Professor Ruggles Gates also supports this view. The biological objection is based upon the fact that, in these crosses, groups of inherited characteristics remain associated or " segregate," with the result that the offspring has a "chaotic constitution." ... Each variety of man or of animal, in the course of time, acquires a constitution adapted

[26] Lowe, Roy, "The Educational Impact of the Eugenics Movement." *International Journal of Educational Research,* 27:8 (1998), 647–60.

[27] Aikman, Kenneth B., "Race Mixture," *The Eugenics Review,* 25:3 (1933), 161.

> to its particular mode of life and to the diseases to which it is exposed. When such constitutions are mixed by inter-breeding, a new constitution is produced, which is not adapted to the mode of life of either parent and too often is not fitted for any actual environment whatever. As examples of simple skeletal mal-adaptations, we find hybrids with skulls too large to permit of their birth; others with teeth too large for their jaws; and others with either the upper or the lower jaw a misfit with its neighbour. There are, however, many more complicated disabilities, such as altered resistance to disease and disharmonies of the internal secretions. It is found that the greater the difference between the races crossed, the less likely is the result to be beneficial: that the Caucasian is nearer to the Mongolian than either is to the Negro, and that the Dark Caucasian is nearer to the Mongolian than is the Fair Caucasian, and so the Dark Caucasian cross is the less harmful of the two. (pp. 161 and 162).

Further to this, Aikman added:

> Is the environment of the hybrid likely to be as good as that of the child of pure race? The answer is, No! Often it will be worse even than that of the race of the inferior parent. Too often the hybrid is illegitimate, hating his white father and despising his black mother. But even if his parents are married and there is no racial prejudice against mixed marriages where they live, it is exceedingly unlikely that the environment will be good, for at least one of the parents is almost certain to be reckless, improvident, disinclined to settle down, and with poor ideals of parenthood. … The United States presents these problems on the largest scale and has devoted much research to them. Indeed, in many States the American view is crystallized into laws absolutely forbidding marriage between white and coloured persons. Furthermore, as the statistics of divorce show, family life in the United States is less stable than it was. I attribute this instability, in very large measure, to the mixed blood of the bulk of her citizens. (P. 162).

Aikman also saw adverse political implications of race mixture, arguing that:

> … immigration of different races leads to the complication of a whole host of administrative problems which are all too difficult already in

> modern civilization. One need only instance the segregation of races, as in the "Jim Crow" cars on railways in the Southern States; the racial friction which often expresses itself in lynchings; the economic problems and trade disputes due to wage-cutting and to different standards of living; the legal problems, often of the most distressing kind, due to laws in the United States rendering illegal marriages between white and coloured persons, and the profound effect upon the life of the nation produced by the Negroes and hybrids. It is not generally realized how great is this effect already. It is likely to become even greater. Not only because the number of people with some negro blood in their veins is increasing (and I would remind you that there are some twelve million Negroes and coloured persons in the States), but also because the Negro is increasing in material prosperity and in education. It will become progressively more difficult to limit his political power in the Southern States and his political power in the North is much greater than it was before the war. (P. 163).

Aikman's views were outspoken, but perhaps chimed with those of Walter Ashby Plecker (1861–1947), the first registrar of Virginia's Bureau of Vital Statistics, who helped create the Virginia Racial Integrity Act of 1924 and others who worked on similar legislation. The eugenics movement, however, saw itself as the brain behind these measures, rather than as the technician who engineered them, and it is interesting to gauge some of the self-perception of the movement's leaders from the following 1940 letter to the editor of *Eugenics Review*. Written by Cyrus H. Eshleman of Ohio, this letter is titled "Eugenics and Mongrelization". Here, Eshleman states[28]:

> SIR,-In order that the eugenics movement shall advance successfully, the eugenics organizations must dissociate their endeavours from the widespread propaganda for race amalgamation and mongrelization. There is little wisdom in breeding selectively among individuals if the results are to be nullified by indiscriminate mixing of the races. ...
>
> There are about twelve million Negroes, who have a small fraction of widely diffused white blood, due mainly to miscegenation on the southern plantations before the Civil War. But there is practically no

[28] Eshleman, Cyrus H., "Eugenics and Mongrelization," *The Eugenics Review*, 32:1 (1940), 28.

> Negro blood in the one hundred and ten million whites, who are almost purely of European descent and have absolutely no intention of amalgamating with the Negroes. The white race is unquestionably uniquely beautiful and is in many respects of superior intelligence. To mix the white features with other races would destroy the white beauty forever. The white race should maintain its purity and should further develop its characteristics. ... The cruel persecution of the Jews in Germany caused a temporary reaction in favour of race solidarity, but with the adjustment of the Jewish problem in some manner, the real attitude of the white race will become more outspoken and unmistakable. The eugenics organizations must act along these lines, else their efforts will fail and new organizations will be formed to strive for the true eugenic ideals. (pp. 28 and 29).

Eshleman's statement defines race mixture, race pollution, miscegenation, and monrgelization as key public health problems or risks. In so doing, it espouses ideas that could have originated from Nazi Germany.

It is interesting to note that the editor of *Eugenics Review* decided to print Eshleman's letter, yet felt compelled to add a personal comment to Eshleman's correspondence stating that:

> Mr. Eshleman's statement that 'the white race is unquestionably uniquely beautiful' must be respected as an expression of his own aesthetic judgment, but it may be doubted whether, for instance, all Chinese ladies and gentlemen would completely subscribe to it. More than ordinary caution is required in discussions that involve the physical characteristics of one's own group and therefore of emotional values about which it is difficult to be entirely objective. 'We-feeling,' or 'ethnocentrism' as the sociologists have called it, is a deep pit into which the unweary are all too prone to tumble. (pp. 29 and 30).

We must assume that key members of the eugenics movement, did indeed see themselves such as neutral, objective scientists, irrespective of the fact that uncritical generalizations about racial characteristics and facilities stood at the core of their belief system.

In the post-war period, when the crimes of Nazism came to be known, leaders of the Eugenics movements, perhaps unsurprisingly, attempted to distance themselves from Nazi racism. As a consequence, many of the prejudiced, biased, and discriminatory views of the discipline were rephrased in more *sotto voce* terms. The core beliefs of eugenics in this mature phase, however, remained largely unchanged and the mainstream eugenics movement is implicated in adversely affecting the lives of individuals in many ways,[29] and also in creating pseudo-intellectual justifications for delaying necessary social reforms in parts of the US and other countries.[30]

To be fair, during the post-war period, some members of the movement also came to retract some of the views of earlier leaders. However, what was said was insufficient and fell far short from a necessary retraction and unequivocal apology. Here we quote from a paper titled "Race Mixture: A Social or a Biological Problem?" published in the *Eugenics Review in* 1949, where the author Dickinson states[31]:

> First, then, as to the theory of disharmony which is advanced in opposition to miscegenation. Its principal exponents are Davenport and Steggerda, who postulate an inheritance, following race crossing, of conflicting characteristics of the two parent groups, which may result in the birth of organic misfits in the second generation after crossing or later. The possibility is envisaged of offspring with, say, a large frame and small viscera, or long legs and short arms, and conversely in each case. Again, it has been alleged that the mixture of two groups, one with large teeth and jaws and the other with small teeth and jaws may result in offspring combining, say, large teeth in small jaws. ... Mj0en, transferring his experiments to the human sphere, studied Lapp Norwegian crossings and again found a "lack of balance" among the hybrids. But

---

[29] See, e.g., Pearson, Susan J., "Birth Registration and the Administration of White Supremacy," *Modern American History,* 5:2 (2022), 117–41; Lombardo, Paul A., "Miscegenation, Eugenics, and Racism: Historical Footnotes to Loving v. Virginia," *UC Davis L. Rev.,* 21 (1987), 421; Gilliam, J. Casey. "White and Everything Else: Promotion the 1924 Virginia Racial Integrity Act.," Undergraduate Thesis, University of Lynchburg (2011).

[30] Goldfield, David, *Black, White, and Southern: Race Relations and Southern Culture, 1940 to the Present,* Baton Rouge, Louisiana, LSU Press (1991). Maloney, Thomas N., "Wage Compression and Wage Inequality between Black and White Males in the United States, 1940–1960," *The Journal of Economic History,* 54:2 (1994), 358–81.

[31] Dickinson, A., "Race Mixture: A Social or a Biological Problem?," *The Eugenics Review,* 41:2 (1949), 81.

> again Castle urged that social factors which must be taken into account. Thus, these hybrids are subjected to considerable disabilities in the cultural and social spheres, as is so often the case with mixed populations living in close contact with the relatively pure parent groups, and it becomes impossible to isolate the biological factor which could be held to contribute to an indisputable hybrid lack of mental balance. Further, before condemning miscegenation on the grounds of physical deterioration in the subjects studied, and before comparisons are made between the hybrid and the parent populations, the characters of the individuals mating must be investigated. Were they typical of the stocks from which they were drawn? Did the mating take place from choice or otherwise? Was it clandestine or open? The union of two poor specimens of their respective races will usually result in offspring inferior to the average of the parent populations. All of which merely goes to show that biological considerations are by no means all in all, that social factors, difficult to measure though they may be, must be taken into account when comparing parent populations and hybrids in respect of physical and mental qualities. (P. 82).

Having gone through several versions of the same argument, the author then states, "It is difficult to escape the conclusion that the seemingly insoluble problem of race mixture is far less biological in character than it is social and psychological; but it is hardly less difficult for that." (P. 85) This obviously is hardly a conclusive stance against previous fallacious science and the toxic policy conclusions derived from it. Dickinson instead follows the "we may have been wrong with some details" but "we were right in principle" approach typical of much post-war eugenics.

Exit Eugenics?

To be clear, by the 1960s, some academics publishing in the *Eugenics Review* sought to present serious and largely unbiased research. However, this endeavor was hindered by some of the core premises of the discipline. One example of this is the article "Genetics and Race" written in 1963 by G. Ainsworth Harrison (1927–2017), who was lecturer at the University of Liverpool, and became professor of Biological Anthropology, while also serving as president of the Royal Anthropological Institute.[32] Discussing variations in skin and eye color, Harrison noted that[33]:

> To it, can now be added a number of physiological variables such as basal metabolic rate, vascular responses in the hand to cold, vital capacity and age of menarche. It also includes many of the marked differential sensitivities to disease such as the geographical variations in liability to hypertensive disease, and the lower incidence of mouth, lip and skin cancers, and higher incidence of cancers of the cervix uteri in Negroes as compared with Europeans.
>
> … The most difficult problem involved in considering the geographical distribution in these characters is to determine the extent to which the environment is directly responsible for the variation. In some cases it would seem that environmental factors are the sole cause and that the variation, therefore, has no racial significance at all. It is common knowledge that the dietary and infectious diseases have ramifying effects on body habitus, and even such an obviously adaptive trait as the variation in red blood cell count with altitude is, in large part at least, attributable to direct environmental effects. … Cradling habits, for instance, may affect adult head shape. Indeed, the extent to which such a frequently studied feature as the cephalic index is environmentally labile is still unknown. (pp. 139 and 140).

The problem with this advanced and seemingly enlightened version of race research seems to have been that it was reluctant to investigate issues of social and economic inequality. In other words, the question as to which factors lead to stark differences in dietary habits or to differential levels of exposures to infectious disease remained largely unexplored. Pre-occupation with race thus tended to obscure what should have been a readiness to objectively examine health differences among races from a social epidemiological perspective.

---

[32] Nick, M. T., "Professor Geoffrey Ainsworth Harrison June 8, 1927–September 14, 2017," (2018), https://policycommons.net/artifacts/1689349/professor-geoffrey-ainsworth-harrison -june-8-1927/2421001/ (accessed 03 May 2023).

[33] Harrison, G. Ainsworth, "Genetics and Race," *The Eugenics Review,* 55:3 (1963), 139.

In any case, by the mid to late 1960s, eugenics or race research had lost most of its glamour. It had failed to address or ameliorate what appeared to be race-specific health problems, largely on account of the fact of a persistent blindness to social and economic inequalities; instead making itself a supporter of false claims regarding innate inequalities of races and their cultures.[34] It had also failed to recognize that "it is morally objectionable for governments or institutions or any third party to compel or coerce anyone's reproductive behavior. The right to reproduce without interference from third parties is one of the fundamental freedoms recognized by international law and moral theories from a host of ethical traditions."[35]

In the final analysis, what can be said about race science, scientific racism, racialism, and eugenics, is that they caused immeasurable suffering to innocent individuals who were guilty of nothing more than having some distinguishing physical characteristics. Meanwhile, these pseudo-disciplines contributed virtually nothing to public health and medicine.[36]

---

[34] Ipgrave, Benedict, *et al.*, "From Small Beginnings: To Build an Anti-eugenic Future," *The Lancet,* 399:10339 (2022), 1934–5.

[35] Caplan, Arthur L., Glenn McGee, and David Magnus, "What is immoral about eugenics?," *BMJ,* 319:7220 (1999), 1284.

[36] Some recent publications have discussed possible links between eugenics and some forms of modern genetics although the positive contribution of the latter discipline to medical science is far clearer. Epstein, Charles J., "Is Modern Genetics the New Eugenics?," *Genetics in Medicine,* 5:6 (2003), 469–75.

Chapter Five

War

Public Health and War: A Kaleidoscope of Contradictions

This chapter discusses the often-contradictory relationship between the conduct of war and public health concerns. Obviously, the destruction of human life is a large component of the conduct of war,[1] while public health activities are expected to be targeted toward the preservation of life. Armed conflict, however, does not merely affect the health and well-being of combatants. It has broader and often far-reaching effects on various population groups and/or even the population of countries and regions as a whole. Likewise, combatants are not harmed by combat alone. A major factor contributing to the deaths of members of military forces was disease, which often emerged from a failure to protect the health of troops outside combat. This chapter looks at historical writings on the relationship between armed conflict and the secondary public health risks it creates. In this context, we describe as secondary public health risks the disease risk experienced by soldiers and their families outside combat.

---

[1] Some theoreticians of war have actually spoken of *Vernichtungskrieg* or annihiliation war which is meant describe a level of material and human damage sufficient to cause the enemy to exist or function as a state. See, e.g., Honig, Jan Willem, "The Idea of Total War: From Clausewitz to Ludendorff," *The Pacific War as Total War: Proceedings of the 2011 International Forum on War History*, Tokyo, National Institute for Defence Studies (2011).

These indirect effects which follow involvement in combat but do not necessarily relate directly to combat-related physical injury.

Again, we examine key historical texts in order to trace the evolution of thinking on the relationship between armed conflict and public health risk. Geographically, our focus is also again on the US, mainly because the literature on this theme coming from this country is extensive and accessible. Chronologically, we focus on the period from the end of the US Civil War in the of 1860s to the 1950s, when public health threats of the Second World War were still being assessed, while nuclear weapons posed a qualitatively new form of threat. As before, our analysis builds on many excellent studies which examine a similar set of topics.[2]

The US fought one of the first modern wars[3] during a period of time which saw the beginning of some key medical discoveries.[4] The US Civil War, which lasted from 1861 to 1865, affected the way combat medicine and medicine in general were practiced in crucial ways. Although "physicians were practicing in an era before the germ theory of disease was established, before sterile technique and antisepsis were known, with very few effective medications, and often operating 48 to 72 hours with no sleep,"[5] many medical advances occurred in battlefield medicine and in terms of responses to the broader challenges this war presented to the nation. Lessons from the US Civil War, in turn, influenced public health responses during later wars, including those taking place during the Great War of 1914 to 1918, which the English writer H.G. Wells thought to be the "war to end all wars."[6] Our relatively brief and sketchy history of the

---

[2] See, e.g. Levy, Levy, Barry S., and Victor W. Sidel, eds., *War and Public Health*, Oxford, Oxford University Press (2008).

[3] Hagerman, Edward, *The American Civil War and the Origins of Modern Warfare: Ideas, Organization, and Field Command*, Bloomington, Indiana, Indiana University Press (1992).

[4] Weiss, Erik D., "The Second Sacrifice: Costly Advances in Medicine and Surgery during the Civil War," *The Yale Journal of Biology and Medicine,* 74:3 (2001), 169.

[5] Reilly, Robert F., "Medical and Surgical Care during the American Civil War, 1861–1865," *Baylor University Medical Center Proceedings,* 29:2 (2016), 138–42.

[6] Wagar, W. Warren. *HG Wells: Traversing Time*, Middletown, Connecticut, Wesleyan University Press (2004).

armed conflict and public health risk relationship, however, does not primarily focus on medical advances in contexts of adversity. Our interest is in how thought-leaders of their time generally viewed the relationship between armed conflict and health contexts. Public health in wartime contexts can exhibit deeply contradictory tendencies. On the one hand, war can encourage efforts to improve public health.[7] On the other hand, social tensions can become more pronounced during war, while the willingness to advocate in social improvement declines. Similarly, discrimination against minority groups can grow to alarming or catastrophic levels.[8] This chapter, like the previous ones, does not center on these historical experiences *per se* but rather focuses on ideas and concepts which key writers in the area used to explore links between armed conflict and health, whichever form these links took. In this sense, we are again interested in how these risks were perceived, which risks were prioritized, and which responses were thought to be appropriate and why.

The US Civil War and Early Thinking on Conflict and Health Risks

Some of the first systematic investigations of the impact of armed conflict on public health occurred in the wake of the US Civil War of the 1860s. This was triggered, in part, by the high level of non-combat losses on both sides of this conflict. Although weaponry had become more dangerous, disease was also a major killer, with diarrhea, dysentery, and typhoid running rampant through army camps. An 1879 publication with the title *Medical and Surgical History of the War of the Rebellion* prepared under

[7] See, e.g., Quirke, Viviane, and Jean-Paul Gaudillière, "The Era of Biomedicine: Science, Medicine, and Public Health in Britain and France after the Second World War," *Medical History,* 52:4 (2008), 441–52. Elena, Sklyarova, "Crimean War and Establishing of Public Health System in Great Britain," *Научный альманах стран Причерноморья* 1:9 (2017), 24–9.

[8] See, e.g. Dadrian, Vahakn N., "The Role of Turkish Physicians in the World War I Genocide of Ottoman Armenians," *Holocaust and Genocide Studies,* 1:2 (1986), 169–92; Tone, John Lawrence, *War and Genocide in Cuba, 1895–1898*, Chapel Hill, North Carolina, Univ of North Carolina Press (2006).

Joseph K. Barnes, Surgeon General, US Army by Joseph Janvier Woodward, Surgeon, US Army stated that[9]:

> 157,004 white soldiers are known to have died from disease, and that there were also 23,347 deaths the causes of which are not recorded. If it is assumed that these deaths from unrecorded causes were distributed between disease and wounds in the same proportion as those in which the cause is recorded, viz: one and seven — tenths deaths from disease to each death from wounds, 14,700 deaths from disease must be added to the number just given, making a total of 171,704 deaths from disease among white troops, 42,318 of which are simply reported as dead of disease ... . If it is supposed that the deaths from diarrhæa and dysentery among these deaths from unspecified diseases bear the same proportion ... [as] those deaths in which the particular disease is recorded, viz: one to three and one-half, 12,091 deaths from these disorders must be added to the number already given, making a total of 49,885 deaths from diarrhea and dysentery among the white troops. ... The 6,764 deaths among colored troops ... represent the deaths from diarrhea and dysentery out of a total of 27,499 deaths in which the disease is specified. It has been shown that the total number of deaths from disease among colored troops was 29,212; that the proportion of deaths from disease to deaths from wounds was eight and eight-tenths to one; and that there were 837 deaths from unknown causes. Dividing these deaths from unknown causes between disease and wounds in the same proportion as those from known causes, and adding, the total number of deaths from disease is found to be 29,964, of which 2,465 are not distributed among the particular diseases. If the proportion of deaths from diarrhæa and dysentery was the same among these as among the others, viz: one to four, 616 deaths must be added to the number given above, making a total of 7,380 deaths from these disorders among the colored troops. Adding this number to the deaths among white troops, as estimated above, gives 57,265 as the number of deaths from diarrhea and dysentery ... and even this, for the reasons indicated, must be regarded as less than the actual mortality from these diseases. (P. 3)

[9] Woodward, Joseph Janvier, *et al.*, *The Medical and Surgical History of the War of the Rebellion (1861–65): pt. II. Medical History*. Vol. 1. Washington, DC, US Government Printing Office (1879), p. 3.

Later, estimates of Civil War deaths were somewhat higher and put the total number of those who died of accidents or disease at 230,000 to which must be added 25,000 to 30,000 dying in Confederate prisons and 26,000 to 31,000 dying in Union prisons as compared to about 204,000 dying of combat wounds.[10] In other words, non-combat deaths exceeded deaths caused by combat by about 40 per cent for white soldiers, with deaths from diarrhea and dysentery playing a major role. Our 1879 source document, meanwhile, also indicates that deaths from disease among African American troops were vastly more numerous than those among white soldiers. This suggests that unequal treatment had major adverse effects on soldiers' health.

The Professionalization of Military Medicine

Some years later, when comparing death rates of the Spanish-American War (1898) with those of the earlier US Civil War, then US Surgeon General, George Sternberg, came to the conclusion that deaths from combat and disease had been reduced considerably.[11] However, again, health problems affecting troops were still a major cause of deaths. Sternberg noted that:

> As compared with the Civil War and with other great wars during the present century, the mortality from wounds and disease among our troops during the war with Spain has been low. Our wounded have, to a large extent, had the advantage of prompt treatment with antiseptic dressings and a very considerable proportion of those who were not killed outright have recovered without any mutilating operation or septic complication. The mortality from disease has also been comparatively low, but unfortunately during the first months of the war, that scourge of new levies of new troops — typhoid fever — prevailed in many of our camps and claimed numerous victims. It is well known to sanitarians

[10] For a critical discussion of these figures, see Faust, Drew Gilpin, ""Numbers on Top of Numbers": Counting the Civil War Dead," *The Journal of Military History,* 70:4 (2006), 995–1009.

[11] Sternberg, George M., "Sanitary Lessons of the War," *Journal of the American Medical Association,* 32:23 (1899), 1287–94.

> and military surgeons that as a general rule more soldiers succumb to disease than are killed by the bullets of the enemy, and our recent war has not been an exception in this regard. (P. 1287).

Sternberg stated optimistically that, "As we now know the cause of typhoid fever, the biologic characters of the typhoid bacillus, and the physical and chemic agents by which this bacillus may be destroyed, sanitarians have no difficulty in formulating rules relating to its prevention, which if strictly followed, would, to a great extent at least, protect our armies from its ravages."[12] This was in fact only partly true. The British Army had indeed introduced an effective typhoid vaccine in 1896, but it took until 1909 that a comparable typhoid vaccine was created and subsequently comprehensively administered by the US Army.[13] So Sternberg had in fact misrepresented the danger typhoid still posed to members of US armed forces stationed in Cuba and similar areas. Unsurprisingly, Sternberg also did not question the motives for this war, the commencement of which had hinged on the misrepresentation of the cause of an explosion on a US naval vessel in Havana harbor.[14]

In a sense, Sternberg's misrepresentation of some of the medical aspects of the Spanish-American war exemplifies two of the key problematic aspects of the armed conflict and health relationship. These include the often unquestioning acceptance of war goals and strategies by those involved in health matters, and the embellishment of the effectiveness of measures taken to protect combatants or affected civilians from health risks.

Some years later, the US federal government's role in public health related activities expanded, as preparations for the first World War came under way. This involved activities led by the newly founded US Public Health Service. Officially established under the name Public Health Service in 1912, the organization's mission moved from an initial focus on

---

[12] *Ibid.*, p. 1288.

[13] Adler, Richard, and Elise Mara, *Typhoid Fever: A History*, North Carolina, McFarland (2016).

[14] The explosion on the battleship Maine was caused by an internal source, but the US navy claimed that it was due to an action by the Spanish navy and escalated this to a declaration of war. Rickover, Hyman George, *How the Battleship Maine was Destroyed. Naval History Division*, Virginia, Navy History Division, Department of the Navy (1976).

communicable diseases to a broad focus to encompass non-communicable diseases.[15] When the US eventually entered World War One in April 1917, it expanded its military medical services twenty-fold, enrolling 29,602 doctors as reserve officers.[16] Advances made by the US Public Health Service during this period were summarized as follows in a 1919 review in *Public Health Reports*[17]:

> … in a report dated February 4, 1917 … a board of officers of the United States Public Health Service formulated a program of activities which could be undertaken by the service in order to assist in the prosecution of the war. Among these are mentioned: The sanitation of ports and places within the United States in order to prepare them for camps of mobilization, concentration, or training for the Army or Navy.
>
> The sanitary supervision of mobilized industrial force medical and surgical relief to sick, wounded, or disabled soldiers and sailors at relief stations of the service. Medical and surgical relief to mobilized industrial workers. Laboratory operations, including, both research and manufacture of serums and vaccines. … at the close of the fiscal year, June 30, 1917, the service consisted of 538 professional personnel, 1,506 other personnel, a total of 2,044; at the close of the fiscal year, June 30, 1918, the professional personnel amounted to 1,472, and the other personnel to 3,515, a total of 4,987. (pp. 1243 and 1244).

Research has suggested that the US was comparatively well prepared to deal with the medical problems of wartime mobilization and demobilization.[18] The overwhelming force with which the Spanish Flu

[15] Rogers, Jerry R., James M. Symons, and Thomas J. Sorg, "The History of Environmental Research in Cincinnati, Ohio: (From the US Public Health Service to the US Environmental Protection Agency)," in Craig L. Patterson, Scott D. Struck, Daniel J. Murray, eds., *World Environmental and Water Resources Congress 2013: Showcasing the Future*, Virginia, American Society of Civil Engineers (2013), 33–7.

[16] Bennett, J. D. C, "Medical Advances Consequent to the Great War 1914–1918," *Journal of the Royal Society of Medicine,* 83:11 (1990), 738.

[17] Warren, Benjamin S. and Charels F. Bolduan, "War Activities of the United States Public Health Service (1919) [with Commentary]," *Public Health Reports,* 121 (2006), 117–31.

[18] Ginn, Richard V.N., *The History of the US Army Medical Service Corps*. Vol. 30. Washington, D.C., US Government Printing Office (1997); and also the early assessment in

affected the US and other countries, however, neutralized many of the potential gains from these approaches, while the War exacerbated this pandemic.[19]

Estimates suggest that the US experienced about 53,000 combat deaths and about 117,000 total military deaths during the First World War which puts the rate of non-combat deaths at about 55 per cent.[20] German losses for this War were 1,531,048 killed, 4,211,569 wounded, and 155,013 dying from disease, to which 762,796 deaths from food shortages must be added.[21] This produces a much higher ratio of non-combat deaths to combat deaths for Germany of about 67 per cent. Overall, improved medical care for soldiers in this War did little to reduce high number of deaths, but then the nature of weaponry, trench warfare, food blockades,[22] and the Spanish flu[23] all contributed to a massive death toll.[24]

Post-Conflict Hopes and Delusions

The end of World War One encouraged several then prominent academics to draw broad lessons about how healthcare provision to troops, and society more generally, could be improved. One of those writing about these issues was the famous Yale economist Irving Fisher (1867–1947), who was probably at this time the most prominent US economist alive.

Ireland, Merritte Weber, and Charles Lynch. *The Medical Department of the United States Army in the World War*. Vol. 4. Washington, D.C., US Government Printing. Office (1928).

[19] Erkoreka, Anton, "Origins of the Spanish Influenza Pandemic (1918–1920) and its Relation to the First World War," *Journal of Molecular and Genetic Medicine: An International Journal of Biomedical Research* 3:2 (2009), 190.

[20] DeBruyne, Nese F. and Anne Leland, "*American War and Military Operations Casualties: Lists and Statistics*," Library of Congress, Congressional Research Service (2015).

[21] Bennett "Medical Advances Consequent to the Great War", p. 738.

[22] Janicki, David A. "The British Blockade during World War I: The Weapon of Deprivation." *Inquiries Journal/Student Pulse,* 6:06 (2014).

[23] Oxford, John S., *et al.*, "World War I may have Allowed the Emergence of "Spanish" Influenza,." *The Lancet Infectious Diseases,* 2:2 (2002): 111–4.

[24] Prost, Antoine. "War losses," *International Encyclopedia of the First World War. Berlin: Freie Universität* 2014. https://encyclopedia.1914-1918-online.net/pdf/1914-1918-Online-war_losses-2014-10-08.pdf (accessed 14 Sept. 2023)

Apart from being recognized as a leading economist, Fisher had a broad range of interests extending from social and health issues to eugenics. In August 1918, he gave an invited paper to the Annual Meeting of the American Public Health Association in Chicago with the title "Health and War", where he speculated about future developments in public health triggered by the experiences of the war. Fisher noted[25]:

> … there is this great problem of health. The war is a means of destroying human life; and therefore in its reaction will probably be the greatest stimulus to life conservation which we have ever experienced. Many a town has never had good fire fighting apparatus until it has had a great fire. We did not make much progress in safety at sea until we had the Titanic disaster. And so we see that the loss of human life which this war has brought has produced a powerful stimulus to toward saving human life. Already the armies and the navies of the belligerent nations have been making use of the very best medical talent available to keep the soldier in health; to prevent his getting typhus; to safeguard him from other epidemics; to provide him with safe drinking water. … At the end of this war we shall have new medical knowledge which we would not otherwise have had. The greatest stimulus to health conservation would be, I believe, health insurance. We ought to establish health insurance throughout the nation, preferably by national action if that be possible, but as it probably is not, then by state action.

Fisher, in other words, believed that the war had helped drive medical innovation and would, now that it was coming to its end, help promote broad social innovation in the area of public health. Fisher, of course, could not have foreseen the utterly devastating outbreak of the Spanish Flu (1918–1920) which dampened hopes for future improvements in public health, just as the Great Depression from 1929 to 1939 did in subsequent years.[26]

[25] Fisher, Irving, "Health and War," *American Journal of Public Health,* 8:8 (1918), 559–63.

[26] Fisher actually gained some notoriety for falsely predicting that there would be no depression. See Thornton, Mark, "The great depression: Mises vs. Fisher," *The Quarterly Journal of Austrian Economics,* 11:3 (2008), 230–41.

However, his lecture was a key testimony of the optimistic and progressive thinking which had characterized the early interwar years.

Expanding the Range of Military Medicine

Once the Spanish Flu pandemic had run its course, the attention of public health experts and medics more generally turned to some of the less well understood phenomena of the "Great War"; notably shell shock and similar psychological effects. Exposure to combat action had left thousands of soldiers to suffer from panic and impaired ability to reason, sleep, walk, or talk.[27] The term shell shock was coined by British psychologist Charles Samuel Myers,[28] who opposed the view that these symptoms reflected a desire to malinger, or were the sign of physical injury.

One of the more interesting contributions to this field includes a 1921 report entitled *Psycho-Analysis and the War Neuroses*, which was published as part of the newly created *International Psycho-Analytical Library* series.[29] The introduction to this collection of essays was provided by Sigmund Freud who stated that:

> The war neuroses, in so far as they differ from the ordinary neuroses of peace time through particular peculiarities, are to be regarded as traumatic neuroses, whose existence has been rendered possible or promoted through an ego-conflict. ... The conflict takes place between the old ego of peace time and the new war-ego of the soldier, and it becomes acute as soon as the peace-ego is faced with the danger of being killed through the risky undertakings of his newly formed parasitical double. Or as one might put it, the old ego protects itself from the danger to life by flight into the traumatic neurosis in defending itself against the new ego which it recognises as threatening its life. The National Army was

[27] Hochschild, Adam, *To End All Wars: A Story of Loyalty and Rebellion, 1914–1918*, Boston, Massachusetts, Houghton Mifflin Harcourt (2011).

[28] Myers, Charles Samuel, "Contributions to the Study of Shell Shock: Being an Account of Certain Disorders of Speech, with special reference to their Causation and their Relation to Malingering," *Lancet*, 188:4854 (1916), 461–8.

[29] Ferenczi, Sandor, *et al.*, *Psycho-analysis and the War Neuroses*, No. 2. London, International Psycho-Analytical Press (1921).

> therefore the condition, and fruitful soil, for the appearance of war neuroses; they could not occur in professional soldiers, or mercenaries. (P. 3)

Freud's analysis was interesting in that he postulated that for members of a national army (draftees), armed conflict was an unnatural experience which would cause psychological contradictions and conflicts. This analysis marked a significant step forward in terms of its perception of the war and public health relationship. Armed conflict, for an ordinary civilian could not be normal or natural, it would be inevitably alienating and traumatic. As such, it was also likely to result in psychological tensions of neuroses, whether these manifested themselves in anxiety and withdrawal or aggression and addiction.

The idea that psychology and psychiatry, in particular, had a significant role to play in addressing health problems resulting from armed conflict gained ground in the interwar years and had a considerable following during and after the Second World War. Thus, a 1942 article by George Blakeslee on "Neuropsychiatry In War Time" published in the *Bulletin of The New York Academy of Medicine* stated that a "well-organized and specialized neuropsychiatric service" had become a major "component part of the medical department in any army." Blakeslee concluded that: "[once] fighting was over … there were still psychiatric tasks to do … ."[30] In other words, when psychological damage of some of those fighting in wars was diagnosed and acknowledged, there was a group of people with long-term care needs, not just in terms of physical injury but also in terms of psychological damage and trauma.

The sheer scale of World War Two and the severity of the fighting and destruction involved, not only led to the recognition that individuals could suffer from long-term psychological damage in addition to physical injury, but it also caused researchers to think about the broader social impact of armed conflict on family and society. One example of this is a 1943 article on *Public Health and the Family in World War II* which appeared in *The Annals of the American Academy of Political and Social*

---

[30] Blakeslee, George A., "Neuropsychiatry in War Time," *Bulletin of the New York Academy of Medicine,* 18:12 (1942), 775.

Science.[31] In this interesting piece, the author Charles Taft, who served as director of Community War Services at the Federal Security Agency, picked up on a number of intriguing themes. He started off with the observation that armed conflict caused break ups of the normal pattern of living, which contributed to the health hazards resulting from physical and mental stresses of the war. In other words, normal family life often acted as a buffer which could mitigate some of the stresses of armed conflict. He also noted that the absence of the husband altered the role of the homemaker, usually in the sense of putting even greater than usual demands on her. Taft further observed that in general:

> … the Nation's health has remained good. No major outbreak of epidemic disease occurred in 1942. In some common diseases, such as typhoid fever and influenza, the record is better than in peace years. Where an increase has been found in the incidence of a communicable disease, as is the case with endemic typhus, efforts of the Public Health Service to limit its spread have been intensified. (P. 146).

Taft concluded that the US experience was positive overall but emphasized that there were important issues which had to be a concern for general health promotion. Specifically, he observed that:

> Probably no other health program which the war has engendered so closely touches the very heart of the family as that for maternal and infant care for wives and infants of men in the armed forces …. Until the end of 1942, maternal and infant mortality rates had continued to decrease since initiation of the maternal and child health program provided for in the Social Security Act. Recently there are indications of some increases in infant mortality in some areas. No one can arbitrarily say that this is a result of war conditions, but it seems logical to suppose that it may be. Certainly, the induction of men into the armed forces has resulted in new problems in maternity and child health. Wives have followed their soldier husbands to be near them in the vicinity. (P. 148).

---

[31] Taft, Charles P., "Public Health and the Family in World War II," *The Annals of the American Academy of Political and Social Science,* 229:1 (1943): 145–9.

Apart from an analysis of conventional public health indicators around contagious diseases and infant mortality, Taft provided an early account of some of the social changes which were to follow. Female-headed households with absentee fathers needed additional financial support as well as easy access to family medical care. Taft's analysis represents an important example of a widening of thinking around the impact of armed conflict on society which involved paying special attention to homemakers, their needs, and their expanded role.

Solidifying Wartime Public Health

Although most publications on contagious disease prevention in the US during World War Two were fairly upbeat, some studies identified specific war-related public health risks. Thus, a 1944 article in the *American Journal of Public Health* discussed salmonellosis as a war-time public health problem.[32] Authored by a team working from the Division of Communicable Diseases at the Massachusetts Department of Public Health, Boston, Mass, this paper observed:

> Under war conditions, the control of diarrheal diseases, which are a constant threat to the health of our armed forces, industrial workers, and other civilians, is one of the problems demanding increasing attention by health departments. Overcrowding in rapidly expanding industrial centers, an ever-growing shortage of labor and a constantly shifting population, are some of the many factors operating in a wartime environment, which tend to increase the incidence of these infections. (P. 1944).

Careful investigation of carriers and cases, led these authors to conclude that: "The stress of war conditions demands better control of diarrheal diseases. Salmonella organisms are important causes of such diseases". In other words, there was a recognition that extra resources had to be deployed under wartime conditions to prevent the outbreak of food-based infections, and that this involved carefully laboratory observation of "persistent convalescent carriers,

---

[32]Rubenstein, A. D., *et al.*, "Salmonellosis as a Public Health Problem in Wartime," *American Journal of Public Health and the Nation's Health,* 34.8 (1944): 841–853.

subclinical, and unrecognized cases are more important sources of infection than permanent carriers". (P. 1944).

Food hygiene was more difficult to maintain during war-time conditions for a host of reasons, and one of the ways of doing so was to increase levels of control, testing, inspection, and training. However, this option was only open to a few countries, such as the US, where an upscaling of such primarily civilian public health measures was deemed necessary and affordable.

Apart from highlighting the increased risks from well-known infectious diseases like salmonellosis during war-time conditions, the US public health literature from the mid-1940s also observed an increased incidence in the outbreak of lesser known and relatively rare diseases. One example of this was Vincent's Infection or acute necrotizing ulcerative gingivitis, a non-contagious infection of the gums. Modern understanding of the disease links it to malnutrition and viral respiratory infections as well as immune defects among young adults especially in institutional settings, including armies. A 1945 article in the *American Journal of Public Health* concluded that: "Since in 14 states the rules and regulations governing quarantine and isolation for communicable diseases do not define Vincent's infection or Vincent's angina, there surely is a wealth of misunderstanding as to the clinical picture that the disease presents".[33] In other words, this dangerous disease which occurred in military settings was poorly understood, while little effort was made to understand why it occurred in these settings or how it could be prevented. It is worth noting that institutional or military settings which bring together a large number of men have remained a public health concern with unexplained high levels of otherwise rare diseases, such as multidrug-resistant pulmonary tuberculosis.[34]

Amongst initially unexpected post-mobilization diseases of World War Two were otherwise well-known chronic arthritis and related-rheumatic diseases. These illnesses were known to affect individuals

[33] Sebelius, Carl L., "Vincent's Infection — A Wartime Disease: Reporting of Vincent's Infection by State Health Departments," *American Journal of Public Health and the Nation's Health,* 35:5 (1945), 451–6.

[34] See, e.g., Lee, Sei Won, *et al.*, "Multidrug-resistant Pulmonary Tuberculosis among Young Korean Soldiers in a Communal Setting," *Journal of Korean Medical Science,* 24:4 (2009), 592–95.

engaged in repetitive physical work in outdoor settings.[35] Hence, their occurrence among veterans was not surprising. A 1946 paper published in the *Annals of Internal Medicine,*[36] presented a strong case for the establishment of specialized rheumatism treatment centers for veterans. The author argued that: "During the First World War about 93,000 American soldiers developed some sort of "rheumatism" (mostly suffering from rheumatoid arthritis, rheumatic fever, osteo-arthritis, and muscular rheumatism) ... [while] no special rheumatism centre was officially established by the War Department." (P. 107) This situation apparently now had changed and:

> the Army acknowledged an obligation to the arthritic soldier, not merely as an individual, but as a representative of all his kind. Thus the medical officers serving at the five rheumatism centres are encouraged to improve our clinical knowledge of the rheumatic diseases, to improve, if possible, our methods of treatment, and to present clearly the results to the medical profession. In an effort to fulfill this obligation a number of clinical investigations are being carried out at each of the five centres. Although quite young, the two centres for chronic rheumatic disease are already, so far as we know, the largest rheumatism centres in the world. As treatment centres and carefully supervised schools of rheumatology, they are providing a unique opportunity which should benefit mutually both the rheumatic soldier and his medical officer. (P. 114).

Rheumatic diseases were among several chronic diseases which affected demobilized soldiers of the US army, and it is interesting to note that following World War Two, the US military acknowledged its obligation to provide care for affected veterans, much more so than it had done during the Great War. Clearly, there had been changes in perspective, where there was now a greater willingness to accept obligations to care for ex-soldiers and also to conduct research into the diseases that affected them. What precisely caused this change is not entirely clear, but several

---

[35] Copeman, W. S. C., "The Arthritic Sequelae of Pneumatic Drilling," *Annals of the Rheumatic Diseases,* 2:2 (1940), 141.

[36] Hench, Philip S., and Edward W. Boland, "The Management of Chronic Arthritis and Other Rheumatic Diseases among Soldiers of the United States Army," *Annals of Internal Medicine,* 24:5 (1946), 808–25.

potential reasons come to mind: The US came out of World War Two much richer than it had done in the previous war. The post World War Two period was not plagued by a major pandemic like the Spanish Flu. Instead of the recession which followed World War One, the post-World War Two period was by and large characterized by prosperity. Veterans and some groups of war-affected civilians were therefore treated with some level of generosity both in terms of responses to their healthcare needs and also in terms of other social provisions.[37] This then also led to a situation where the government was more willing to acknowledge public health risks that had been created during the military conflict, ranging from deafness to rheumatic diseases. The respective change in attitude thus included a gradual recognition of the environmental and occupational exposures of veterans.[38]

Another facet of the broadening and modernization of the understanding of public health aspects of armed conflict included a fuller understanding of the special health risks faced by veterans. This is exemplified by a 1946 article on *Combat Exhaustion* which was co-authored by the American pioneer psychiatrist Dr Karl Menninger.[39] Here, the authors highlighted the importance of the totality of networks a soldier-patient relied on and the risk created by disruptions of these group life aspects of military service:

> The group life of the combat soldier becomes his inner life. When his emotional bonds to the group are disrupted he, as a person, becomes disorganized. This disruption of group unity is a principal cause of the personality disorganization. The precipitating factor, especially under combat where there is no adequate recuperative pause, may be anything which alters the structure of the group with subsequent effect on the individual, or some event affecting the individual directly and

[37] Mettler, Suzanne, *Soldiers to Citizens: The GI Bill and the Making of the Greatest Generation*. Oxford, Oxford University Press (2005).

[38] Richards, Erin E., "Responses to Occupational and Environmental Exposures in the US military — World War II to the Present," *Military Medicine,* 176:suppl_7 (2011), 22–8.

[39] Bartemeier, Leo H., *et al.*, "Combat exhaustion," *The Journal of Nervous and Mentaldisease,* 104:5 (1946), 489–525.

> subsequently his relation to the group. Precipitating events may have a double meaning in evoking old, buried and displaced emotions. (P. 430).

There is ample evidence that the recently established "risk centered" approaches to therapy design and selection made inroads into military medicine by the mid-1940s. Here, we cite from a 1946 article on *Advances on the Treatment of Rheumatic Fever,*[40] in order to illustrate the increasingly prominent use of risk terminology at the time:

> Our Conclusions on Sulfonamide Prophylaxis for Rheumatic Patients. — Although the exact value of sulfonamide prophylaxis for rheumatic fever appears still to be a matter for some debate, for the present the arguments in favor of this procedure appear to be much stronger than those so far advanced against it. The patient and his family may be put to some expense and trouble in the conduct of this treatment and there is a slight risk of toxicity from sulfonamides. But these disadvantages appear to be quite justified in the expectation of reducing materially the chances for acute exacerbations, for prolonged invalidism or even for an early death from rheumatic carditis or from subacute bacterial endocarditis, which … so often occur when rheumatic fever is allowed to pursue its usual course.

And further on:

> When sulfamerazine and other improved sulfonamides become widely available the chances of significant toxicity, already small, should be materially reduced. Then even more than now will the risks from the disease, treated otherwise, be obviously greater than those inherent in chemoprophylaxis. Approaching the ideal agent would, of course, be a potent oral preparation of penicillin. (pp. 495–6, underline added).

In other words, a recommended therapy selection was justified on account of a balancing of medication risks with benefits, while a future

[40]Rosenberg, Edward F., and Phllip S. Hench, "Recent Advances in the Treatment of Rheumatic Fever; with Special Reference to Sulfona. Mide Prophylaxis and Intravenous Salicylate Therapy," *Medical Clinics of North America,* 30:3 (1946), 489–509.

improvement in the quality of the medication, and hence a reduction in medication risk was expected. As military medicine in the US increasingly came to grip with the wider and long-term consequences of conventional warfare, news about the nuclear arms race and related evaluations of the Hiroshima and Nagasaki bombings turned public attention to the public health implications of nuclear conflict.

By the 1950s, discussions about the risks and dangers of warfare posed to public health increasingly emphasized the possibility and potential consequences of nuclear conflict. One part of this concern was fed by closer post-war examinations of the Hiroshima and Nagasaki bombings.[41] The other major impetus for nuclear worry was created by near daily news about weapons testing, the threat of nuclear proliferation, and the failure to negotiate credible restrictions of the ongoing nuclear weapons race. The military establishment of the US, on the whole, attempted to de-emphasize the specific threats created by nuclear weapons, while emphasizing their similarity to conventional arms.[42] This is exemplified by the following paper from 1950, which was given by a Captain of the US Navy as address to the Atlanta Graduate Medical Assembly, Atlanta, Georgia[43]:

> Great quantities of ionizing radiation in the form of gamma rays, neutrons, alpha and beta particles, and radioactive fission products are liberated during the explosion of the bomb. It is this ionizing radiation that has captured the popular interest and beclouded the thinking of many imaginative minds. To these, radiation deaths appear to be more deliberate and conclusive than deaths from other causes. I have no desire to deemphasize or minimize the importance of radiation casualties. Nine thousand of these occurred in Hiroshima. This was approximately 15 per cent of the total deaths. Eighty-five per cent, however, of those who died would have died had there been no incidence of radiation. These people

---

[41] In 1945 The United States had detonated two atomic bombs over the Japanese cities of Hiroshima and Nagasaki killing between 90,000 and 146,000 people in Hiroshima and 39,000 and 80,000 people in Nagasaki.

[42] Tannenwald, Nina, "Stigmatizing the Bomb: Origins of the Nuclear Taboo," *International Security,* 29:4 (2005), 5–49.

[43] Aston, Melville J., "The Atomic Bomb versus Survival," *The Military Surgeon (United States),* 106:4 (1950), 270–75.

> were killed also by blast trauma as well as by burns, a sort of supersaturation of death as it were. Too much emphasis has been placed on the frightful effects of ionizing radiation and too little thought given to the great number of those who died from blast and burn injuries. Public confusion and unwarranted fears have developed to the point where many of our people would consider it most hazardous to enter a bombed area to carry out rescue operations. This happened at Hiroshima and Nagasaki as well. It should not happen here. Fears of the danger of exposure to residual radiation should be dispelled. (P. 271).

The tenor of this paper was quite typical of the widespread strategy of US military and civil defense authorities to underplay the qualitative difference between nuclear and conventional warfare. It paralleled efforts to convince the public that these weapons posed only a limited threat if adequate defensive measures were taken.[44] These approaches led to the dissemination of somewhat contradictory images and messages during the Cuban missile crisis of 1962, when the threat posed the US by these nuclear weapons was emphasized.[45] The advent of this crisis was shown by later researchers to have had widespread public health effects, with many adolescents in the US and Europe being significantly concerned about the threat of Nuclear War.[46]

War and Public Health Risks: A Summary

The primary focus of this chapter was not on the risks to public health armed conflicts generate *per se*. Rather we tried to assess some of the views of influential writers on what challenges and opportunities war

---

[44] Jacobs, Bo, "Atomic kids: Duck and Cover and Atomic Alert Teach American Children How to Survive Atomic Attack," *Film & History: An Interdisciplinary Journal of Film and Television Studies,* 40:1 (2010), 25–44.

[45] Paterson, Thomas G., and William J. Brophy, "October missiles and November elections: The Cuban missile crisis and American politics, 1962," *The Journal of American History,* 73:1 (1986), 87–119.

[46] Goldenring, John M., and Ron Doctor, "Teenage Worry about Nuclear War: North American and European Questionnaire Studies," *International Journal of Mental Health,* 15:1-3 (1986), 72–92.

would create for those who concerned themselves with public health risks. Several loosely connected themes came to the fore. Firstly, we noted that early writings on public health aspects of armed conflict picked up on the surprisingly high number of soldiers' deaths from accident and disease when compared to those related to combat wounds. This was documented extensively during the US Civil War when deaths from disease exceeded the number of deaths from combat wounds by about 40 per cent. While the emerging germ theory of disease suggested that some of this could be prevented through sanitary measures and the antiseptic treatment of wounds, military medicine was still far removed both from an effective understanding of the causes of diarrhea and dysentery outbreaks and effective approaches to the antiseptic treatment of wounds and injuries. The far greater rate of non-white soldiers dying during the Civil War from causes other than combat, meanwhile, indicates that unequal exposure to health risks was likely aggravated during this conflict. War may have increased racial inequality among soldiers rather than reducing it. While there may have been many causes for this, it is clear that an immoral and irresponsible white hierarchy was all too willing to create, or tolerate, conditions where diseases affecting blacks thrived.[47]

Military medicine, of course was at its infancy during the Civil War and it was only during the Spanish-American War that it came to be seen as a core activity of the military command structure. At this time, military medicine focused on the immediate needs of wounded soldiers, such as the provision of antiseptic dressings, while gradually embracing longer term agendas like the development of vaccines against diseases such as typhoid fever. World War One saw a professionalization of health services for military personnel as well as public health services more generally. However, the unexpected outbreak of the Spanish Flu pandemic (1918–1920) followed by the Great Depression (1929–1939) undermined many of the gains which had been made in terms of the understanding and management of health risks during periods of armed conflict. Nonetheless, important innovations took place in terms of how public health risks of

---

[47] Humphreys, Margaret, *Intensely Human: The Health of the Black Soldier in the American Civil War,* Baltimore, Maryland, Johns Hopkins University Press (2008).

armed conflict were understood. This included, for example, first efforts to uncover and address psychological dimensions of armed conflicts and the risks they posed to combatants.

The sheer scale of World War Two and the victory of the US as a prosperous super-power, brought a further professionalization of military medicine as well as a significant broadening of the understanding of the public health risks created by war. This included the realization that public health risks extended to families, as well as the realization that social networks mitigated the impact of the effects of war on individual combatants and thus could act as a buffer. As a consequence, services available to ex-soldiers and their families were expanded considerably, and a far wider range of physical or psychological medical conditions were recognized as being war-related. In parallel, the modern language of medical risks became integrated into military medicine. Meanwhile, the invention and proliferation of nuclear weapons gave the idea of nuclear war risk a prominent dimension in public debate,[48] often despite efforts by elite military circles to downplay the paramount risks to public health these weapons posed.[49]

War and Public Health Risks: Key Themes

The relationship between war or armed conflict and thinking about public health risks is probably one of the most complex and most revealing areas of tension. Based on the mission of their discipline, we should expect public health officials to object vehemently to most, if not all, forms of armed conflict; and some practitioners have in fact taken this line in recent

---

[48] See, e.g., Hoffman, F. Owen, A. Iulian Apostoaei, and Brian A. Thomas, "A Perspective on Public Concerns about Exposure to Fallout from the Production and Testing of Nuclear Weapons." *Health Physics,* 82:5 (2002), 736–48; Kramer, Bernard M., S. Michael Kalick, and Michael A. Milburn. "Attitudes toward Nuclear Weapons and Nuclear War: 1945–1982," *Journal of Social Issues,* 39:1 (1983), 7–24.

[49] Gavin, Francis J., "Same as it Ever Was: Nuclear Alarmism, Proliferation, and the Cold War," *International Security,* 34:3 (2010), 7–37; Meyer, David S., "Framing National Security: Elite Public Discourse on Nuclear Weapons during the Cold War," *Political Communication,* 12:2 (1995), 173–92.

years.[50] The analysis presented here delineates a long journey where military medicine, as a sub-discipline of public health, was initially assigned a growing place in improving care for combatants. The large number of non-combat deaths occurring during the US Civil War as well as later wars, such as World War One, explains the increasing occupation of war-related public health with infectious disease prevention which occured in parallel with improvements in the care for war wounded. Two aspects are interesting to note in this context. The first is the tendency of official sources to overestimate progress made in the protection of soldiers. The second is the persistence of inequalities among combatants of different races, which is evidenced by the far greater number of deaths from disease and accidents among soldiers of African American origin during the US Civil War. The First World War, additionally highlights the vulnerability of populations to war-related actions such as blockades, as well as links between major armed conflicts and the outbreak of pandemics such as the Spanish Flu.

Apart from the recognition of these sequelae of armed conflict, the First World War also marks a watershed in the understanding of the public health implications of conflict, by highlighting the role of non-physical psychological injury to soldiers. This opened the door to novel concepts of war-related health problems such as combat fatigue, combat stress, and a widening of the concept of war-related injury more generally. It also encouraged to some of the first critical anti-war statements by medics, when members of the circle around Sigmund Freud highlighted the "abnormality" of armed conflict for ordinary citizens, and tied this to numerous harmful effects.

The Second World War led to a further widening of recognized war injuries as well as a broadening of the understanding of the social effects of this military conflict and its implication in terms of the health needs of the population. The Cold War and the introduction of nuclear weapons,

---

[50] See Toole, Michael J., Steven Galson, and William Brady, "Are War and Public Health Compatible?," *The Lancet,* 341:8854 (1993), 1193–6. and Wiist, William H., *et al.*, "The Role of Public Health in the Prevention of War: Rationale and Competencies," *American Journal of Public Health,* 104:6 (2014), e34–e47.

lastly, reintroduced behavioral patterns that harked back to the early days of modern warfare, when the implications of armed conflict, involving these weapons on soldiers and civilians was grossly underestimated. Overall, given the stakes of conflict, particularly in relation to potential nuclear conflict, it is striking how little influence the field of public health had in questioning risks and opposing confrontational policies of the Cold War.

Summary Section

Manipulation, Risk, Health, and Risk Literacy

The COVID-19 pandemic has raised serious questions about the ability of public health experts to predict, prepare for, and mitigate novel public health risks. Accordingly, it has been argued that the COVID-19 outbreak has been aggravated by endemic weaknesses in the way public health systems perceive, respond to, and cope with novel risks.[1] These weaknesses have been attributed to several problems including existing prejudices and misjudgments.[2] We would, however, argue that they also relate to deeper philosophical and conceptual aspects of the risk and public health nexus, as it has evolved over the past centuries. The history of public health included periods when the discipline supported social change

[1] See Villa, Simone, *et al.*, "The COVID-19 Pandemic Preparedness... Or Lack Thereof: From China to Italy," *Global Health & Medicine,* 2:2 (2020): 73–77; and also Rudan, Igor, "A Cascade of Causes that led to the COVID-19 Tragedy in Italy and in other European Union Countries," *Journal of Global Health,* 10:1 (2020): 1–10; and Tangcharoensathien, Viroj, Poonam Singh, and Anne Mills, "COVID-19 Response and Mitigation: A Call for Action." *Bulletin of the World Health Organization,* 99:2 (2021): 78. Sacco, Pier Luigi, and Manlio De Domenico, "Public Health Challenges and Opportunities after COVID-19," *Bulletin of the World Health Organization,* 99:7 (2021), 529.

[2] See Royo, Sebastián, "Responding to COVID-19: The Case of Spain," *European Policy Analysis,* 6:2 (2020): 180–190; and also Yearby, Ruqaiijah, and Seema Mohapatra. "Systemic Racism, the Government's Pandemic Response, and Racial Inequities in COVID-19," *Emory LJ* 70 (2020), 1419.

and advocated housing, sanitation, and labor reform efforts.[3] However, it also included lengthy periods when it was characterized by a persistent lack of critical thinking, an unwillingness to recognise new risks, and a readiness to serve powerful elites while neglecting the rights and needs of minority groups and the weak more generally.[4] While research has contextualized some of the stigmatizing aspects of disease within broader concepts of social risk,[5] little effort has been made to systematically relate the pathological aspects of some public health initiatives and policies to patterns of risk perception and risk description.

This book has sought to investigate the relationship between risk thinking and public health within historical and thematic contexts. This work has included what we would describe as pathological episodes which involved the fabrication of health arguments in support of immigration-phobia and racism. In examining the risk and public health nexus, we have made a number of observations. These include, firstly, the relatively slow absorption of the language of risk and the idea of weighing the costs and benefits of uncertain actions within medical writing. We attribute this, in part, to delays in the development of techniques for the analysis of mass observations in healthcare, which, in turn, had to do with a scarcity of reliable and informative data which would have been of relevance to medics or those interested in public health more generally. Simply put, medical statistics was a prerequisite for the application of risk concepts to medical thinking and decision making, but for a long time, neither statistics as technique, nor relevant population data relating to health issues were sufficiently advanced and reliable to do this effectively. Sadly, when

---

[3] See Fairchild, Amy L., *et al.* "The EXODUS of Public Health What History Can Tell Us About the Future," *American Journal of Public Health* 100:1 (2010), 54–63; and also Anser, Muhammad Khalid, *et al*, "Identifying the Potential Causes, Consequences, and Prevention of Communicable Diseases (including COVID-19)," *BioMed Research International,* 2020 (2020), 1–13.

[4] See Pernick, Martin S., "Eugenics and Public Health in American history," *American Journal of Public Health* 87:11 (1997), 1767–72; and also Stern, Alexandra Minna, "Sterilized in the Name of Public Health: Race, Immigration, and Reproductive Control in Modern California." *American Journal of Public Health* 95:7 (2005), 1128–38.

[5] Cooper, Elizabeth. "Social Risk and the Transformation of Public Health Law: Lessons from the Plague Years," *Iowa L. Rev.*, 86 (2000), 869.

statisticians turned toward health related topics, some researchers did so, not to improve the situation of patients, but rather in order to support their own prejudices, particularly as they related to the assumed inferiority of certain population groups and the risks this might pose to society at large. These patterns of a misuse of risk discourses in relation to health which sought to exclude, condemn, and marginalize the weak, repeated itself in a number of contexts, where the risk and public health nexus played major roles, such as discourses around immigration, race, and to lesser degree risk assessments in relation to armed conflict.

Both of these observations (a) the relatively slow absorption of risk thinking in public health and (b) its often socially regressive application, raise serious questions about the nature of modern medical discourse in Western societies, and in particular the lack of critical reflection among many thought leaders and inventors in the medical area. There are several different ways in which these questions can be framed, and none are sufficiently precise to lend themselves to easy or clear-cut answers:[6] Why were notions of public health risk so readily misused by those who wanted to restrict immigration or curtail the rights and prospects of recent immigrants? Why did only a small number of public health experts object to this? Why were notions of racial inequality so readily embraced by medically literate individuals? And, again why did medicine and public health do so little to oppose the dangerous ideas of eugenics? Lastly, why did professionals in areas of medicine and public health pay so little attention to the crass inequality in the number of deaths from diseases of African American soldiers as compared to white soldiers during many armed conflicts? And, why, once military medicine became more professionalized, did it so often underestimate the risks and horrors of armed conflict for military personnel and civilians alike.

Some facets of the evolution of risk science as a theoretical discipline bear similarities with other branches of mathematics and philosophy in that there are distinct episodes of progression of understanding and

---

[6] In a way, questions about the root causes of the often "pathological" relationship between public health and risk mimic some of the characteristics of "wicked problems" or questions, in that they are highly complex, wide ranging, have no definitive formulation and no set answer or solution.

theoretical refinements.[7] This too can be said about applications of risk modelling and statistics in relation to medicine.[8] When it comes to the political use of notions of risk in relation to potentially socially divisive issues, we find less of this progressive spirit and more of its opposite. As a historical genre, non-rational notions of risk predate "rationalistic" versions of uncertainty analysis which helped the discipline progress.[9] In their oldest form, some of these archaic types of risk thinking are associated with the primal human fear of unforeseeable, non-preventable, uncontrollable, and unmitigable catastrophe that can evoke panic and other irrational and ineffective responses associated with persecution and scapegoating, dark rites, and even human sacrifice.[10] In its more modern form, it is associated with post-enlightenment writers who focused on imagined dangers and often associated these with specific human groups, technologies, and forms of organization.[11]

---

[7] See, e.g., Feduzi, Alberto, Jochen Runde, and Carlo Zappia, "De Finetti on Uncertainty," *Cambridge Journal of Economics,* 38:1 (2014), 1–21.

[8] Damen, Johanna A., *et al.* "Performance of the Framingham Risk Models and Pooled Cohort Equations for Predicting 10-year Risk of Cardiovascular Disease: A Systematic Review and Meta-analysis." *BMC Medicine,* 17:109 (2019), 1–16.

[9] For a discussion of the of 'rationalistic' risk analysis written before Pascal's main works, see Franklin, James, *The Science of Conjecture: Evidence and Probability before Pascal.* Baltimore, Johns Hopkins University Press (2001); Daston, Lorraine, *Classical Probability in the Enlightenment*, Princeton, Princeton University Press, NJ (1995) elaborates on later developments.

[10] Mary Douglas is perhaps one of the first modern scholars to investigate the role of 'irrational' rites as a means through which pre-modern and modern societies responded and respond to threats. See Douglas, Mary, *Purity and Danger: An Analysis of Concepts of Pollution and Taboo*, London, Routledge (2003).

[11] The philosopher Lewis Mumford (1895–1990), spoke evocatively of this literature as representing a backlash against the enlightenment in which "renewed admiration of barbarism became visible, shortly after the middle of the nineteenth century: the racial theories of Gobineau, the cult of violence expressed by the nihilists, [a]nd the glorification of brutality in Carlyle's defence of Governor Eyre, the repressor of the Jamaican insurrection. … To rape, to torture, to hate to kill became a method of redemption: in fantasy if not in fact." See Mumford, Lewis, *The Condition of Man*, New York, NY Harcourt, Brace and Comp. (1944), p. 366.

Accordingly, writings about dangerous classes, crowds, nationalities, races, and peoples figured prominently in the nineteenth century and early twentieth century historiography of risk. This was widely absorbed in early writings on public health, as the discipline began to grapple with ideas of risk and uncertainty. As a consequence, areas such as immigration and racial diversity became fertile grounds for fearmongers and those wishing to exclude minorities and newcomers. In some cases, false blame of minorities for diseases became a prelude to violence as well as a justification for systematic discrimination.[12] Public health, as a discipline, of course, was not the only source of pseudo-scientific arguments aimed at asserting danger or threat to society. Nonetheless, as a discipline, it contributed to archaic fears, which motivated irrational waves of fear and hate of the "other" or the "unknown."

The Black Death, which ravaged Europe from the 1340s to the 1350s, is said to have killed between 30 to 60 per cent of Europe's population and an unknown number of people in the Middle East, being possibly the worst pandemic to befall humanity.[13] It had a profound impact on European society and culture, weakening existing feudal structures[14] as well as leading to the scapegoating of Jews and other minorities.[15] While the Black Death affected a vast geographic area, other epidemics triggered near apocalyptic transformations on a smaller geographic scale. Thus, the arrival of the Spanish on Hispaniola and in Central

---

[12] See, e.g., Kraut, Alan M., *Silent Travelers: Germs, Genes, and the Immigrant Menace*. Baltimore, Maryland, JHU Press (1995). This highlights historical patterns of immigrant blame for public health problems.

[13] Alchon, Suzanne Austin, *A Pest in the Land: New World Epidemics in a Global Perspective*, Albuquerque, New Mexico, University of New Mexico Press (2003).

[14] Some of the European writers whose work was influenced by the Black Death include Chaucer, Boccaccio and Petrarch. As to its social impact, David Herlihy (1997) suggests that the concomitant population decline not only undermined existing feudal ties but also transformed economies by forcing them to adopt labor-saving technologies. See Herlihy, David, *The Black Death and the Transformation of the West*, Cambridge, MA, Harvard University Press (1997).

[15] See, e.g., Gottfried, Robert S., *Black Death: Natural and Human Disaster in Medieval Europe*, London, The Free Press (1983).

America caused a crippling outbreak of smallpox among the native populations.[16]

The specific vulnerability of urban populations to epidemic was recognized by writers in England during a series of plague epidemics which affected London in 1603, 1625, 1636, and for the last time in 1665.[17] These plagues disproportionately affected the poor who lived in squalid conditions and often suffered from inadequate nutrition. The last and worst of these plagues, the Great Plague of 1665 was eventually put to an end by one of the greatest urban conflagrations of its time, the 1666 Great Fire of London which is said to have led to the destruction of 90 per cent of the city's houses. Like other disasters before it, the Fire of London led to breakdowns in law and order with recently arrived Dutch and French immigrant populations being subject to mob violence.[18] Interestingly, only six deaths were recorded as having resulted from the fire, which represented fewer fatalities than had been caused by mob violence and lynching.[19]

Some historical accounts of disasters reflect what Mary Douglas has described as a want to blame, where such blame can relate to certain behaviors, individuals, or groups of individuals. At its most basic level, this desire to blame can involve the drawing of erroneous correlations of cause and effect between the actions of society as a whole, or elements within society, and the onset of a disaster or disease. During the Black Death of the 1340s and 1350s, similarly, European Jews were blamed for causing the disease

---

[16]The view that the Mexican population was decimated in 1520 by a smallpox epidemic has been questioned by some authors including Brooks, Francis J., "Revising the Conquest of Mexico: Smallpox, Sources, and Populations," *The Journal of Interdisciplinary History,* 24:1 (1993), 1–29.

[17]It is estimated that the 1603 epidemic killed circa 30,000 Londoners, that of 1625 killed 35,000, the 1625 outbreak claimed 10,000, and the Great Plague of 1665 may have led to 80,000 deaths; see Porter, Roy, *London, a Social History*, Cambridge, MA, Harvard University Press, 1998.

[18]Ibid.

[19]The tradition of naming various disasters such as the London Fire of 1666 as "Great" is partly a reflection of eurocentric attitudes whereby European historians uncritically accept the significance attributed to disasters occurring in the Western hemisphere by contemporary authors — even though some of these disasters pale into insignificance when compared to non-European events such as the 1556 Shaanxi earthquake.

either by poisoning wells or simply by attracting God's Wrath.[20] During the 1666 Great London Fire, the search for scapegoats among Catholics and foreigners was reinforced by the fact that the fire began in a neighborhood crowded with French and Dutch tradespeople.

One plausible expectation has been that such irrational blame behavior would disappear with progress in medicine and public health. Mary Douglas, however, has suggested that such an assumption is not necessarily warranted as blame can help some groups maintain social hierarchies and order.[21] This view has been extended by Raymond Lau who argues that the moralization of danger continues today, only that danger now comes in the form of risk, which constitutes "a new blaming system and today's 'forensic vocabulary' equivalent to past sin or taboo."[22] As previous chapters of this book have indicated, "blaming" or "moral othering" and disease outbreaks do not necessarily follow sequential patterns, which means that blaming can occur without a disease outbreak yet having happened or harm yet having occurred. Perhaps more importantly, with risk being frequently socially constructed, what is considered blame-worthy behavior by a dominant social group, may in fact represent the entirely legitimate conduct or actions of less privileged individuals or groups.

Another equally complex interpretation of risk, public health, and blame is that the mere threat of disease can create windows of uncertainty which allow existing entrenched interests to manipulate collective behavior (or at least, to attempt to do so). We are likely to observe such behavior especially where the impetus to manipulate through the medium of risk and uncertainty is inspired by some form of desire for material gain or a desire to avoid material loss.[23] Concretely, this can mean that blaming in the absence of expectations that certain accusations or causations are evidenced. Blaming in relation to health risks, however does not necessarily

---

[20] See e.g., Gottfried, *The Black Death,* pps. 73–4.

[21] See Douglas, *Purity and Danger.*

[22] See Lau, Raymond W.K., "The Contemporary Culture of Blame and the Fetishization of the Modernist Mentality." *Current Sociology,* 57:5 (2009): 661–83.

[23] This argument has been developed more fully in Beck, Matthias, Darinka Asenova, and Gordon Dickson, "Public Administration, Science, and Risk Assessment: A Case Study of the UK Bovine Spongiform Encephalopathy Crisis." *Public Administration Review,* 65:4 (2005), 396–408.

have a direct and easily discernible social function. Rather, it can be a learned response which arises opportunistically within contexts in which there is uncertainty about an object (such as a technology or a group of individuals) or its immediate environment (such as the setting aside of a site for the development for low-income housing). In such a case, a privileged center group may be able and willing to stimulate a belief system which attributes risk or danger to the "risk" object.[24] This type of irrational blaming, accordingly, is likely to occur if several conditions are met. There has to be agency, in the sense of the presence of an established center group which seeks to blame and is powerful, materially well resourced, or socially connected enough to do so. This has to be coupled with some level of real or socially constructed uncertainty about the blame object (or its context) to allow the "blamers" not to be immediately discredited. Lastly, there has to be a sufficient material or ideological impetus for the "blamers" to devote resources to their actions.[25] Once these, or similar, conditions are met, and self-censorship by enlightened public health professionals does not take place, we might observe responses to perceived public health risks which entail irrational elements of blame. The partial grounding of public health expertise within the medical sciences can historically be observed to act as a double-edged sword. On the one hand, linkage to medical science can add power to blame even if the underlying causation lacks evidence, merely by invoking fears of a clear and present danger to public health. On the other hand, it can act, if grounded in sufficient scientific rigor, to its detriment by raising questions about the factual evidence base of a blame.

For much of the late part of the 1800s as well as the early part of the 1900s historians have tended to describe the US as an elite dominated society, where minorities and newcomers were routinely victimized by blame and discriminatory policies, which were frequently justified on account of public health considerations. Thus, Richard Hofstadter's widely-read book *Social Darwinism in American Thought, 1860–1915* argued that late nineteenth century US political and social philosophy was

---

[24]This concept of social center and periphery groups borrows from Galtung, Johan, "A Structural Theory of Imperialism," *African Review* 1:4 (1972): 93–138.

[25]A potential contributory factor would be the absence of effective counter-mobilization by the blaming target.

dominated by a reactionary belief system which emphasized and promoted racism, competition, and nationalism. This belief system, according to Hofstadter, had developed gradually through the works of Herbert Spencer, who exerted a major influence on the industrialist Andrew Carnegie and the social philosopher William Graham Sumner, and created a biological justification of laissez faire which assumed that unrestrained capitalism ensured the survival of the nation.[26] Some recent interpretations of these ideologies, such as the works of Johann Van der Dennan expanded on this view and by suggesting that the *zeitgeist* of the period allowed for various popular and intellectual currents to be absorbed into a flexible pseudo socio-biological framework.[27] The emergent melee of an insidious stream of pseudo-scientific publications alleged the inferiority of individual peoples and races, the superiority of others and, in some instances, the presence of a racial hierarchy amongst the populations of the earth.[28] Perhaps because of its vast extent and past popularity, the disciplinary evolution of this literature and its link to writings about health and health risk is relatively poorly understood.[29] This is helped by a number of factors, including the length of time over which this literature developed as well as its conceptual and disciplinary heterogeneity.[30]

---

[26] Hofstadter, Richard, *Social Darwinism in American Thought*, Boston, Beacon Press (1992) [originally published in 1944].

[27] See, van der Dennen, van der Johan Matheus Gerardus, *The Origin of War: The Evolution of a Male-Coalitional Reproductive Strategy, Vols. 1 & 2*, San Rafael, CA, Origin Press, (1995).

[28] Daniel K Kevles observes that protestant racial obsessions in the United States involved not only the dividing line between whites and blacks, but also alleged differences between "the old-stock white Anglo Saxon, Protestant majority" and "the numerous Catholic and many Jewish immigrants from Eastern and Southern Europe." See Kevles, Daniel J., *In the Name of Eugenics: Genetics and the Uses of Human Heredity*, No. 95. Cambridge, MA, Harvard University Press (1995).

[29] One of the few attempts to assess different aspects of racism across multiple countries is Finzsch, Norbert, and Dietmar Schirmer, eds., *Identity and Intolerance: Nationalism, Racism, and Xenophobia in Germany and the United States*, Cambridge, Cambridge University Press, 2002.

[30] One of the last efforts to revive the idea of racial polygenism in the US was the publication of Carlton S. Coon, *The Origin of Races*, New York City, Knopf (1996). This received a predictably hostile reception by the senior geneticists and anthropologists of the time. See Jackson, John P., ""In Ways Unacademical": The Reception of Carleton S. Coon's The Origin of Races," *Journal of the History of Biology*, 34 (2001), 247–85.

One of the key examples of this coalescence of blame is the creation of the field of eugenics. This was inspired initially by the work of the Victorian English polymath Francis Galton. As noted by Daniel Kevles, Galton derived the term eugenics from a Greek root meaning "good by birth;" with Galton's principal "scientific" goal being to give "the more suitable races or strain of blood a better chance of prevailing speedily over the less suitable."[31] This led to the creation of regional and national eugenics societies and chapters, endowed academic chairs, as well as in the US, the enactment of legislation promoting racial segregation and the sterilization of allegedly "unfit" persons.[32] The political and legislative activities of American eugenicists in particular centered on three areas of activity. These included interference with marriage, mandatory sterilization, and race-based restrictions on immigration.

Outside the creation of eugenics as a discipline, which appears to have thrived on a peculiar confluence of racist thinking, misguided concerns for public and population health and, especially in the US, the continuance of separate white political and social institutions, there is little clarity as to the origins of racist writing and its massive popularity in Western nations during the late 19th and early 20th centuries. One possible explanation which has been forwarded in the past is that the racist bend within public health emerged from the need to justify colonial exploration and exploitation. This exploitation is said to have generated a desire to rationalize slavery and other excesses by labelling other races as inferior, unhealthy, and as representing health risks of some form or another. Other interpretations have suggested that the rise of racism within public health during the 19th century emerged as a response to increased economic competition among native and immigrant groups in countries such as the US, Canada, Australia, and New Zealand, which had seen pronounced increases in immigration.[33] Both hypotheses are supported by historical evidence. The

---

[31] Kevles, op. cit., at p. xii, citing Galton.

[32] American eugenicists also sometimes referred to their work as "scientific racism." However, the usage of this term is less clear than that of eugenics.

[33] Although Kevles does not focus on the macro-level socio-political forces which may have supported the growth of eugenics in the late nineteenth and early twentieth century, his preface to the 1995 edition of his book emphasizes the role of political and economic competition as a reason for the receptiveness of the US to these ideas.

Spanish Jews, known as Marranos, who had been forced to convert to Christianity in the late 15th century, were subject to continuous prosecution often on account of their economic success but were also seen as threat to Christendom on account of their lack of purity of blood. Similarly, when the French naturalist Louis LeClerc, Comte Buffon developed the idea that racial characteristics were due to climate variation, he had already infused these theories with notions of European superiority which were used by later writers to justify slavery within the French Empire.

Public health centered support for slavery and discrimination more generally, however, was rarely purely defensive. Instead, racial mixing or racial influx, be it through already present or through immigrant population, was often viewed and described in crisis terms. These crisis-centered viewpoints of race gave rise to a number of political and social sub-agendas. In summary, on the micro level, racist fearmongering of the late 19th and early 20th century saw threats to "racial integrity" as arising from several sources. These included, "feeble" genetic elements within existing racial groups, which could contaminate the existing genetic stock of all races at any time, even without racial crossbreeding taking place. Alleged unequal mechanisms of procreation, whereby less fit elements or racial groupings within society were assumed to be more likely to succumb to sexual urges and therefore to bear a greater number of children were said to help this. Next, the composition of population was said to be damaged by mechanisms which prevented "worthy" elements of society from procreating for reasons such the time they spend on learning and studying. Lastly, it was assumed that sexual aggression or sexual potency were more pronounced among certain races or individuals, which again allowed them to procreate faster than more "worthy" elements of society.

According to some of the key writers of this time, these micro level dangers or eugenic hazards were compounded and aggravated by macro-level factors which American authors of the time frequently cast in terms of a "racial struggle" or a "race war." At its core, the "racial struggle" literature assumed that the white race was not only threatened by innate tendencies of "lesser races" or "lesser individuals" to procreate locally or globally at a faster rate, but that additionally, these tendencies overlapped with deliberate moves through which "inferior" groups sought to enhance their global position. Accordingly, 19th century anti-immigrationists in the US argued that the arrival of Asian, Italian, and Southern and Eastern European immigrants was not only a threat to the racial integrity of the nation but further proclaimed that this immigration was part of a deliberate policy of these nations to weaken existing US domestic elites and ultimately to replace these with indecisive puppet regimes. In this context, it was specifically argued that these Asian immigrants not only threatened the integrity of the US as a white nation but also acted as a vanguard to a broader future racial conflict, which was to engulf America and the Asiatic nations of the Pacific region. Lastly, anti-assimilationists in the South proclaimed that any sharing of wealth or power with the descendants of slaves would aggravate the already existing racial threat of rapid "Negro" procreation and argued that therefore, any measures to give these groups greater equality had to be opposed.

Regarding the issue of academic opposition to racist beliefs, Yudell cogently observes how from the 1930s to the 1950s onwards, the works of the biologists Theodosius Dobzhansky and L.C. Dunn, together with those of the anthropologists Ruth Benedict and Ashley Montagu, popularized the idea that race was not the immutable constant which previous writers thought it to be.[34] Perhaps the most important of these interventions was Dunn and Dobzhansky publication in 1946 of *Heredity, Race, and Society.*[35] As a piece of popular science writing, Dunn and Dobzhansky's *Heredity, Race, and Society* was a major success primarily because it filled a void in terms of providing a modern explanation of human evolution. This void had become all the more obvious because previous racist theories of polygenism and the ideas of a hierarchy of races which it entailed had become thoroughly discredited after World War Two. Selling millions

[34]Yudell, Michael. *Making race: Biology and the Evolution of the Race Concept in 20th century American Thought.* Columbia University, 2008.

[35]L. C. (Leslie Clarence) Dunn (1893–1974) was Professor of Genetics at Columbia University. His co-author and life-long collaborator, the Russian American scholar Theodosius Dobzhansky (1900–1975) was a Professor of Genetics at California Institute of Technology, Professor of Zoology at Columbia University and Professor of Zoology at Rockefeller University. Dobzhansky, Theodosius Grigorievich, and Leslie C. Dunn. *Heredity, Race and Society.* New York, NY, New American Library, 1959.

of copies and being translated in several languages, Dunn and Dobzhansky's *Heredity, Race, and Society* essentially suggested that individuals were "not the embodiment of some ideal type or norm, but rather a unique and unrepeatable realization in the field of quasi-infinite possible genetic combinations."[36] This led them to conclude that genetic variation, rather than race, provided the biological foundation of human individuality. In so far as race existed at all, this was based on the fact "that populations or groups of populations differ from each other in the frequencies of some genes."[37]

Moreover, Dobzhansky in particular suggested that "the number of races and the boundaries between them [were] largely arbitrary, because rarely if ever are populations the same species separated by sharp discontinuities in their genetic makeup."[38] This recognition of race as a deeply flawed concept was confirmed, among others, in the works of Francis Collins and Craig Venter in connection with the announcement of the completion of a draft sequence of the human genome.[39] Specifically, the analyses of the human genome provided the hitherto strongest argument for the fact that human genetic diversity could not be captured by the traditional concepts of race, with all humans having genome sequences that are 99.9% identical.

Dunn and Dobzhansky's work on the genetics of race was complemented by the research of progressive anthropologists, such as Ruth Benedict and Ashley Montagu.[40] Ruth Benedict challenged traditional ideas of race in her 1942 publication *Race and Racism.* Benedict's *Race and Racism* specifically suggested that there was no distinctive superiority

---

[36] Ayala, Francisco J., "Theodosius Dobzhansky: January 25, 1900-December 18, 1975," *Biographical Memoirs. National Academy of Sciences (US),* 55 (1985): 163–213, p. 167

[37] Ibid., at p. 168.

[38] Ibid., at p. 169.

[39] Collins and Ventner's work was presented at President Clinton's Rose Garden Ceremony in 2000. At the time of this ceremony, Collins was head of the National Human Genome Research Institute and Venter was President of Celera Genomics.

[40] Ruth Benedict (1887–1948) was Professor of Anthropology at Columbia University. The British born academic Ashley Montague (1905–1999) was Professor of Anthropology at Rutgers University in New Jersey; Benedict, Ruth. *Race and Racism*, London, Taylor & Francis (1983).

among peoples and races and argued that differences in material wealth or cultural activity could be explained by the presence of favorable conditions at certain junctures in time. Similarly, Ashley Montague's 1942 publication *Man's Most Dangerous Myth: The Fallacy of Race* argued that given that humans faced similar environmental conditions and challenges, there was no reason to expect mental differences across populations or population groupings.[41]

It remains interesting to note that the contribution of public health as a discipline to the rejection of racist stereotyping was limited when compared to the works of anthropologists such as Montague or Benedict. Again, this related quite possibly to the risk-centered nature of the latter phase of epidemiological thinking, which tended to emphasize differences across population categories as compared to their common characteristics. These criticisms notwithstanding, it has to be said, that the mainstream public health research became increasingly evidence focused, which prevented it from supporting questionable political claims and allowed researchers to adopt a more reflective stance toward desirable role of the discipline in relation to new diseases such as AIDS.[42]

[41] See Montagu, MF Ashley. *Man's Most Dangerous Myth: The Fallacy of Race*. Columbia University Press, 1945. Montague gained fame through his input into the 1950 UNESCO statement on race; see Hazard Jr, Anthony Q., "A Racialized Deconstruction? Ashley Montagu and the 1950 UNESCO Statement on Race," *Transforming Anthropology,* 19:2 (2011), 174–86.

[42] See, e.g., Goldin, Carol S., "Stigmatization and AIDS: Critical Issues in Public Health," *Social Science & Medicine* 39:9 (1994), 1359–1366; see also Valdiserri, Ronald O., "HIV/AIDS Stigma: An Impediment to Public Health," *American Journal of Public Health,* 92.3 (2002), 341–2.

Select Bibliography

Agnoletti M and Simone NS. (2014) In *The Basic Environmental History, Vol. 4*, Cham, Springer.

Adler R and Mara E. (2016) In *Typhoid fever: A history*, Jefferson (ed.), NC, McFarland.

Aikman KB. (1933) Race mixture. *The Eugenics Review*, **25**(3), 161.

Anser MK, *et al.* (2020) Identifying the potential causes, consequences, and prevention of communicable diseases (including COVID-19). *BioMed Research International*, 2020, 1–13.

Alchon SA. (2003) In *A pest in the land: New world epidemics in a global perspective*, University of New Mexico Press, Albuquerque, NM.

Aston MJ. (1950) The atomic bomb versus survival. *The Military Surgeon (United States)*, **106**(4), 270–275.

Ayala FJ. Theodosius Dobzhansky: January 25, 1900 December 18, 1975. *Biographical Memoirs National Academy of Sciences (US)*, **55**(1985), 163–213.

Baker LD. (2000) Daniel G. Brinton's success on the road to obscurity, 1890–1899. *Cultural Anthropology*, **15**(3), 394–423.

Barkan E. (1992) In *The retreat of scientific racism: Changing concepts of race in Britain and the United States between the world wars*, Cambridge, Cambridge University Press.

Barker D. (2001) A new model for the origins of chronic disease. *Medicine, Health, Care and Philosophy,* **4**(2001), 31–35.

Barr DP. (1955) Hazards of modern diagnosis and therapy: The price we pay. *Journal of the American Medical Association*, **159**(15), 1452–1456.

Barreto ML, Maria GT and Eduardo HC. (2006) Infectious diseases epidemiology. *Journal of Epidemiology & Community Health*, **60**(3), 192–195.

Barry CJ. (1958) Some roots of American nativism. *The Catholic Historical Review*, **44**(2), 137–146.

Bartemeier LH, *et al.* (1946) Combat exhaustion. *The Journal of Nervous and Mental Disease*, **104**(4), 358–389.

Bartrip PWJ. (2002) The home office and the dangerous trades: Regulating occupational disease in Victorian and Edwardian Britain. *Clio Medica*, **68**, 1–344.

Bateson HC. (1950) In *Medical Statistics*, Washington, DC, Army Medical Department Research and Graduate School.

Beck M, Asenova D and Dickson G. (2005) Public administration, science, and risk assessment: A case study of the U.K. Bovine spongiform encephalopathy crisis. *Public Administration Review*, **65**(4), 396–408.

Beecher HK and Donald PT. (1954) A study of the deaths associated with anesthesia and surgery: Based on a study Of 599,548 anesthesias in ten institutions 1948–1952, inclusive. *Annals of Surgery*, **140**(1), 2.

Benedict R. (1983) In *Race and Racism*. London, Taylor & Francis.

Bennett JDC. (1990) Medical advances consequent to the great war 1914–1918. *Journal of the Royal Society of Medicine*, **83**(11), 738–742.

Berkman LF, Ichirō K and Glymour MM. (2014) Social epidemiology. *Oxford University Press.*

Bernell S and Howard SW. (2016) Use your words carefully: What is a chronic disease? *Frontiers in Public Health*, **4**, 159.

Berta WB and Baker R. (2004) Factors that impact the transfer and retention of best practices for reducing error in hospitals. *Health Care Management Review*, **29**(2), 90–97.

Biddiss MD. (1976) The politics of anatomy: Dr Robert Knox and victorian racism. *Proceedings of the Royal Society of Medicine, Section of the History of Medicine*, **69**, 245–250.

Blakeslee GA. (1942) Neuropsychiatry in war time. *Bulletin of the New York Academy of Medicine*, **18**(12), 775.

Board of Supervisors of the City and Country of San Francisco. (1885) *Report of the Special Committee of the Board of Supervisors of San Francisco on the Condition of the Chinese Quarter of That City*, San Fransisco, CA, AL Bancroft & Company, 163.

Bodmer W, *et al.* (2021) The outstanding scientist, RA Fisher: His views on eugenics and race. *Heredity*, **126**(4), 565–576.

Bottoms DM. (2013) In *An aristocracy of color: Race and reconstruction in California and the West, 1850–1890, Vol. 5*. Norman, OK, University of Oklahoma Press.

Bradford A. (1965) Association or causation. *Proceedings of the Royal Society of Medicine*, **58**, 295–300.

Brand, Ulrich, *et al.* (2008) In *Conflicts in environmental regulation and the internationalisation of the State: Contested terrains*. London, Routledge.

Bratt O. (2002) Hereditary prostate cancer: Clinical aspects. *The Journal of Urology*, **168**(3), 906–913.

Brennan TA, *et al.* (1991) Incidence of adverse events and negligence n hospitalized patients: Results of the Harvard medical practice study I. *New England Journal of Medicine*, **324**(6), 370–376.

Brinton DG. (2020) in *Races and Peoples*. Raleigh, NC, BoD–Books on Demand.

Brown KL. (2013) *Plutopia: Nuclear families, atomic cities, and the great soviet and American plutonium disasters*. Oxford, Oxford University Press.

Brooks FJ. (1993) Revising the conquest of Mexico: Smallpox, sources, and populations. *The Journal of Interdisciplinary History*, **24**(1), 1–29.

Budil I. (2013) Robert Knox: Racial imagination, transcendental anatomy and Western colonial expansion. *UWB Papers, University of West Bohemia*.

Byrd WM and Clayton LA. (2001) Race, medicine, and health care in the United States: A historical survey. *Journal of the National Medical Association*, **93**(3 Suppl), 11S–34S.

Caldwell D. (1971) The negroization of the Chinese stereotype in California. *Southern California Quarterly*, **53**(2), 123–131.

California Legislature Senate Special. (1876) In *Chinese immigration: The social, moral, and political effect of Chinese immigration. testimony taken before a Committee of the Senate of the State of California, appointed April 3d, 1876*. Sacramento, CA, State Printing Office.

Cambrosio A, *et al.* (2009) Biomedical conventions and regulatory objectivity: A few introductory remarks. *Social Studies of Science*, **39**(5), 651–664.

Caplan AL, McGee G and Magnus D. (1999) What is immoral about eugenics? *British Medical Journal*, **319**(7220), 1284.

Carter CO. (1966) The population explosion. *The Eugenics Review*, **58**(1), 53.

Carter KC. (1985) Ignaz Semmelweis, Carl Mayrhofer, and the rise of germ theory. *Medical History*, **29**(1), 33–53.

Comer SD. (1936) The growing need for a national eugenic program. *Bios*, 176–187.

Cooper E. (2000) Social risk and the transformation of public health law: Lessons from the plague years. *Iowa Law Review*, **86**, 869.

Copeman WSC. (1940) The arthritic sequelae of pneumatic drilling. *Annals of the Rheumatic Diseases*, **2**(2), 141.

Dachert A. (1931) Positive eugenics in practice: An account of the first positive eugenic experiment. *The Eugenics Review*, **23**(1), 15.

Dadrian VN. (1986) The role of Turkish physicians in the World War I genocide of Ottoman Armenians. *Holocaust and Genocide Studies*, **1**(2), 169–192.

D'Agostino Sr, Ralph B, *et al.* (2013) Cardiovascular disease risk assessment: Insights from Framingham. *Global Heart*, **8**(1), 11–23.

Darwin L. (1934) The eugenic predicament. *The Eugenics Review*, **25**(4), 266.

Davie N. (2011) Dissecting the races of men: Robert Knox, anatomy and racial theory in Britain, 1820–1870. *Sexe, race et mixité dans l'aire Anglophone*, 19–42.

De C. Ward R. (1910) National eugenics in relation to immigration. *The North American Review*, **192**(656), 56–67.

De Syon GP. (2008) In *Science and Technology in Modern European Life*, St Barbara, CA, ABC–CLIO.

DeBruyne NF and Leland A. (2015) *American war and military operations casualties: Lists and statistics*. Congressional Research Service, Washington, United States.

Decker RJ. (2014) Citizenship and its duties: The immigration restriction league as a progressive movement. *Immigrants & Minorities*, **32**(2), 162–182.

Defense Technical Information Center. (1987) *History of the Army Nuclear Test Personnel Review (ANTPR)*, Fort Belvoir, VA.

Delzell DAP and Poliak CD. (2013) Karl Pearson and eugenics: Personal opinions and scientific rigor. *Science and Engineering Ethics*, **19**(3), 1057–1070.

van der Dennen JMG. (1995) In *The Origin Of War: The Evolution of a Male-Coalitional Reproductive Strategy, Vols. 1 & 2*, San Rafael (ed.), CA, Origin Press.

Dennis RM. (1995) Social darwinism, scientific racism, and the metaphysics of race. *Journal of Negro Education*, 243–252.

Dewbury A. (2007) 7. The American school and scientific racism in early American anthropology. *Histories of Anthropology Annual*, **3**(1), 121–147.

Dickinson A. (1949) Race mixture: A social or a biological problem? *The Eugenics Review*, **41**(2), 81.

Diez–Roux AV. (1998) Bringing context back into epidemiology: Variables and fallacies in multilevel analysis. *American Journal of Public Health*, **88**(2), 216–222.

Dobzhansky TG and Leslie CD. (1959) In *Heredity, race and society*. New York, NY, New American Library.

Doll R and Peto R. (1976) Mortality in relation to smoking: 20 years' observations on male British doctors. *British Medical Journal*, **2**(6051), 1525–1536.

Doll R, *et al.* (2004) Mortality in relation to smoking: 50 years' observations on male British doctors. *British Medical Journal*, **328**(7455), 1519.

Douglas M. (2003) In *Purity and danger: An analysis of concept of pollution and taboo*, London, Routledge.

Elena S. (2017) Crimean war and establishing of public health system in Great Britain. *Научный альманах стран Причерноморья*, **1**(9), 24–29.

Epstein CJ. (2003) Is modern genetics the new eugenics? *Genetics in Medicine*, **5**(6), 469–475.

Erkoreka A. (2009) Origins of the Spanish influenza pandemic (1918–1920) and its relation to the first world war. *Journal of Molecular and Genetic Medicine: An International Journal of Biomedical Research*, **3**(2), 190.

Eshleman CH. (1940) Eugenics and mongrelization. *The Eugenics Review*, **32**(1), 28.

Everitt B. (1999) In *Chance rules: An informal guide to probability, risk and statistics*, Cham, Springer.

Fairchild AL, *et al.* (2010) The EXODUS of public health what history can tell us about the future. *American Journal of Public Health*, **100**(1), 54–63.

Fang J-q and Lu Y. (2003) In *Advanced Medical Statistics*. Singapore, World Scientific.

Faust DG. (2006) Numbers on top of numbers: Counting the civil war dead. *The Journal of Military History*, **70**(4), 995–1009.

Feinstein AR. (1972) The need for humanised science in evaluating medication. *The Lancet*, **300**(7774), 421–423.

Ferenczi S, *et al.* (1921) In *Psycho–analysis, war neuroses*, London, The International Psycho-Analytical Press.

Finzsch N and Dietmar S. (2002) In *Identity and intolerance: Nationalism, racism, and xenophobia in Germany and the United States*. Cambridge University Press.

Fisher I. (1918) Health and war. *American Journal of Public Health*, **8**(8), 559–563.

Freeden M. (1979) Eugenics and progressive thought: A study in ideological affinity. *The Historical Journal*, **22**(3), 645–671.

Galton F. (1904) Eugenics: Its definition, scope, and aims. *American Journal of Sociology*, **10**(1), 1–25.

Galtung J. (1972) A structural theory of imperialism. *African Review*, **1**(4), 93–138.

Gardner FT. (1950) The little acorn: Hugh Huger Toland, 1806–1880. *Bulletin of the History of Medicine*, **24**(1), 61–69.

Gates RR. (1923) *Heredity and eugenics, Vol. 10*. New York, NY Macmillan Company.

Gavin FJ. (2010) Same as it ever was: Nuclear alarmism, proliferation, and the Cold War. *International Security*, **34**(3), 7–37.

Gawande AA, *et al.* (1999) The incidence and nature of surgical adverse events in Colorado and Utah in 1992. *Surgery*, **126**(1), 66–75.

Gaynes RP. (2011) In *Germ theory: Medical pioneers in infectious diseases*. New York, NY, John Wiley & Sons.

Gigerenzer G, *et al.* (1990) In *The empire of chance: How probability changed science and everyday life*. Cambridge, Cambridge University Press.

Gilliam EW. (1886) Chinese immigration. *The North American Review*, **143**(356), 26–34.

Gilliam JC. (2011) White and everything else: Promotion the 1924 Virginia Racial Integrity Act.

Ginn RVN. (1997) In *The History of the US Army Medical Service Corps, Vol. 30*, Washington, D.C., US Government Printing Office.

Girdwood RH. (1974) Death after taking medicaments. *British Medical Journal*, **1**(5906), 501–504.

Glasgow SM. (2005) In *The private life of public health: Managing chronic disease in an era of neoliberal governmentality*. University of Maryland, College Park.

Gold M. (2011) In *Forbidden citizens: Chinese exclusion and the US congress: A legislative history*, Washington, DC, The Capitol Net Inc.

Goldenring JM and Doctor R. (1986) Teen-age worry about nuclear war: North American and European questionnaire studies. *International Journal of Mental Health*, **15**(1–3), 72–92.

Goldfield D. (1991) In *Black, white, and southern: Race relations and southern culture, 1940 to the present*, Baton Rouge (ed.), LA, LSU Press.

Goldin CS. (1994) Stigmatization and AIDS: Critical issues in public health. *Social Science & Medicine*, **39**(9), 1359–1366.

Goldin C. (1994) The political economy of immigration restriction in the United States, 1890 to 1921. In *The regulated economy: A historical approach to political economy*. Chicago, IL, University of Chicago Press, 223–258.

Gosney ES. (1934) Eugenic sterilization. *Scientific American*, **151**(1), 18–53.

Gottfried RS. (2010) In *Black death*, New York, NY, Simon and Schuster.

Grant M. (1921) In *The passing of the great race: Or, the racial basis of European history*. New York, NY, C. Scribner's sons.

Hagerman E. (1992) *The American civil war and the origins of modern warfare: Ideas, organization, and field command, Vol. 715*, Bloomington, IN, Indiana University Press.

Hall LI. (1922) *Immigration and other interests of Prescott Farnsworth Hall*, New York, NY, Knickerbocker Press.

Hall PF. (1904) Selection of immigration. *The Annals of the American Academy of Political and Social Science*, **24**(1), 169–184.

Hall PF. (1913) In *Immigration and its Effects upon the United States*. New York, NY, H. Holt.

Hanley A. (2022) Migration, racism and sexual health in postwar Britain. In *History Workshop Journal, Vol. 94,* Oxford Academic.

Hanson C. (2012) *Eugenics, literature, and culture in post–war Britain*. Routledge.

Harrison GA. (1963) Genetics and race. *The Eugenics Review*, **55**(3), 139.

Hazard Jr, Anthony Q. (2011) A racialized deconstruction? Ashley Montagu and the 1950 UNESCO Statement on Race. *Transforming Anthropology*, **19**(2), 174–186.

Hench PS and Boland EW. (1946) The management of chronic arthritis and other rheumatic diseases among soldiers of the United States army. *Annals of Internal Medicine*, **24**(5), 808–825.

Herlihy D. (1997) *The Black Death and the transformation of the West*. Cambridge, MA, Harvard University Press.

Higham J. (2002) In *Strangers in the land: Patterns of American nativism, 1860–1925*. New Brunswick, NJ, Rutgers University Press.

Hochschild A. (2011) In *To end all wars: A story of loyalty and rebellion, 1914–1918*.

Hoffman FO, Apostoaei AI and Thomas BA. (2002) A perspective on public concerns about exposure to fallout from the production and testing of nuclear weapons. *Health Physics*, **82**(5), 736–748.

Hoffman FL. (1896) Race traits and tendencies of the American Negro. *American Economic Association*, **11**(1–3), 1–329.

Hofstadter R. *Social darwinism in American thought*. Boston, MA, Beacon Press, (1992, originally 1944).

Honig JW. (2011) The idea of total war: From Clausewitz to Ludendorff. In *The Pacific War as Total War: Proceedings of the 2011 International Forum on War History*, Tokyo: National Institute for Defence Studies.

Howard–Jones N. (1975) In *The scientific background of the international sanitary conferences, 1851–1938*, Geneva, World Health Organization.

Humphreys M. (2008) In *Intensely human: The health of the black soldier in the American civil war*, Baltimore, MD, Johns Hopkins University Press.

Illich I. (1975) Clinical damage, medical monopoly, the expropriation of health: Three dimensions of iatrogenic tort. *Journal of Medical Ethics*, **1**(2), 78.

Illich I. (2003) Medical nemesis. *Journal of Epidemiology and Community Health*, **57**(12), 919–922.

Illich I. (1975) The medicalization of life. *Journal of Medical Ethics*, **1**(2), 73–77.

Ingraham HS. (1958) Statistics and medical knowledge. *American Journal of Public Health and the Nations Health*, **48**(11 Pt 1), 1449–1459.

Inkret WC, Meinhold CB and Taschner JC. (1995) A brief history of radiation protection standards. *Los Alamos Science*, **23**(1995), 116–123.

Institute of Medicine. (2002) In *The future of the public's health in the 21st century*, Washington, DC, National Academies Press.

Ipgrave B, *et al.* (2022) From small beginnings: To build an anti–eugenic future. *The Lancet*, **399**(10339), 1934–1935.

Jackson JP. (2001) In ways unacademical: The reception of Carleton S. Coon's the origin of races. *Journal of the History of Biology*, **34**, 247–285.

Jackson JP, Weidman NM and Rubin G. (2005) The Origins of Scientific Racism. *The Journal of Blacks in Higher Education*, **50**(50), 66–79.

Jacobs B. (2010) Atomic kids: Duck and cover and atomic alert teach American children how to survive atomic attack. *Film and History: An Interdisciplinary Journal of Film and Television Studies*, **40**(1), 25–44.

Janicki DA. (2014) The British blockade during World War I: The weapon of deprivation. *Inquiries Journal*, **6**(6).

Jasen P. (2002) Breast cancer and the language of risk, 1750–1950. *Social History of Medicine*, **15**(1), 17–43.

Jousilahti P, *et al.* (1996) Body weight, cardiovascular risk factors, and coronary mortality: 15-year follow-up of middle-aged men and women in Eastern Finland. *Circulation*, **93**(7), 1372–1379.

Kanazawa M. (2005) Immigration, exclusion, and taxation: Anti–Chinese legislation in gold rush California. *The Journal of Economic History*, **65**(3), 779–805.

Kanjanarat P, Winterstein AG, Johns TE, Hatton RC, Gonzalez–Rothi R and Segal R. (2003) Nature of preventable adverse drug events in hospitals: A literature review. *American Journal of Health–system Pharmacy*, **60**(17), 1750–1759.

Kevles DJ. (1995) In *In The Name of Eugenics: Genetics and the Uses of Human Heredity*, Cambridge, MA, Harvard University Press.

Knox R. (1850) In *The races of men: A fragment*. London, H. Renshaw.

Knox R. (1862) In *The races of men: A philosophical enquiry into the influence of race over the destinies of nations*, Lonson, H. Renshaw.

Kohn LT, Corrigan JM and Donaldson MS. (2000) Errors in health care: A leading cause of death and injury. In *To Err Is Human: Building a Safer Health System*, Washington, DC, National Academies Press (US).

Kramer BM, Kalick SM and Milburn MS. (1983) Attitudes toward nuclear weapons and nuclear war: 1945–1982. *Journal of Social Issues*, **39**(1), 7–24.

Kraut AM. (1994) In *Silent Travellers, Germs, Genes, and the "Immigrant Menace"*, New York, NY, Basic Books.

Kuhl S. (2002) In *The Nazi Connection: Eugenics, American Racism, and German National Socialism*, Oxford, Oxford University Press.

Kuller LH. (1987) Relationship between acute and chronic disease epidemiology. *The Yale Journal of Biology and Medicine*, **60**(4), 363.

Last JM. (1985) Medicine and health: Reducing the hazards of health care. *World Health Forum*, **6**, 135–142.

Lau RWK. (2009) The contemporary culture of blame and the fetishization of the modernist mentality. *Current Sociology*, **57**(5), 661–683.

Le Fanu J. (2011) In *The Rise and Fall of Modern Medicine*. London, Hachette UK.

Lee E. (2007) The "Yellow Peril" and Asian Exclusion in the Americas. *Pacific Historical Review*, **76**(4), 537–562.

Lee E. (2002) The Chinese exclusion example: Race, immigration, and American gatekeeping, 1882–1924. *Journal of American Ethnic History*, 36–62.

Lee E. (2019) In *America for Americans: A history of xenophobia in the United States*, New York, NY, Basic Books.

Lee E. (2003) In *At America's Gates: Chinese Immigration During the Exclusion Era, 1882–1943*, Chapel Hill, University of North Carolina Press.

Lee SW, *et al.* (2009) Multidrug-resistant pulmonary tuberculosis among young Korean soldiers in a communal setting. *Journal of Korean Medical Science*, **24**(4), 592–595.

Leonard TC. (2009) American economic reform in the progressive era: its foundational beliefs and their relation to eugenics. *History of Political Economy*, **41**(1), 109–141.

Lesch JE. (2007) In *The first miracle drugs: How the sulfa drugs transformed medicine*, Oxford, Oxford University Press.

Leslie C. (1990) Scientific racism: Reflections on peer review, science and ideology. *Social Science and Medicinei*, **31**(8), 891–905.

Levy BS and Sidel VW. (2008) In *War and Public Health*. Oxford, Oxford University Press.

Lewis T. (1934) Diseases of the heart described for practitioners and students. *The Journal of Nervous and Mental Disease*, **79**(2), 222.

Lew–Williams B. (2018) In *The Chinese must go: Violence, exclusion, and the making of the alien in America*, Cambridge, MA, Harvard University Press.

Lofgren CA. (1988) In *The Plessy case: A legal–historical interpretation*, Oxford, Oxford University Press.

Lombardo PA. (1987) Miscegenation, eugenics, and racism: Historical footnotes to Loving v. Virginia. *University of California Davis Law Review*, **21**(2), 421–452.

Loudon ISL. (1981) The origins and growth of the dispensary movement in England. *Bulletin of the History of Medicine*, **55**(3), 322–342

Lowe R. (1998) The educational impact of the eugenics movement. *International Journal of Educational Research*, **27**(8), 647–660.

Lucey DS. (2014) 'These schemes will win for themselves the confidence of the people': Irish independence, poor law reform and hospital provision. *Medical Historyi*, **58**(1), 46–66,

Ludmerer KM. (1972) Genetics, eugenics, and the immigration restriction act of 1924. *Bulletin of the History of Medicine*, **46**(1), 59–81.

Lutton W. (1996) 1876 California report on Chinese immigration. *The Social Contract*, **6**(3).

Lynch HT. (1991) Hereditary breast cancer. *Annals of Medicine*, **23**(5), 475–477.

Magnello EM. (2006) Victorian vital and mathematical statistics. *BSHM Bulletin*, **21**(3), 219–229.

Magnello E and Hardy A. (2002) *The Road to Medical Statistics, Vol. 67*, Amsterdam, Rodopi.

Malmer B, Henriksson R and Grönberg H. (2003) Familial brain tumours — genetics or environment? A nationwide cohort study of cancer risk in spouses and first-degree relatives of brain tumour patients. *International Journal of Cancer*, **106**(2), 260–263.

Maloney TN. (1994) Wage compression and wage inequality between black and white males in the United States, 1940–1960." *The Journal of Economic History*, **54**(2), 358–381.

Markel H. (2000) 'The eyes have it': Trachoma, the perception of disease, the United States Public Health Service, and the American Jewish immigration experience, 1897–1924. *Bulletin of the History of Medicine*, **74**(3), 525–560.

Markel H. (1993) Cholera, quarantines, and immigration restriction: The View from Johns Hopkins, 1892. *Bulletin of the History of Medicine*, **67**(4), 691–695.

Mayer D. (2004) In *Essential evidence–based medicine, Vol. 1*, Cambridge, Cambridge University Press.

Meyer DS. (1995) Framing national security: Elite public discourse on nuclear weapons during the Cold War. *Political Communication*, **12**(2), 173–192.

McCulloch J and Tweedale G. (2008) In *Defending the indefensible: The global asbestos industry and its fight for survival*. Oxford, Oxford University Press.

Mercer A. (2014) In *Infections, chronic disease, and the epidemiological transition: A New perspective*, Martlesham, Boydell & Brewer.

Merchant EK. (2017) A digital history of anglophone demography and global population control, 1915–1984. *Population and Development Review*, 83–117.

Mettler S. (2005) Soldiers to citizens: The GI bill and the making of the greatest generation. Oxford, Oxford University Press on Demand.

Miles SH. (2015) Kaci Hickox: Public health and the politics of fear. *The American Journal of Bioethics*, **15**(4), 17–19.

Mold A, *et al.* (2019) In *Placing the Public in Public Health in Post–War Britain, 1948–2012*. Cham, Springer Nature.

Molina N. (2006) Medicalizing the Mexican: Immigration, race, and disability in the early–twentieth–century United States. *Radical History Review*, **94**(2006), 22–37.

Montagu AF. (1998) In *Man's Most Dangerous Myth: The Fallacy of Race*. Lanham, MD, AltaMira Press.

Moore PG. (1983) In *The Business of Risk*, Cambridge, Cambridge University Press.

Moreno JD. (2013) In *Undue risk: Secret state experiments on humans*. London, Routledge.

Moser RH. (1961) Diseases of medical progress. *Clinical Pharmacology & Therapeutics*, **2**(4), 446–522.

Mouat FJ and Snell HS. (1889) In *Hospital Construction and Management*, London, J. & A. Churchill.

Moriyama IM, *et al.* (1958) Inquiry into diagnostic evidence supporting medical certifications of death. *American Journal of Public Health and the Nations Health*, **48**(10), 1376–1387.

Mumford L. (1944) In *The Condition of Man*, New York, NY Harcourt, Brace and Comp.

Myers CS. (1916) Contributions to the study of shell shock: Being an account of certain disorders of speech, with special reference to their causation and their relation to malingering. *Lancet*, **188**(4854), 461–468.

Ngai MM. (2003) The strange career of the illegal alien: Immigration restriction and deportation policy in the United States, 1921–1965. *Law and History Review*, **21**(1), 69–108.

Nightingale F. (1863) In *Notes on hospitals*, London, John W. Parker and Son, West Strand.

O'Brien GV. (2003) Indigestible food, conquering hordes, and waste materials: Metaphors of immigrants and the early immigration restriction debate in the United States. *Metaphor and Symbol*, **18**(1), 33–47.

Oppenheimer GM. (2010) Framingham heart study: The first 20 years. *Progress in Cardiovascular Diseases*, **53**(1), 55–61.

Oppenheimer GM. (2006) Profiling risk: The emergence of coronary heart disease epidemiology in the United States (1947–70). *International Journal of Epidemiology*, **35**(3), 720–730.

Oxford JS, *et al.* (2002) World War I may have allowed the emergence of "Spanish" influenza. *The Lancet Infectious Diseases*, **2**(2), 111–114.

Parascandola M. (2011) Causes, risks, and probabilities: Probabilistic concepts of causation in chronic disease epidemiology. *Preventive Medicine*, **53**(4-5), 232–234.

Payne MM. (2001) Charles Theodore Dotter: the father of intervention. *Texas Heart Institute Journal*, **28**(1), 28.

Paul RW. (1938) The origin of the Chinese issue in California. *The Mississippi Valley Historical Review*, **25**(2), 181–196.

Pearce N. (1996) Traditional epidemiology, modern epidemiology, and public health. *American Journal of Public Health*, **86**(5), 678–683.

Pearl R. (1930) In *Introduction to Medical Biometry and Statistics*. Philadelphia, PA, W.B. Saunders.

Pearson K and Moul M. (1925) The problem of alien immigration into Great Britain, illustrated by an examination of Russian and Polish Jewish children. *Annals of Eugenics*, **1**(1), 5–54.

Pearson SJ. (2022) Birth registration and the administration of white supremacy. *Modern American History*, **5**(2), 117–141.

Perea JF. (1996) In *Immigrants out!: The new nativism and the anti–immigrant impulse in the United States, Vol. 76*, New York, NY, NYU Press.

Pernick MS. (1997) Eugenics and public health in American history. *American Journal of Public Health*, **87**(11), 1767–1772.

Petersen A and Lupton D. (1996) In *The new public health: Health and self in the age of risk*, London, Sage.

Pfaelzer J. (2008) In *Driven out: The Forgotten War Against Chinese Americans*, Berkeley, CA, University of California Press.

Pickstone JV. (1992) *Medical Innovations in Historical Perspective*. New York, NY, St. Martin's Press.

Pilgrim D. (2008) The eugenic legacy in psychology and psychiatry. *International Journal of Social Psychiatry*, **54**(3), 272–284.

Pitt B, *et al.* (1997) Randomised trial of losartan versus captopril in patients over 65 with heart failure (evaluation of losartan in the elderly study, elite). *The Lancet*, **349**(9054), 747–752.

Popenoe P and Johnson RH. (1918) In *Applied Eugenics*. New York, NY, Macmillan.

Popenoe P. (1922) Intelligence and race: A review of some of the results of the army intelligence tests — II. The Negro. *Journal of Heredity*, **13**(7), 295–298.

Porter D. (2005) In *Health, civilization and the state: A history of public health from ancient to modern times*, London, Routledge.

Porter D. (2011) In *Health citizenship: Essays in social medicine and biomedical politics*, Berkeley, CA, University of California Press.

Porter R. (1998) In *London, a Social History*. Cambridge, MA, Harvard University Press.

Pringle M. (2000) The shipman inquiry: Implications for the public's trust in doctors. *The British Journal of General Practice*, **50**(454), 355.

Prinzing F. (1916) *Epidemics resulting from Wars, Vol. 3*. Oxford, Clarendon Press.

Prost A. (2014) In *War losses*. International Encyclopaedia of the First World War, Berlin: Freie Uuniversität.

Quirke V and Gaudillière JP. (2008) The era of biomedicine: Science, medicine, and public health in Britain and France after the Second World War. *Medical History*, **52**(4), 441–452.

Rehbock PF. (1990) Transcendental anatomy. *Romanticism and the Sciences*, 130–143.

Reilly RF. (2016) Medical and surgical care during the American Civil War, 1861–1865. *Baylor University Medical Center Proceedings*, **29**(2), 138–142.

Remington PL and Brownson RC. (2011) Fifty years of progress in chronic disease epidemiology and control. *CDC Morbidity and Mortality Weekly Report (MMWR)*, **60**(4), 70–77.

Richards EE. (2011) Responses to occupational and environmental exposures in the US Military — World War II to the present. *Military Medicine*, **176**(Suppl 7), 22–28.

Rickover HG. (1976) In *How the battleship Maine was destroyed.* Wahington, D.C., Naval History Division, Department of the Navy.

Ripley WZ. (1909) Race progress and immigration. *The Annals of the American Academy of Political and Social Science*, **34**(1), 130–138.

Roberts S. (2009) In *Infectious fear: Politics, disease, and the health effects of segregation*. Chapel Hill, NC, University of North Carolina Press.

Rogers JR, Symons JM and Sorg TJ. (2013) The history of environmental research in Cincinnati, Ohio: (From the US public health service to the US environmental protection agency). *World Environmental and Water Resources Congress 2013: Showcasing the Future.*

Rosenberg EF and Hench PS. (1946) Recent advances in the treatment of rheumatic fever: With special reference to sulfona, mide prophylaxis and intravenous salicylate therapy. *Medical Clinics of North America*, **30**(3), 489–509.

Rothstein WG. (2003) In *Public health and the risk factor: A history of an uneven medical revolution*. Rochester, NY. University of Rochester Press.

Royo S. (2020) Responding to COVID-19: The Case of Spain. *European Policy Analysis*, **6**(2), 180–190.

Rubenstein AD, Feemster RF and Smith HM. (1944) Salmonellosis as a public health problem in wartime. *American Journal of Public Health and the Nations Health*, **34**(8), 841–853.

Rudan I. (2020) A cascade of causes that led to the COVID-19 tragedy in Italy and in other European Union countries. *Journal of Global Health*, **10**(1).

Sacco PL and De Domenico M. (2021) Public health challenges and opportunities after COVID-19. *Bulletin of the World Health Organization*, **99**(7), 52.

Salyer LE. (1995) *Laws harsh as tigers: Chinese immigrants and the shaping of modern immigration law*. Chapel Hill, NC, University of North Carolina Press, (1995).

Sandmeyer EC. (1991) In *The anti–Chinese movement in California*, Champaign, IL, University of Illinois Press.

Sargent Senator Aaron A. (1877) Report of the joint special committee to investigate Chinese immigration, *Senate Rept*, 689.

Scharf I. (1999) Tired of your masses: A history of and judicial responses to early 20th century anti–immigration legislation. *University of Hawaii Law Review*, **21**, 131.

Schlich T and Tröhler U. (2004) *The risks of medical innovation: Risk perception and assessment in historical context*. London, Routledge.

Schlich T. (2004) Objectifying uncertainty: History of risk concepts in medicine. *Topoi*, **23**(2), 211–219.

Scholz H. (2002) Some historical aspects of the development of cardiovascular drugs. *Zeitschrift für Kardiologie*, **91**(4), iv34–iv42.

Schumacher M. (2016) Entwicklung Klinischer Studien von Paul Martini bis Heute. *Drug Research*, **66**(S 01), S5–S7.

Schwantes CA. (1997) From anti–Chinese agitation to reform politics: the legacy of the knights of labor in Washington and the Pacific Northwest. *The Pacific Northwest Quarterly*, **88**(4), 174–184.

Sebelius CL. (1945) Vincent's infection — a wartime disease: Reporting of Vincent's infection by state health departments. *American Journal of Public Health and the Nations Health*, **35**(5), 451–456.

Shah N. (2001) *Contagious divides: Epidemics and race in San Francisco's Chinatown, Vol. 7*, Berkeley, CA, University of California Press.

Sheynin OB. (1982) On the history of medical statistics. *Archive for History of Exact Sciencesi*, **26**(3), 241–286.

Siegfried A. (1926) American emigration and eugenics. *The Eugenics Review*, **18**(3), 217.

Skolbekken J–A. (1995) The risk epidemic in medical journals. *Social Science & Medicine*, **40**(3), 291–305.

Smith RA. (2014) Types of mankind: Polygenism and scientific racism in the nineteenth century united states scientific community.

Sokal RR and Rohlf FJ. (2000) In *Biostatistics*, New York, NY, Freeman & Co.

Starr C and Whipple C. (1984) A perspective on health and safety risk analysis. *Management Science*, **30**(4), 452–463.

Starr C. (1969) Social benefit versus technological risk: What is our society willing to pay for safety? *Science*, **165**(3899), 1232–1238.

Stern AM. (2005) Sterilized in the name of public health: Race, immigration, and reproductive control in modern California. *American Journal of Public Health*, **95**(7), 1128–138.

Sternberg GM. (1899) Sanitary lessons of the war. *Journal of the American Medical Association*, **32**(23), 1287–1294.

Stoddard L. (1922) In *The revolt against civilization: The menace of the under man*. New York, NY, Chapman & Hall, 1922.

Stout AB. (1862) In *Chinese immigration and the physiological causes of the decay of a nation*. San Francisco, CA, Agnew & Deffebach, printers.

Stout AB. (1837) In *A thesis on the cataract: With some remarks on the eye*, New York, NY, Henderson Greene.

Stout AB. (1868) In *Hygiene, as Regards the Sewerage Of San Francisco*, San Francisco, CA, Roman & Company.

Taft CP. (1943) Public health and the family in World War II. *The Annals of the American Academy of Political and Social Science*, **229**(1), 145–149.

Tangcharoensathien V, Singh P and Mills A. (2021) COVID-19 response and mitigation: A call for action. *Bulletin of the World Health Organization*, **99**(2).

Tannenwald N. (2005) Stigmatizing the bomb: Origins of the nuclear taboo. *International Security*, **29**(4), 5–49.

Thornton M. (2008) The great depression: Mises vs. Fisher. *The Quarterly Journal of Austrian Economics*, **11**(3), 230–241.

Tone JL. (2006) In *War and Genocide in Cuba, 1895–1898*, Chapel Hill, NC, University of North Carolina Press.

Toole MJ, Galson S and Brady W. (1993) Are war and public health compatible? *The Lancet*, **341**(8854), 1193–1196.

Trauner JB. (1978) The Chinese as medical scapegoats in San Francisco, 1870–1905. *California History*, **57**(1), 70–87.

Tucker WH. (2002) In *The Funding of Scientific Racism: Wickliffe Draper and The Pioneer Fund*, Champaign, IL, University of Illinois Press.

Turda M. (2022) Legacies of eugenics: Confronting the past, forging a future. *Ethnic and Racial Studies*, **45**(13), 2470–2477.

Ummel D. (2016) Dream or nightmare? The impact of American eugenics, past and present. *CrossCurrents*, **66**(3), 389–398.

Valdiserri RO. (2002) HIV/AIDS Stigma: An Impediment to Public Health. *American Journal of Public Health*, **92**(3), 341–342.

Villa, Simone, *et al.* (2020) The COVID-19 pandemic preparedness... or lack thereof: from China to Italy. *Global Health & Medicine*, **2**(2), 73–77.

Vincent C. (2011) In *Patient safety*, New York, NY, John Wiley & Sons.

Wagar W. (2004) In *HG Wells: Traversing time*. Middletown, CT, Wesleyan University Press.

Walshe K and Offen N. (2001) A very public failure: Lessons for quality improvement in healthcare organisations from The Bristol Royal Infirmary. *British Medical Journal, Quality & Safety*, **10**(4), 250–256.

Wardell W. (1974) Assessment of the benefits, risks and costs of medical progress. *Benefits and Risks in Medical Care, London, Office of Health Economics*, 93–104.

Warren BS, *et al.* (2006) War activities of the United States public health service (1919) [with Commentary]. *Public Health Reports*, 116–131.

Watterson A and Beck M. (2022) An exploratory study of Beryllium and UK soft touch regulation: An enduring example of weaknesses of UK occupational health and safety governance. *International Journal of Environmental Research and Public Health*, **19**(19), 12771.

Weber M and Lynch C. (1928) In *The Medical Department of the United States Army in the World War, Vol. 4*, Washington, D.C., US Government Printing. Office.

Weingart NS, *et al.* (2000) Epidemiology of medical error. *British Medical Journal*, **320**(7237), 774–777.

Weiss ED. (2001) The second sacrifice: Costly advances in medicine and surgery during the civil war. *The Yale Journal of Biology and Medicine*, **74**(3), 169.

Weisz G. (2014) In *Chronic disease in the twentieth century: A history*, Baltimore, MD, Johns Hopkins University Press.

Wellborn M. (1912) The events leading to the Chinese exclusion acts. *Annual Publication of the Historical Society of Southern California*, 9(1/2), 49–58.

Wiist WH, *et al.* (2014) The role of public health in the prevention of war: Rationale and competencies. *American Journal of Public Health*, **104**(6), e34-e47.

Wilson LL and Fulton M. (2000) Risk management: How doctors, hospitals and MDOs can limit the costs of malpractice litigation. *Medical Journal of Australia*, **172**(2), 77–80.

Withering W. (2014) *An Account of The Foxglove, and Some of Its Medical Uses (1785)*, Cambridge, Cambridge University Press.

Woodward JJ, *et al.* (1879) In *The Medical And Surgical History of The War of the Rebellion (1861–65): pt. II. Medical History, Vol. 1*, Washington, DC, US Government Printing Office, 3.

Yearby R and Mohapatra S. (2020) Systemic racism, the government's pandemic response, and racial inequities in COVID-19. *Emory Law Journal*, **70**, 1419.

Young RJC. (2005) In *Colonial desire: Hybridity in theory, culture and race*, London, Routledge.

Yudell M. (2008) In *Making race: Biology and the evolution of the race concept in 20th century American thought*, Columbia University.

www.ingramcontent.com/pod-product-compliance
Ingram Content Group UK Ltd.
Pitfield, Milton Keynes, MK11 3LW, UK
UKHW021824231025
3372IPUK00001B/2

9 789814 689526